ROUTLEDGE LIBRARY EDITIONS:
EDUCATION MANAGEMENT

Volume 19

THE CHANGING GOVERNMENT OF EDUCATION

THE CHANGING GOVERNMENT OF EDUCATION

Edited by
STEWART RANSON AND JOHN TOMLINSON

Routledge
Taylor & Francis Group
LONDON AND NEW YORK

First published in 1986 by Allen & Unwin

This edition first published in 2018
by Routledge
2 Park Square, Milton Park, Abingdon, Oxon OX14 4RN

and by Routledge
711 Third Avenue, New York, NY 10017

Routledge is an imprint of the Taylor & Francis Group, an informa business

British Library Cataloguing in Publication Data
A catalogue record for this book is available from the British Library

ISBN: 978-1-138-48720-8 (Set)
ISBN: 978-1-351-04158-4 (Set) (ebk)
ISBN: 978-1-138-48797-0 (Volume 19) (hbk)
ISBN: 978-1-138-54545-8 (Volume 19) (pbk)
ISBN: 978-1-351-04078-5 (Volume 19) (ebk)

Publisher's Note
The publisher has gone to great lengths to ensure the quality of this reprint but points out that some imperfections in the original copies may be apparent.

Disclaimer
The publisher has made every effort to trace copyright holders and would welcome correspondence from those they have been unable to trace.

The Changing Government of Education

Edited by

STEWART RANSON
and
JOHN TOMLINSON

For the
Institute of Local Government Studies
University of Birmingham

ALLEN & UNWIN
London Boston Sydney

**George Allen & Unwin (Publishers) Ltd,
40 Museum Street, London WC1A 1LU, UK**

George Allen & Unwin (Publishers) Ltd,
Park Lane, Hemel Hempstead, Herts HP2 4TE, UK

Allen & Unwin, Inc.,
8 Winchester Place, Winchester, Mass. 01890, USA

George Allen & Unwin Australia Pty Ltd,
8 Napier Street, North Sydney, NSW 2060, Australia

First published in 1986

British Library Cataloguing in Publication Data

The Changing government of education.
1. Educational sociology – Geat Britain
2. Education and state – Great Britain
I. Ranson, Stewart II. Tomlinson, J. R. G.
III. University of Brimingham. *Institute of Local Government Studies*
370.19'0941 LC191.8.G7
ISBN 0–04–352216–5
ISBN 0–04–352217–3 Pbk

Library of Congress Cataloging-in-Publication Data

The Changing government of education
'For the Institute of Local Government Studies, University of Birmingham,'
1. School management and organization – Great Britain – Addresses, essays, lectures. 2. Education and state – Great Britain – Addresses, essays, lectures. I. Ranson, Stewart. II. Tomlinson, John. III. University of Birmingham. Institute of Local Government Studies.
LB2901.C43 1986 379.41 85–26673
ISBN 0–04–352216–5 (alk. paper)
ISBN 0–04–352217–3 (pbk.: alk. paper)

Set in 10 on 11 point Sabon by Computape (Pickering) Ltd, N. Yorkshire
and printed in Great Britain by
Anchor Brendon Ltd, Tiptree, Essex

To our parents
Betty
Ken *and* Louise

The worth of a State, in the long run, is the worth of the individuals composing it; and a State which postpones the interests of *their* mental expansion and elevation to a little more of administrative skill, or of that semblance of it which practice gives, in the details of business; a State which dwarfs its men, in order that they may be more docile instruments in its hands even for beneficial purposes – will find that with small men no great thing can really be accomplished; and that the perfection of machinery to which it has sacrificed everything will in the end avail it nothing, for want of the vital power which, in order that the machine might work more smoothly, it has preferred to banish. (John Stuart Mill, *On Liberty*, 1859)

Contents

Foreword

In the months since these chapters were drafted the crisis which they identify within the Education Service has deepened. The following trends have continued

- the impoverishment of the service, starved of funds necessary for books, curriculum development, the maintenance of school buildings, as well as decent salaries for the teaching profession,
- the denigration of local authorities, teachers and the public service in general, which is demoralizing and alienating those who are striving to meet the needs of young people during a period of social change
- the accelerating privatization of the service both directly, in the case of 'post 16' education, with the development of the Youth Training Scheme sponsored by employers, and indirectly, as parents are driven to subsidize their children's learning in the crumbling fabric of our schools
- the reinforcement of a narrow, utilitarian, vocational preparation of young people, accelerating the reintroduction of 'tripartism' in education.
- the fragmentation of authority within education and between education and the training agencies, leading increasingly to confusion and disarray.

This crisis is now finally eroding the foundation-stones of purpose and power laid by the 1944 Education Act. The 'Butler' Act established as a primary purpose the *universal right* of all young people to receive a comprehensive education which was not dependent upon their parents' wealth, power or status; and it created a framework of governmental power in which the state, local authorities, teachers and parents could work in *partnership* to fulfil that goal. Now, those purposes of a noble public education service providing equal opportunities for all are derided while the partnership is being dismembered.

A vociferous debate is now emerging nationally about the future role and organization of education. The government of education has become the central issue for the service. The publication of this book is timely. It can shape the terms of the debate. It offers analysis and prescription which can re-establish public education on firm ground for the difficult decade to come.

S. R. and J. T.
Greenriggs, April, 1986

Introduction

STEWART RANSON AND JOHN TOMLINSON

Education has been the most complex and burdened of services. As the keystone of public policy-making and social reform in the postwar period education has been expected to fuel economic growth, facilitate equality of opportunity and afford social justice to the deprived: to educate has been to bring a new world out of the old. To accomplish this burdensome collective vision education has had to manage the most complex network of relationships which cuts across institutions, communities, services, authorities and levels of government. A rising birth rate, economic growth and political will coalesced in the expansion of the education service during the 1960s and early 1970s. But education now occupies a changed and more fragmented world: the confluence of forces has altered. Demographic and economic contraction, eroded beliefs about the contributions which education can make and the disquiet of parents and politicians have combined to produce a more severe and pessimistic context. This changing environment has enormous implications for the management of the service. Its vision and objectives are being questioned and simplified, while the complex, often ambiguous, traditional framework of decision-making – with its assumptions about *who* should be involved, *whose* values should count and *how* decisions should be arrived at – is being clarified, concentrated and centralized. In short, the traditional balance of autonomy, power and accountability in education is being redefined.

This book is an attempt to contribute to an understanding and analysis of this changing pattern of power and decision-making in education, and in particular the relations between the centre and the locality. This Introduction will describe the distinctive pattern of government by partnership in education since the Second World War. The 'settlement' established by the Education Act 1944 distributed powers and duties between the department, the local authority, institutions and parents, so that none should have a controlling voice, but that each became a partner to the service.

The changed context of education – demographic, economic, professional and political – has placed this traditional partnership under considerable strain. Because the experience and interpretations of change often vary according to the perspective of the several partners, we have invited contributions from the Department and the local authorities, from teachers and parents, so that we can grasp more immediately the pressures experienced in different parts of the service. In Part 2 of the book a number of specialists have been invited to take the discussion forward by analysing the problems and initiatives that are developing within key policy sectors – in curriculum and assessment, in the professionalism of teachers, in planning and in finance.

Part 3 of the book will review the major scenarios for resolving the current dilemmas in the government of education. The first argues that education should become more overtly a national service: the strains in the partnership can be resolved by concentrating power at the centre. The second proposes a community service which would decentralize decision-taking to schools and their local communities. A third scenario argues for strengthening of the local authority. We shall evaluate these scenarios before promoting our own reconstruction of the government of education.

PARTNERS AND POWER IN THE SETTLEMENT OF 1944

The architect of the Education Act 1944, R. A. Butler, believed that there was nothing radical in his legislation and that it only 'recast the existing system'. His achievement was for the first time to *create* an integrated national system; to integrate disparate interests while allowing for their separate identity. This was, nevertheless, a source of ambiguity. It was intrinsic to a settlement which sought to systematize yet divide powers and responsibilities between partners to the service. The Act sought to shift the balance of power towards the centre and created for the first time a minister ostensibly with absolute powers. The previous president of the Board of Education merely had 'superintendence of matters relating to education',[1] but the 1944 Act installed a minister who was 'to promote the education of the people of England and Wales and the progressive development of institutions devoted to that purpose and to secure the effective execution by local authorities *under his control and direction*, of the national policy' (our emphasis). Butler's hope that the minister 'should lead boldly and not follow timidly'[2] reflected a strong feeling at the time that 'some concentration of power at the centre was essential in order to promote a fairly even standard of educational provisions throughout the whole country'.[3] Indeed the explanatory memorandum of 1943 sought to justify the strengthening of the central power in terms of a 'recognition of the principle that the public system of education, though locally administered, is the nation's concern.'[4] It seems clear that this strengthening of the centre was equally designed to mean a 'contraction of local decision-making powers and a reduced capacity on the part of the local authorities "to make what they liked" of parliamentary legislation when now constrained and monitored by a more powerful central administration'.[5]

Although the Act sought to shift the balance of power towards the centre, it only provided the minister with limited and specific powers; for example, the power to approve changes in the nature of individual institutions; to settle disputes between LEAs and between LEAs and their school governors; and to arbitrate between LEAs and parents over admission to schools. The central authority would not own or build any schools, it would not provide or employ the teachers, nor supply books and equipment for schools, nor prescribe how they might be used. These responsibilities were still to reside with the LEA who were to be the *providing* authority with control of 'secular instruction' in the schools. But they were to be much more besides, for the initiative for change and development was to lie with them. Butler illustrated the point while talking of development plans during the committee stage of the Bill:[6]

> here we see the new machinery of the administration of education and this new machinery means that the initiative or enterprise, the variety and diversity to which we attach so much importance in English education, shall be provided at the instance of the local authority and shall differ in various areas, but that once the Minister has had the opportunity of approving the development plan and has made his orders, it shall be mandatory upon the [local] authority to carry out that plan.

The key tasks of winning resources, of providing and maintaining institutions and of developing curriculum and teaching methods came to be divided between the three critical partners to the service: between the centre, locality and institutions; between ministers, councillors and governors; and between officials, officers and teachers. The upshot of the 1944 Act is thus what Briault[7] chooses to call a 'distributed' system of decision-making, planning and responsibility so as to form essentially a triangle of tension, of checks and balances. The manifold participants were to form, as Weaver[8] has put it, 'a complex web of interdependent relationships'.

The lack of clarity about the relationships, the absence of definition, suggested the need for 'partnership'. Celebrating the jubilee of the creation of the centralized department, the ministry stressed the importance of 'the progressive parnership between the central department, the local education authorities and the teachers'.[9] The secretary to the Association of Education Committees, Sir William Alexander, as always emphasized the significance of smooth and flexible partnership in education.

Bogdanor has suggested that it was difficult to identify a 'controlling voice' in education:[10]

> the 'efficient secret' of the system, to adapt Bagehot, was that no *one* individual participant should enjoy a monopoly of power in the decision-making process. Power over the distribution of resources, over the organisation and content of education was to be diffused amongst the different elements and no one of them was to be given a controlling voice.

Recently ministers at the Department of Education and Science (DES) have concurred that their powers were very much circumscribed[11]: thus Shirley Williams believed that 'there isn't much direct power in the hands of the Secretary of State except in a number of rather quirky fields; there is [however] a lot of direct influence'; and Gerald Fowler as Minister of State for Education agreed that ministerial power was constrained although influence could create or change 'a climate of opinion'.

A number of writers, however, argue that although the system of government in education distributes fundamentally different powers and duties between the partners, it nevertheless remains possible to attribute balance of influence and power. According to some, education has been a decentralized service.[12] Regan,[13] however, argues that the centre has been the strongest partner standing in a relation of deep involvement to the service, while Kogan[14] concluded that the only ultimate certainty in the complex structures of educational policy-making was that the 'DES wields determinant authority and great power'.

Although it may be appropriate to identify partners who have been more powerful in a complex educational system, we shall argue[15] that the balance of influence and power has varied over time. The attribution of dominance requires to be located historically. Three approximate periods of dominant influence can be identified since the Second World War: an early period (roughly 1945–55) specifies a phase of central dominance; a middle period (1955–75) has been one of local dominance; while the present period (from 1975) witnesses an acceleration towards the restoration of central control.

THE EARLY POSTWAR PERIOD

In the early postwar years it is arguable that the Ministry of Education was clearly the dominant partner. This can be supported by an interpretative account of the 1944 Act which it is suggested intended to give the minister directive powers. This interpretation is grounded not in a reading of section 1 alone, but in association with sections 11–13 and section 100:

(1) section 11 required every local education authority (LEA) to produce a development plan for the whole LEA;
(2) section 12 enshrined the plan in a development order which the LEA had to follow and from which it could not depart;
(3) section 13 specified how an LEA could tinker with its system (clearly there would have to be occasional changes) by submitting proposals to the minister;
(4) section 100 stated that the minister would pay grant to LEAs directly in the form of specific grants.

The 1944 Act 'was aimed at radical change' according to Halsey, Heath and Ridge.[16] Sections 11 and 12 were only meant to last a limited time, but they were about transforming secondary education. We talk glibly about secondary education before the war, but the 1944 Act through these sections was the revolutionary change to introduce secondary education. Sections 13 and 100 were further key direction controls. Those who drafted the Act, which was to be the instrument of these radical changes, clearly saw the minister as absolutely central to the educational system and gave him important powers to direct the other partners.

Things did not quite work out as the drafters of the Act intended. A number of LEAs produced a development plan, but not a single development order was ever made. The reason lay in the rapidity of economic and social change. The gap between the world as conceived by the framers of the Act and the world as it is (early postwar austerity, sluggish growth and a substantially expanding birth rate) began to grow. The world was too fluid, too under-resourced, to allow the plans any overall relevance. For some years, however, the lacunae between plans and reality did not undermine the power and influence of the centre in education. The department continued to pursue the plans to monitor in some detail the development of individual LEAs, while control of recurrent education expenditure of particular authorities through the specific education grant enabled officials of the department to scrutinize LEA expenditure in detail and disallow particular items for grant purposes if necessary. Moreover, the minister gave detailed advice through administrative circulars and issued elaborate codes of guidance.

MIDDLE POSTWAR PERIOD

The balance of power began to shift as the years passed and the local authorities gained power at the expense of the centre. Studies[17] showed that there was enormous scope for LEA autonomy and discretion:[18]

> not only on matters of style – for example, type of secondary education provided, the content of the curriculum and the age of transfer from primary school . . . but also in terms of the amount of resources used in the education service, for example, teaching staff, age and standard of buildings, equipment and facilities.

Ironically, in view of the LEA's opposition, it was that change in the arrangements for central grant which most loosened the central hold. In 1958 the grant funding arrangements changed with the introduction of general grant (later to be superseded by rate support grant), thus ending the close scrutiny by the department of LEA recurrent expenditure. The centre also ceded detailed control of capital expenditure. Guidance too in the form of circulars and administrative memoranda became less detailed.

It is, however, in studies of comprehensive secondary reorganization that the shifting balance of power becomes clearly apparent. First, the initiatives were often made by local rather than central government:[19]

> in fact, a number of LEAs had either reorganised or were seriously considering doing so well before central government was committed to such a course of action. Indeed, until 1965 the role of central government whether Labour or Conservative controlled, was usually to inhibit and delay local initiative in the area . . . When national government introduced its own plans in the mid-sixties it drew heavily on the experience of those authorities.

Secondly, LEAs were able to negotiate considerable discretion to suit local circumstances. Thirdly, there was the ability of the LEA to win out in a test of power, that is, to achieve objectives in the face of opposition and resistance.

The cases of Tameside and Enfield illustrate the ability of an LEA (in the case of the former authority) and a local action group (in the case of the latter authority) to frustrate the intentions of the secretary of state in the courts and win.[20] In short, the attempt to promote comprehensive schools illustrated the essential weakness of the centre when confronted with resolute opposition.

The financial and educational changes we have discussed demonstrate the diminishing power of the centre. A number of other, broadly political, factors contributed to the process over time. First, the teachers' unions became more militant in pursuit of their professional claims – cf. Coates;[21] secondly, the rapid growth of political organization and of corporate management in many local authorities contributed to an increase in the centralization and concentration of decision-making, so that the dialogue that central departments such as the DES had with local services came increasingly to be mediated by the local authority in general at a political and official level; and thirdly, the voice of the consumer came to be articulated more clearly and vociferously. The body politic of education in particular, and local government in general, became more organized and aggressive in pursuit of sectional claims. But at the same time, it became more fragmented and therefore more difficult for the centre to connect with and to control.

A CHANGED WORLD

The confluence of forces which had worked to expand the education service in the 1960s had changed radically by the late 1970s. Demographic and financial contraction, change in the nature of work and employment, together with altered beliefs about the polity and education's place within it, all amounted to a considerable reversal of fortune for the service.

The birth rate has only just begun to rise following a downward path since 1964. The implications of this contraction for education have been profound. The school population which grew to a peak of 9 million in 1977 will probably fall below 7·5 million by 1990.[22] The decline reached the 16–19 age-group in 1984, which by 1993 will be a quarter below its present level. For LEAs such as Manchester or Sheffield, or Birmingham or London, the impact of declining school rolls has been dramatic. With the prospect of nearly half the number of 15-year-olds in schools in the late 1980s as against a decade earlier, these authorities more than others have been forced once more to reorganize their schools.[23]

The problems of managing falling school rolls have been considerably exacerbated by the severity of the economic recession and its impact upon public expenditure. The reversal of financial fortunes has affected education dramatically. Between 1955 and 1975 education had enjoyed 'an unrivalled record of growth'.[24] But from the mid-1970s spending on education began to level off and from 1979 began to decline sharply. Peston, analysing the public expenditure White Paper for 1982, argued that the planned expenditure for education when considered in real terms would imply reductions that would 'take education back to a position similar to what it was in the late 1950s or early 1960s'.[25] In other words, right back to the beginning again!

Further draconian cuts are revealed moreover in the 1984 expenditure White Paper. When a proper allowance is made for inflation and salary settlements, the new figures imply for local government as a whole cuts of £3 billion or 13 per cent between 1984 and 1987. Education on the same principles can expect a cut of 12 per cent over the period. The government will no doubt argue that school rolls will also fall by 13 per cent at secondary level. This suggests that pupil–teacher ratios will merely be held constant. Yet in the early 1980s the government conceded the argument of local education administrators that, paradoxically, managing schools with declining rolls was a *more* expensive business. An 'operating margin' was required and momentarily given. This margin has now been eliminated, leaving LEAs to bear the full cost of staffing even a basic curriculum. Moreover, to base the total financial plan upon falling rolls in one sector ignores the growth needed in primary and further and higher education.

Until now the full force of the cuts upon education has been softened in many LEAs by the protection of the local authority. Local government has allowed considerable 'overspending' on education.[26] With the implementation of rate-capping legislation, the last loophole for local government to protect education and other services – the capacity to raise their rates – has been closed. More dramatic cuts and redundancies can then be expected in the education service.

The recession and the fiscal crises it has produced are more severe than anything experienced since the 1930s. Yet however important these economic changes are, they are overshadowed by even more significant structural changes in employment. The revolution in the nature of work created by the new technologies seems finally to be emerging. Massey and Meegan[27] have produced a powerful account of the mechanisms of industrial intensification, rationalization and technical innovation which explains the anatomy of job loss. This contraction and restructuring of the economy and labour market has affected the school-leaving age-groups more severely than any other. Unemployment has risen four times as quickly among young people as among the population as a whole. In the recent past 50 per cent of the age-group could not only expect to leave school and find work, but also to alternate jobs until they discovered a suitable employment experience. Now the transition from school to work is likely for many young people to include an intermediary stage of special training sponsored by the Manpower Services Commission (MSC), preceded and followed by the experience of futile job search, unemployment and a loss of morale.

The shedding of surplus labour – young and old – through the restructuring of employment is already beginning to raise fundamental social and political questions about preparation and access to work, and about dependence upon the state and thus personal identity, dignity and citizenship. These cyclical and structural changes in the economy parallel and reinforce fundamental changes in society. Social trends show an ageing society, more fragmented family patterns – often reflecting the changing relations between men and women – and a multicultural society striving for more equality of opportunity amid growing boredom, anxiety and alienation and the establishment of a more politicized world as differences sharpen about ways of resolving economic and social problems.

A changed political context for the education service has accompanied demographic and economic contraction. Whereas – in our earlier postwar period – the service had basked in the glow of public esteem and expectation, now it confronted a chillier climate. The ambitions of producing new manpower skills or of delivering a fairer and more equal society seem to have been disappointed. The consensus which had supported educational reform began to fragment as the right-wing 'Black Paper' group challenged the standards achieved by comprehensive schools. The crisis at the William Tyndale School reflected public concern about what teachers were up to in schools.

At the centre of these challenges was a belief that schools should be more accountable to the society which they served. Teachers should be held to account for the content and purposes of schooling. During the 1970s industrialists, politicians and parents were increasingly criticizing schools for being too self-absorbed and preoccupied with the social development of young people rather than preparing them for the transition from school to work. A 'more relevant' curriculum was advocated. The criticisms of the DES made by the Organization for Economic Co-operation and Development (OECD) 'examiners' and subsequent initiatives of the MSC reinforced a concern for the curriculum at the centre. These challenges coincided with internal analyses by officials and the HMI at the department. In 1976 this work had its (leaked) public expression in a memorandum known as the Yellow Book (the work for which had begun as early as 1974). It argued that the weakness of secondary education was that it underprepared young people for employment: 'the time may now be ripe for change as the national mood and government policies have changed in the face of hard and irreducible facts'.

THE LATE POSTWAR PERIOD AND THE RESTRUCTURING OF EDUCATION

Inevitably these transformations in the context of education have had enormous consequences for the service. The purposes of education, the curriculum, planning procedures and resourcing have all had to be reviewed and questioned in the light of the economic and social changes. Most important, the partnership and its traditional distribution of duties and responsibilities have been brought into question. Ministers and the department have been challenged to provide a new lead to curriculum development, to institutional arangements, teacher training and methods of examining and reporting on schooling, thus to the quality of the educational experience offered to young people. Yet the centre, bereft of funds and the necessary statutory instruments, had become manifestly unable to secure the implementation of its policies through persuasion alone. The secretary of state and the DES moved to arrest the decline in *its* influence and to reassert control.

Any fundamental redirection of education, and of 14–19 provision in particular, required the support and legitimation of ultimate sources of power. James Callaghan's premiership initiated and developed this basic review and redirection of the service. His speech at Ruskin College in October 1976 expressed concern that the needs of industry and commerce were not being met by education and called for a national debate on the service. The Green Paper[28] summarizing the debate reinforced the themes outlined by the Prime Minister:

> that the school system is geared to promote the importance of academic learning and careers with the result that pupils, especially the more able, are prejudiced against work in productive industry and trade; that teachers lack experience, knowledge and understanding of trade and industry; that curricula are not related to the realities of most pupils' work after leaving school; and that pupils leave school with little or no understanding of the workings, or the importance, of the wealth producing sector of our economy.

The education service was answerable to the society which it served and should therefore be responsive to such criticisms. It was 'vital to Britain's economic recovery and standard of living that the performance of manufacturing industry is improved and that the whole range of government policies, including education, contribute as much as possible to improving industrial performance and thereby increasing national wealth'.

Restructuring would require complex changes to key components of the education system; institutions would have to be rationalized, finance redirected; and, critically, the curriculum and examinations would need to be recast. The DES believed that control of the curriculum was central to its purpose: 'our focus must be on the strategic questions of the content, shape and purposes of the whole educational system and absolutely central to that is the curriculum.' Attention focused on the 16–19 sector because of its strategic location between secondary schooling and the world of work (or the prospect of unemployment), and because it was less hedged around by statutory constraints, it was more amenable to policy initiative and change. The point was underlined by a senior official:[29]

> the 16–19 area is one of the key means of changing the educational system and of achieving the relevance we desire because it sits at the watershed between school and work. If we can achieve things with the new 17+ examination that will give us an important lever to vocationalise or to re-vocationalise the last years of public schooling. That will be a very important, and significant step, indeed.

Given a firm view from the department about the conception and direction that education should take in a period of change, the hidden contradictions of the DES could, however, become manifest: responsible for change but unable to secure policy implementation for its conception of change. A DES initiative presupposed greater control for the centre than perhaps existed and a capacity to lead, intervene and shape change which did not obtain. The DES moved to reassert control over its partners.

This interventionist strategy of the DES to the problems of managing contraction imposed further strains upon the education partners. We now turn to these partners and to their own experience and interpretation of the pressures faced in managing a changed context.

NOTES: INTRODUCTION

1 W. O. Lester Smith, *Government of Education* (Harmondsworth: Penguin, 1965), p. 133.
2 F. B. Sullivan, *Lord Butler: The 1944 Act in Retrospect* (Milton Keynes: Open University Press, 1980), p. 16.
3 Lester Smith, op. cit., p. 11.
4 P. H. J. H. Gosden, *The Development of Educational Administration in England and Wales* (Oxford: Oxford University Press, 1966), p. 115.
5 M. Archer, *Social Origins of Educational Systems* (London: Sage, 1979), p. 583.
6 In J. A. G. Griffith, *Central Departments and Local Authorities* (London: Allen & Unwin, 1966), p. 98.
7 E. Briault, 'A distributed system of educational administration', *International Review of Education*, vol. 22, no. 4 (1976), pp. 429–39.
8 T. Weaver, *Tenth Report from the Expenditure Commitee 1975–76*, HC 621, p. 379.
9 Lester Smith, op. cit., p. 12.
10 V. Bogdanor, 'Power and participation', *Oxford Review of Education*, vol. 5, no. 2 (1979), pp. 3–15.
11 See T. Weaver, *Department of Education and Science: Central Control of Education?* (Milton Keynes: Open University Press, 1979).
12 J. A. G. Griffith, *Central Departments and Local Authorities* (London: Allen & Unwin, 1966).
13 D. Regan, *Local Government and Education* (London: Allen & Unwin, 1977).
14 M. Kogan, *Educational Policy Making* (London: Allen & Unwin, 1975).
15 See S. Ranson, 'Changing relations between centre and locality in education', *Local Government Studies*, special issue on 'Partners and power in education', vol. 6, no. 6 (1980), pp. 3–23.
16 A. H. Halsey, A. F. Heath and J. N. Ridge, *Origins and Destinations* (Oxford: Clarendon Press, 1980).
17 See, for example, B. Davies, *Social Needs and Resources in Local Services* (London: Michael Joseph, 1968); and E. Bryne, *Planning and Educational Inequality* (Slough: NFER, 1974).
18 D. Pyle, 'Resource allocation in education', *Social and Economic Administration*, vol. 10, no. 2 (1976), p. 111.
19 P. James, *The Reorganisation of Secondary Education* (Slough: NFER, 1980), p. 113.
20 See, for example, Kogan, *The Politics of Educational Change* (London: Fontana, 1978); and Griffith, *The Politics of the Judiciary* (London: Fontana, 1977).
21 R. D. Coates, *Teacher Unions and Interest Group Politics* (Cambridge: Cambridge University Press, 1972).
22 DES, 'Report on education numbers 92 and 96, Trends in school population', *Department of Education and Science* (November 1979).
23 DES, 'Education for 16–19 year olds', *Department of Education and Science* (January 1980).
24 T. E. Chester, 'Priorities for education', *National Westminster Bank Quarterly Reviews* (November 1976), pp. 45–58.
25 M. Peston, 'Sir Geoffrey's framework for decline', *Times Educational Supplement*, 12 March 1982.
26 J. D. Stewart, 'Tying hands in the town hall', *Times Educational Supplement*, 9 December 1983.
27 D. Massey and R. Meegan, *The Anatomy of Job Loss* (London: Methuen, 1982).
28 *Education in Schools, a Consultative Document*, Cmnd 6869 (London: HMSO, 1977).
29 See S. Ranson, 'Towards a tertiary tripartism: new codes of social control and the 17+', in P. Broadfoot (ed.), *Selection Certification and Control* (London: Falmer Press, 1984), p. 224.

PART ONE

Strains among the Education Partners

1

Parliament

CHRIS PRICE

Partnerships are easy on a growth curve; indeed they are probably necessary. The only way successfully to spend money is to have plenty of others to help one do so. The concept in the Education Act 1944 of a central service locally administered was a markedly successful one as long as there was a rising birth rate and, therefore, rising budgets to go with it. It was the combination of the recession and the fall in the birth rate which did more than anything else to erode in the 1980s the concept of partnership in education.

Quite apart from the external pressures however, each of the partners – the local education authorities (LEAs), the teachers, the Department of Education and Science (DES) and the churches – had been coming under internal strains for some time. It was upon this scene that the reorganized Select Committee for Education, Science and the Arts arrived. Of course for the past eleven years parliamentary committees on education had existed; there had been a subcommittee of the Expenditure Committee which exercised some supervision over the DES between 1970 and 1979. But it had suffered under a whole range of disadvantages compared with its successor: first, its powers were limited – it was intended to look primarily at expenditure rather than policy or administration; secondly, it existed on mere annual leases of life at the behest of the whips – if it annoyed the government, its membership or responsibilities could be altered; and thirdly, it was not autonomous – its decisions were subject to the whims of the Expenditure Committee as a whole, where the whips could mount an exercise, if they wished, to bring its recommendations into line. This is not to say that it did not actually inquire into policy or that it did not do good work; but its work was patchy and it was incapable of stamping its mark on the education landscape anywhere near the point where it could reasonably be regarded as a 'partner' in the system. Like the short-lived Crossman Select Committee on Education of the late 1960s, it pointed the way without really arriving at a consistent *raison d'être*.

Moreover, during the 1960s and 1970s the need for a parliamentary element in the education partnership was not so stark. The old partnership of the 1944 Act was still in some sort of shape, if becoming increasingly ramshackle. It is necessary to analyse this breakdown in the confidence and effectiveness of the old partners to understand the increased parliamentary interest in education and the advent of the new Select Committee in 1979. The key to the local authority partnership in education was the Association of Education Committees, effectively run for nearly fifty years by two men, Sir Percival Sharp and Sir William Alexander. That lobby was broken by local government reform of the early 1970s and the determination of both the chief executives and the politicians (of both parties) to curb an educational empire they perceived as having become too powerful. In some authorities education was eating up nearly 70 per cent of the expenditure – but it never commanded 70 per cent of the votes on the local education authority (LEA). The creation of the Local Authority Consultative Committee by Tony Crosland in 1974 did something to bring the education lobby in local government back into partnership. But now that it was irretrievably split between the Association of Metropolitan Authorities (AMA) and the Association of County Councils (ACC), the government could divide and rule far more effectively than ever in the past. Had education been given as a responsibility to the new metropolitan councils in 1974, the story would have been different – a more united front on education and probably the survival of the metropolitan counties in 1984. But during the 1970s the local education lobby lacked an effective central bureaucracy to confront the DES; certainly lacked unity and frequently lacked leadership; was constantly harassed by cuts from central government and treasurer's departments; and lacked too support from the local authorities' political leaders, who were more interested in other subjects. The result was to hand over to the DES much of the control and initiative gained during the 1950s and 1960s, and to divert to parliamentary action matters which often before had been settled locally. By the time the government decided first to control and then to destroy local government in the 1980s, the educational lobby at any rate was too weak to fight back. Moreover, in terms of policy, by such action, the government had rendered the whole idea of partnership nugatory. Once again pressure through Parliament tended to fill the gap.

The story of the teachers is not so different from that of the local authorities. In the 1950s and 1960s, partly because of a lack of expertise in the DES and its predecessor, the Ministry of Education, and partly because of a tradition of leadership from the National Union of Teachers in an undefined but nevertheless quite powerful alliance with the Joint Four, there was a genuine partnership, in which the government had to take account of the teachers' wishes over a wide area and accord to them a very substantial majority shareholding within the school curriculum. But the teachers' lobby also became fatally weakened during the 1970s. The crowding up of teachers' training to cope with the bulge, coupled with the subsequent erosion of teachers' salaries in the Barber boom, all coming in the aftermath of the student revolt of 1968, left a trail of accusations that teachers were no longer delivering the goods to the community as they had in the past. 'Teachers couldn't teach' was the accusation, and in some cases it was correct. During the years of overcrowding they had been trained too feebly and too fast, and then all of a sudden they were paid well under the market rate for the job. Some urban authorities were scouring the streets at home and abroad for teachers. Inevitably a minority were drawn into the schools who could not cope, but could not be removed either. Suddenly teachers, who for decades had earned a very high place in the sympathies of the public, found themselves demoted in public esteem. Their unions were perceived as interested in financial rewards rather than professional competence; a small number of the profession left to found the Professional Association of Teachers (PAT). The war between the National Union of Teachers (NUT) and the National Association of Schoolmasters (NAS) went on; and the question began to be asked by politicians why should the teachers be allowed to maintain their exclusive control of the curriculum? Politicians of both the main parties tended to answer the question in the affirmative. Teachers remained partners in the system, but at a very much reduced level. The events of 1968, which eroded respect for the value of education as a whole, had lost them that 'clinical status' which they had built up over the decades and which most of the other professions managed to hang on to. By 1979, like the LEAs, they were a weakened force within the education system and parliamentary lobbying tended to fill the gap.

The churches (which effectively meant the Church of England and the Roman Catholics) were also no longer the power in the land which once they had been. The 1944 Act gave them the responsibility for finding half the capital expenditure they needed in exchange for being installed as formal partners within the new system. The 1944 settlement which enjoined that every child in the realm should daily sing a hymn and say a prayer and receive weekly instruction in religion was also meant to give meaning and force to this partnership. But then two things happened. First, their 50 per cent capital grant inexorably rose to 85 per cent because they – and in particular the fertile Catholics – could not possibly find the money out of their own resources to cope with the birth rate bulge; and simultaneously, the other religious provisions of the 1944 settlement fell little by little into desuetude. Morning assembly either became secular or disappeared altogether and religious education – the only statutory subject on the curriculum – became the worst taught. So the churches became beleaguered and increasingly junior partners. By 1980 they were in no position to shore up a genuine pluralist educational partnership either.

In this situation, with the traditional partners weakened, dismembered, or split, one might have expected the secretary of state and the DES to have expanded proportionately in power and influence. But in fact nothing of the kind took place. The DES was subject to many of the same pressures under which the local authorities laboured, with the Treasury fixing the budget and then the Department of the Environment, in effect, doing so all over again; and since under the 1944 Act it could not fund local authorities directly, it had to watch helplessly as the Departments of Employment and Industry did so and took over what should have been the education budget. The DES suffered from the additional handicap that it became, almost by tradition, a ministerial dustbin. It became a recipient of a succession of weak Cabinet ministers (and junior ones) who gained office because of what they were expected *not* to achieve rather than the reverse. Weak ministers assisted the

Treasury in holding down public expenditure. (Edward Boyle used a different image; he advised me on one occasion to get out of the specialism because it was the 'graveyard' of politics.) True, from the mid-1970s onwards there was an increasingly successful attempt by the DES to move into the curricular gap left by the teachers. But it was a messy affair which disturbed the partnership to its core, and at first caused more trouble than it was worth.

So by the early 1980s the old partnership was crumbling. One reason why it was in worse shape than it might have been was the lack of any mediating educational forum, where the partners could sort out their complaints. The 1944 Act had made provision for this in section 2 with the words: 'There shall be a central Advisory Committee.' But Labour, under pressure from the civil servants, had decided in the late 1960s that the committee was a nuisance and closed it down after the Plowden Report; and the (illegal) aftermath was continued by all subsequent governments. So the vacuum was complete by the time the Conservatives won the 1979 general election – weak partners and no mediating body in the middle.

It was into this vacuum that the Select Committee effectively stepped. The origin of the new comprehensive system of Select Committees set up in 1979 was a curious and tortuous one. Michael Foot had set up a Procedure Committee in 1976 (when he was Leader of the House) hoping to smother the idea, but it was this committee, supposedly packed to kill the idea, which eventually recommended it. Meanwhile the Conservatives were looking for some policy to balance their contention that under Labour Britain was in danger of becoming a corporate state run by the trade unions. (Never in fact a serious possibility.) So they advocated the Select Committee system in their 1977 manifesto, declaring that: 'Parliament and no other body should stand at the centre of the nation's affairs.' Few members of the new Conservative government were enthusiastic; but Norman St John-Stevas was and used his position as Leader of the House to set up the system before any of his colleagues could sabotage it. Then the Conservatives opted for the chairmanships they wanted, leaving to the Opposition 'unimportant' ones like Education, Health, Housing and Transport. Thus it was that by the end of 1979 I found myself chairman of the Education Select Committee, a body with the potential to command substantial authority within and over the traditional education partnership and to play an important part in helping to establish a new English education consensus.

It started with advantages over the old Central Advisory Council. Its members had security of tenure for the full five years of the Parliament. It had an independent body of clerks who were employed by, and responsible to, not the DES but the House of Commons. It had powers to supplement the clerks, in theory to an unlimited extent, by calling on whatever educational expertise there was in the country which it wished to employ. So though it never became an education system 'partner' in the traditional sense, it had the potential to re-create some of the old partnership and to reassure the old partners that there was an institution in being that could prevent the power of government becoming absolute.

It is probably too early to pronounce definitively on the committee's influence; but it is important to understand the role of the committee not so much in terms of its formal powers, but rather in terms of the aims and objectives which I, at any rate, set myself and with which I suspect most of my colleagues also sympathized.

The primary role of the committee was simply to be there, ready to ask searching questions in public, as soon as the right moment came. No minister or civil servant could take any action, without pausing first to think how that action might shape up under scrutiny from the committee. Almost its most important role was, as the lawyers say, 'in terrorem'.

Secondly, it was a positive boost for the DES civil servants and inspectors. Sinking morale is the most serious infectious disease from which departments of state can suffer – and the DES was suffering seriously in 1979. There were occasional complaints from ministers that we were putting an unwarrantable burden of work upon the DES. I knew the reverse to be the truth. The fact that their actions were being discussed and talked about in the highest forum in the land was a positive incentive to them for more effective work – even if it did mean that from time to time they had to be scrutinized in public about that work.

Thirdly, it was a boost to the partners as a whole – the teachers, the local authorities and the churches. Though each of them kept their traditional direct access to the minister, if that failed, they could always brief the Select Committee and see whether the power of scrutiny, publicity and persuasion in Parliament would work better results.

Fourthly, we became an extremely important extra conduit of educational information and news for the press. In the 1960s almost every daily paper had an education correspondent, often two of them. By 1980 the number was falling; I believe that it might have dropped still further had it not been for the public sessions we held, the briefings which I and others gave in advance of them and the general interest aroused by the regular scrutiny to which ministers and civil servants were subjected.

Finally, through our public sessions, the recommendations in our reports and private contacts (of which there were many) we were able to present to ministers a menu of sensible, 'non-party' courses of action for them to follow. To a greater or lesser degree the creation of the National Advisory Body, legislation for local authority direct funding, the publication of HM Inspectorate annual reports and the shift from norm- to criterion-referencing in examinations all have the influence of the Select Committee behind them. So did the quite marked change in the DES towards openness about their activities at all levels.

The above is a list of the positive influences of the committee. But we also stopped the government making serious mistakes through regular and sometimes aggressive scrutiny of prospective policies. Had there not been a Select Committee, both students' loans (instead of grants) and school vouchers might well have got off the ground and then collapsed in ignominious failure. With the prospect of Select Committee scrutiny at every point, it simply was not worth the candle.

During the period of four years while the committee was in operation the education budget suffered regular annual cuts. There was little that we as a

Select Committee could do about these – except try to make explicit what was happening and how it was affecting standards in the schools. But though we could not stop the cuts, we made it easier through publicity at our sessions and the publication of the HMI reports for others to mitigate their effects. The fact that a national argument developed about the connection between education standards and education expenditure was almost entirely due to the efforts of the Select Committee. So the Select Committee fell into the national role of a consensus-producing body – in touch with government, the media and all the pressure groups and able, on a number of occasions, to work out formulae, which government was not willing to and the pressure groups, individually, were not able to. We had the additional advantage that we could stray over the departmental boundaries of 'education', for example, summoning to give evidence David Young and officials of the Manpower Services Commission (MSC) to explain how the Youth Training Scheme (YTS) and the Technical and Vocational Education Initiative (TVEI) fitted in to education policy. Through their four-year existence all the Select Committees developed 'trading' relations of this kind throughout their four years of existence, each allowing others to invade their territory when it seemed sensible. The Education Committee inquired into the MSC, the Home Office Committee looked at multi-ethnic education, the Health Committee looked at higher education for medical manpower, and so on. We were far less proprietorial about departmental 'territory' than were government departments. Sir Keith Joseph's new enthusiasm for the 'practical curriculum' had much of its origins in the all-party recommendations of the Select Committee.

So the Education Select Committee is not the only House of Commons body with something to say about education; nor have the new Select Committees a monopoly of scrutiny powers. The Public Accounts Committee (PAC) is the most senior of all the Commons committees and has a very specific role – to ensure that public money is spent on what it is meant to be spent on and accounted for properly. Moreover, the comptroller and auditor-general has powers which the staff of other Select Committees do not have: he can go into government departments and look at the books. For this reason all departments tend to take the PAC more seriously than the other committees; they tend to react to its reports rather more rapidly. But because it is fundamentally interested in money rather than policy, from time to time it gets its lines tangled with departmental Select Committees. We recommended an increase in the 'home fee' element of financing higher education because we felt it was one way of identifying institutions which could actually recruit students; the PAC recommended a decrease to discourage them from recruiting over the unenforceable University Grants Committee (UGC) norm. The DES took no notice of us, but succumbed to the Public Accounts Committee. So although the advent of the Education Select Committee has added a new dimension to partnership, it only represents part of 'Parliament's' point of view – if indeed that phrase can be held to mean anything at all. It is seldom that the report of a Select Committee is actually debated on the floor of the House of Commons. There are, from time to time, little flashes of resentment that the nine MPs (now eleven) can represent a 'parliamentary' view. I have never accepted this. However small the sample, the arguments within the Select Committee were almost always a microcosm of the sort of arguments which would have taken place within a larger sample of MPs. With all its inadequacies, the Select Committee was the first forum in which any sort of dialogue between Parliament and the world of education became possible.

So far we have mainly discussed the changing role of Parliament, brought about by the introduction of the Select Committee, and the extent to which we thus influenced ministerial decisions. But the attitude of ministers has always been subject to a range of other influences – some ideological but most of them economic. The past five years have been unprecedentedly contradictory ones for Secretaries of State for Education. Their duties under the law to ensure the provision of a decent education system have constantly clashed with duties to the Chancellor of the Exchequer, denying local authorities the resources to provide an adequate system. As has already been noted, this has put enormous strain on their traditional relationship with LEAs. Had it just been left to education ministers, the relationship would not have deteriorated to such a low point. But as soon as the total control of local authority expenditure in general became a tenet of government policy, the traditional relationship as mapped out in the 1944 Act was doomed. It will not, indeed cannot, ever be the same again. Britain is now in the process of going irretrievably centralist, without any of the French techniques or traditions of making that particular political approach work; I believe it will be disastrous for services far beyond education.

The most obvious phenomenon of this cult of centralism is the use of the MSC (a Heath creation) increasingly to supervise the training of Britain's 'non-academic' adolescents. All the signs are that this will create a quite new form of 'partnership' at the further education level, in which the MSC will seek to be the senior body. It will need all the political effort of the LEAs to maintain the locus in local government; if they do, it will be at the expense of the involvement of the DES.

However, it would be wrong to pronounce the cult of centralism as the only one in this political climate. Simultaneously, there is at work a decentralizing cult, that of privatization. Hitherto it has only touched education at the edges – the assisted places scheme, the encouragement of the private school sector in other ways. But it remains, potentially, a greater threat to the traditional partnership than the centralism of the MSC and the attack on local government.

The 1944 Act was a balance: central policy and central arbitration for disputes, local administration and local elbow-room for development; yet the two were linked – organically, legislatively and administratively. Two random examples are the former Ministry of Education which had to approve every short-list for the post of chief education officer (CEO), and the percentage grant system which operated before 1959 and positively encouraged nudges and winks in particular policy directions.

There can be no such organic relationship between the new DES centralism and the new privatization. It is true that attempts to put such a relationship together have been made in the past. Lord Fleming in 1944, and

Sir John Newsom in 1967, presided over attempts to produce one; both reports were careful, contrived efforts to produce a new English public concordat which ran right across the social spectrum from the Old Etonian privileged to the poor of the cities. But the animal instincts of each entrenched camp ensured that both failed – partly because the radical left smelt a large and dangerous rat, but mostly because insufficient concessions had been made to tempt the private schools to give up the privilege of selecting their own mix of students to enter that rat race towards Oxbridge they prized so much. That quest for a consensus is, I suspect, at an end for ever in England. Future attempts to cut the Gordian knot will be more violent either through the Conservatives regaining faith in vouchers (a battle, for the time being, lost) or through a more radical Labour government than we have yet seen making such private schools as it wishes to preserve an offer they feel unable to refuse.

That said, the present paradoxical pattern of simultaneous privatization and centralism is dangerous to the central concept of the 1944 Act – a *national* service. What we have is an increasingly divided service, driven by private economic forces. Privatized education for the middle class, whether in the overtly 'private' sector or in those increasingly 'parentally privatized' areas of local authority education, and MSC 'national service' for the rest. Between these sectors there is no organic relationship, no partnership – just a class gulf.

Could the Select Committee have done more to emphasize the need for partnership across the divide and the dangers of this split? Perhaps. But it would have been difficult. At the end of the day the Select Committee was a coalition device rather than a consensus one. It was possible to build, within the political currents of the committee, a majority to hold the line here, even unanimity for a particular reform there. A package of building-blocks could be produced in a report which, in the end, possessed more the appearance of consensus than the reality. Any attempt to state a broad principle of the kind which commanded genuine unanimity in 1944 was in danger of failing the test of acid scrutiny from left and right. It was easier either to stick to the building of concrete majorities for concrete proposals or to find some exquisite form of words to cover up the failure to build such a concrete majority. My personal favourite in this latter category was our unanimous judgement on a single system of examinations at 16+; in the end we reached a formula innocuous enough to be assented to by left and right with equal fervour:

> Reservations have been expressed which reflect the very real problems inherent in the introduction of this new examination. Pilot schemes are already in operation. We believe that there is substance in the concern of our witnesses and others about these problems, and we urge the Secretary of State to ensure, after wide consultation, that what develops is a coherent examination system, giving full opportunities to children of all aptitudes and abilities.

So the power of the committee to mediate a new consensus should not be exaggerated to global proportions. On particular issues, yes – in wider, philosophical terms, very much more difficult. Because there was always a temptation to gloss over issues we could not resolve, we were from time to time guilty of knowingly colluding with incompatibilities.

But that, after all, is the reality of politics as the art of the possible. In the end the climate and the philosophy in which legislation is cast is determined not by grand pronouncements, but rather by the flow of the intellectual tide. By building a little dam in one part of the stream and opening it up in another, we were able, in my opinion, collusion or no, to shift the tide just a little towards faith in an education system, publicly provided in a partnership between government and other institutions, as the cornerstone of English education; and by receiving evidence and producing our reports in a spirit of openness which shone out in contrast to the way most of the institutions of *government* conducted themselves, we in Parliament were able to lift to some extent the morale of those others in England who also believe in that partnership and wish to preserve it. The Select Committee was a worthwhile exercise and I hope it continues to be so.

2

The Department of Education and Science

EDWARD SIMPSON

The traditional model for the role of the centre in the education system in England is that it provides a framework within which other agencies and people run the schools and colleges. Or rather several kinds of framework. There is a framework of institutions – some (like the universities and the Council for National Academic Awards, CNAA) created by Royal Charter, others (like the LEAs themselves) by Parliament or (like the polytechnics or the Advisory Council for the Supply and Education of Teachers, ACSET) by government. There is a framework of law, and another of financial support and financial restraint, which Parliament and the government of the day each have a hand in providing. Most difficult to define precisely, sometimes contentious but indisputably recognized both in law and custom, is a framework of objectives and priorities which the Secretary of State for Education sets out in the government's name. In the best of circumstances this will be offered and accepted as a framework of leadership by the local education service. These frameworks are loose ones. They do not by themselves determine the kind of central–local relationship that will operate within them.

The form of the relationship which was well understood through the period of major expansion in the 1960s was at its zenith with the publication in 1972 of the White Paper, *Education: A Framework for Expansion*. The use of the word 'framework' in the title was not accidental, and each of the kinds of framework mentioned above can be found within it. The White Paper set out a new balance of interrelated priorities for the schools: a carefully defined diminution in the rate of improvement in teacher staffing; a switch of priority to primary schools; and a rapid expansion of nursery education. It affirmed its view of the purposes of higher education, put figures to its judgement of the logistics necessary to fulfil them and indicated the institutional changes that should follow – in particular, from the reduction in the numbers to be trained as teachers and the improvement in their professional preparation. The overall pattern of these developments was woven together over an illustrative ten-year period, and costed to be contained within a rate of growth of expenditure in real terms which was consistent with the government's forward planning at that time.

The proposed new balance of priorities had been extensively canvassed beforehand, notably in a 'what would you do if...?' speech by the secretary of state at the conference of the Association of Education Committees the previous summer. It was confidently expected to command assent, especially in local education authority (LEA) circles, and did so.

But the response to the White Paper was not wholly favourable. In particular, it was criticized, mainly from outside the educational world itself, for having so concentrated on logistics as to exclude consideration of the nature and quality of what lay at the heart of the matter: what was taught, and how. The Prime Minister (Edward Heath) was one of the first then addressing the January 1973 Conference of the Society of Education Officers within a few weeks of the White Paper's publication:

> Those of us who have been concerned in Parliament with the problems of education have concentrated too much in recent years on organisation and finance, on bricks and mortar. I believe that most people in this country are more concerned with what is taught in schools than with how schools are organised.

The department was sensitive to this criticism, but cautious too, remembering the storm that had greeted its establishing, some ten years earlier, a small Curriculum Study Group on the lines of the earlier and admired Development Group for Educational Building (which also contained a significant curricular component). The stimulus to move to some form of action on standards soon overcame this caution and, by the end of 1974, the Assessment of Performance Unit was in train and the permanent secretary at the OECD Education Committee 'did wonder aloud whether the Government could continue to debar itself from what had been termed "the secret garden" of the curriculum'. The centre of gravity of the department's concern was on the move.

Wider events, however, pulled the foundations from under the logistics of the 1972 White Paper. The Middle East war and subsequent oil crisis cancelled the White Paper on public expenditure of January 1974 and cuts in public expenditure plans were substituted; and it was recognized that birth numbers after 1971 were not going to recover but fall more steeply. Taken together, these developments of 1974 were to lead the secretary of state and the department into some very unfamiliar territory.

The concern over the content of school education developed quickly, and extended to critical examination of the aims that the schools set themselves and the standards of performance that they achieved. Mr Callaghan's Ruskin College speech in 1976 called for a public debate in the light of which a Green Paper, *Education in Schools*, was issued in July 1977.

The chapter headings of the Green Paper show how far the centre of gravity of the department's concern had shifted. Standards of achievement were discussed and new work proposed on means of assessing them at national, school and individual pupil level. But the new central concern was with the curriculum. The secretary of state proposed, after further consultations with the LEAs and the teachers' representatives, to ask all LEAs to conduct a review of curricular arrangements in their areas. In the following November Circular 14/77 set this in train.

The Green Paper also dealt extensively with the new developments that were required in connection with teachers. Initial training and in-service training were familiar ground in which to advance new proposals. But the Green Paper went on to wholly new territory in discussing what would be required of LEAs in the management of the teacher force as it contracted. In discussing such questions as redeployment and the selection of teachers for premature retirement (or even, in the last resort, for redundancy or dismissal) the department was into areas which had previously been the LEAs' exclusive concern.

In the following years ministers and the department pressed further into both the curriculum and the teacher employment areas, publishing *A Framework for the Curriculum* and devoting much time and attention to the problems LEAs would face in maintaining curriculum balance and appropriately qualified teaching staffs in schools as their pupil numbers fell. Neither story is yet concluded. But so far the central–local relationship seems to have adapted well to its extension into this very new territory. The ministerial initiatives have been consistent with LEA responsibilities for curriculum and for teacher employment. Understandable concern that a centrally imposed curriculum might be intended has found no ground to take root in, and the 'framework' concept still fits the new developments.

One feature common to the curriculum and the teacher employment work is worth noting. Both lie outside those branches of the department which traditionally have territorial organizations linking them with individual LEAs. It follows that LEA members and officers will know of the secretary of state's and the department's activities here in more general terms, and rather more at arm's length, than when, say, policies on the building or reorganization or closure of schools are discussed with all the immediacy of concrete local cases. A new kind of relationship might be required if more direct discussion were to be needed with individual LEAs on, say, their curricular arrangements or the appropriateness of a teaching staff's qualifications as reported by HM Inspectors following formal inspection.

More serious difficulties have arisen in the central–local relationship where the change from expansion to contraction is the governing factor. During the period of expansion many objectives were expressed in logistics terms and the desired direction of advance was not in dispute; only on the pace of advance was there room for argument. The relationship reflected the assumption that the LEA would provide the impetus to build or to recruit, responding to visible local needs, and that the department's role was to moderate the pace as required by overall financial limits or fair shares. In contraction the main objective may no longer be held in common. Those concerned only to forward the education service's interests may see falling demand as an opportunity for further qualitative improvement, which the government with their wider financial responsibilities will feel obliged not just to moderate, but to deny. The former will see no visible local need to provide an impetus downward; and the latter can initiate no reduction on their own. This kind of difficulty naturally shows most clearly in the financial arrangements between the government and the LEAs.

In law the major change from an education grant to a general or block grant had taken place in 1958. Opponents of that change had warned that it would bring the end of the integral education service we had hitherto known. At first, and indeed for the next fifteen years or so, it seemed that those fears had been groundless, for the change seemed to be more of form than of substance. The LEAs and department alike could confidently identify an education service component within the block grant, based on expenditure assumptions they could both accept, and guidance on expenditure levels and priorities continued to be given by the secretary of state and broadly followed.

The year 1975 marked the beginning of the end of that familiar scene. In the public expenditure White Paper of January 1975 expenditure by local authorities was everywhere subsumed within the respective expenditure totals for the services to which they contributed; the total of planned spending by local authorities was nowhere even added up. Under the cross-examination of the economic crisis, however, the record of growth of local authority expenditure – some 7–8 per cent in real terms in each of the three years since 1971/2 – attracted adverse attention in the Chancellor's budget statement and in successive circulars. Alongside the traditional consideration of individual services and their costs, a new consideration – the level of local authority expenditure as a whole – had come on the political stage: (1) the tension between responsibility for individual services and responsibility for their overall cost and financing is a familiar one in any organization; in relation to local authority spending the problem for the government has the additional subtlety that the ministers responsible for the respective local authority services do not actually run them, nor do the ministers concerned with their financing control either their costs or the income available. So there is (2) a second tension – if the government attaches high importance to restraining the total of local authority expenditure, which cannot be secured without the co-operation of the authorities themselves, can they expect still to express their policies and priorities on services, and their guidance to be followed, as before? – this second question is critical to the central–local relationship in the education service.

The ministers with major concern, and frequently important statutory duties, for services provided by local authorities are education, health and social services, and the Home Secretary. The Secretary of State for the Environment, though also in part a services minister, is the minister for local government affairs generally, and for local government finance in particular, and thus more concerned with expenditure totals than with individual services, as also are Treasury ministers. Under our system of Cabinet government important differences between these ministerial interests can only be resolved at (or just a little below) Cabinet level, which leaves scope for what local authorities have often called 'government speaking with two voices' and what the Layfield Committee criticized as lack of a coherent approach. The December 1975 rate support grant (RSG) circular certainly backed it both ways:

> From an economic point of view, the Government's major concern is with the total level of local authority expenditure ... The importance the Government attach to priorities ranges from areas where the decisions of local authorities need to be related to a clear framework of policies announced by Central Government, to those where Central Government have little or no policy interest. For example, education and the police fall at one end of this range ... The paragraphs on individual services below ... go into greater detail for those policies for which the Government carry a high degree of direct responsibility.

This entrenchment of the Secretary of State for Education's position was, however, short-lived. The government continued to move in the direction of trading its guidance role on services and priorities for a larger voice in total local authority expenditure. The February 1976 public expenditure White Paper quoted the total local authority expenditure in England and Wales in a 'special analysis' annex, and that of January 1979 treated it as an expenditure block in the main text. In the same month's RSG circular the service paragraphs had been demoted to 'considerations the Government had in mind in arriving at the settlement' with no visible injunction to heed them. The ascendancy of concern for the total over concern for the services was secured. Mr Joel Barnett, then Chief Secretary to the Treasury, has written of this change that 'It was more than a bit hard on the Secretary of State for Education, who would then have to take the blame for the inadequacy of education expenditure'.

This shift away from expressed government concern for individual services was perhaps not entirely unwelcome in local authority circles. The growth of corporate management styles in many authorities following the 1974 reorganization, with chief executives taking central responsibility in some at the expense of chief officers for services, was a parallel movement. The Consultative Council on Local Government Finance (CCLGF), created in 1975, showed in its title where its main concern lay; and local authority members chiefly associated with the education service have been under-represented in its membership. The Association of Education Committees (AEC), which for some time had been under pressure from the associations representing local authorities as a whole, succumbed and was wound up in 1976; the Council of Local Education Authorities (CLEA) which the main associations had created in 1974 was not intended to speak and act on behalf of the local education service alone as the AEC did, and has not done so. Taken together, these changes reinforced the government's move progressively to concentrate its dialogue with local government on one subject – money – and along one axis – that between the Secretary of State for the Environment and the local authorities' corporate leaders. Discussions along the traditional axis between the Secretary of State for Education and the local authorities' education leaders, deprived of its financial aspects, was correspondingly weakened.

The Conservative government which came to power in 1979 moved further in the same direction. An early symbolic change was the abolition of the annual rate support grant circular as part of the cutback of circulars and other communications; since 1979 the government have addressed no views directly to local authorities about the services that they provide or the priorities between them. The major change was, however, the introduction of block grant in 1981 and its subsequent modifications.

It seemed at the earlier stages that a degree of government guidance on services and priorities might be reinstated through the new concept of 'grant-related expenditure' (GRE): that is, the level of expenditure for each service that each local authority should (in the government's opinion) incur in order to fulfil the government's policy assumptions in its particular local circumstances. But the government made it clear in various ways that they did not intend the GRE figures for particular services to be interpreted in that way; and since 1983 the importance of GRE in determining shares of grant has been overwhelmed by the importance of 'targets' derived not from local spending needs, but from previous spending practice. With this development, the separation – within government – of responsibility for services from the responsibility for their financing was made still wider. With important measures still before Parliament at the time of writing, the story is yet far from complete.

The Green Paper, *Alternatives to Domestic Rates*, of December 1981 canvassed the possibility of an education block grant regime under which the government's financial contribution to the cost of the local education service would have been calculated separately and paid through a system sharing many of the main block grant features but tailored to the generally more orthodox spending patterns of those local authorities which were LEAs. Had this been pursued, one result would have been to restore the financial aspects of the education service to the axis of discussion between the Secretary of State for Education and the local authorities' education leaders. It is debatable whether the influences exerted from the centre on local spending on education would then have been stronger or weaker than those now exerted by the present block grant system and its accompanying 'penalties'. But their effects would certainly have been less erratic than now for LEAs and also, to greater or less degree, related (as the present effects are not) to the Secretary of State for Education's thinking about the local education service. While it remained on the table this possibility gave rise to some lively and informative debate. Its ending was untidy: simply the absence of further reference to the matter in the 1983 White Paper.

The development of another strand in the relationship is closely linked with the question of in-service training for teachers. It has long been a commonplace that the teacher force should devote a bigger fraction of its time and energy to its own improvement through in-service training. The 'framework' White Paper of 1972, for example, adopted as government policy for the years ahead the 3 per cent fraction which the James Committee had recommended as a desirable first stage. By 1976 in the very different context of both economic and demographic retrenchment there was little to show; yet the need was the sharper if, in addition to self-improvement, the teacher force was to be reduced without unacceptable distortions. In the rate support grant settlement for 1977/8 an additional £7 million of expenditure on teacher employment was built in to the assumed total of local authority spending on education; the extra teachers employed would permit a gradual expansion of in-service training and a start on systematic induction of new entrants. And the corresponding public expenditure White Paper of February 1977 extended this forward to a proposed fourfold increase by 1981. The collective response of the LEAs was to employ all the additional teachers envisaged in 'the Government plans (indeed, in 1977–78 more of them than the Government had provided for) but without increasing the in-service effort: giving higher priority to putting more teachers into the classrooms to meet the "diseconomies of contraction" for which no provision was yet made in the Government's plans'.

The secretary of state and the department took this disagreement very seriously. It was not a matter of political difference, nor of contrary educational objectives: all were agreed on the importance of expanding in-service training. These were circumstances where normally a strong central lead on priorities could expect to be broadly followed. Moreover, the failure to follow the central guidance made the secretary of state vulnerable, in the now fierce competition for resources within government, to the damaging argument that extra money for education might only be diverted away from the purpose the government intended it for; so better deploy it to another service where its application could be assured.

The issue stayed at the forefront throughout 1977. At the consultative council and in meeting the Council of Local Education Authorities (CLEA) leaders the secretary of state argued for a degree of specific grant support for urgent national priorities, and in particular for in-service training; and in May the Green Paper on local government finance (in response to the Layfield Report) formally canvassed the proposition in more general terms. In the course of resisting these overtures the CLEA leaders offered the alternative of a gentleman's agreement to give generous consideration to the government's views on spending priorities. Neither approach could bridge the confidence gap that had opened up, and both foundered.

Through all the fluctuations of public expenditure expectations that followed in 1978 and later years two features stood firm. Successive secretaries of state made clear their conviction that room could – and should – be found for more and better in-service training within the teacher strength available; but equally stubbornly the fraction of release has stuck just above the 1 per cent level; leaving a heavy share of the profession's self-improvement to be borne by the better-motivated teachers in their own time. A move towards dislodging the impasse – or at least to crumble its edges – came with the secretary of state's announcement in 1982 of a limited scheme of government grant support for the release of teachers for further training in certain priority areas. By coincidence, the cost of the first phase of the scheme in the 1983/4 school year is set at £7 million: its success (or not) in achieving its objectives will be important both for the in-service training programme and as a limited experiment in the evolution of the central–local relationship.

Differences between government and LEAs over what was possible (to say nothing of what would be desirable) inevitably became more widespread and more contentious as the pace of the required contraction of the service quickened. But one administrative innovation has at least helped to avoid compounding confusion with contention. This is now familiarly known as the ESG(E).

The ESG(E) is the Expenditure Steering Group (Education), one of the series of such steering groups created under the auspices of the Consultative Council on Local Government Finance in 1976. The local authority side comprises officers and advisers of the local authority associations, drawn from treasurer's as well as education departments. The DES and HM Inspectorate are represented, on the other side of the table, at deputy secretary and under secretary level. A senior Treasury officer attends as an observer. The chairman is one of the DES deputy secretaries.

The steering groups' main task is to assess each year the implications for their respective services of the government's latest expenditure proposals, normally those in the public expenditure White Paper published in the early months of the year. Their reports to the consultative council, generally compiled between April and July, carry the annual cycle forward from the culmination of one public expenditure round to the beginning of the next rate support grant settlement.

Among the steering groups the ESG(E) has established a particularly strong corporate existence and has grown to fulfil a wider role than its bare terms of reference would require. Topical questions with expenditure implications are jointly explored there whenever it is convenient for both sides to do so, with all the advantages of thorough familiarity with the background figures (and of the wary camaraderie born of earlier tussles) that regular meetings and a strong and exceptionally numerate secretariat can provide. The ESG(E) decides little more than the content of its own reports, but meetings between education ministers and the local authority education leaders can often be more succinct and productive (and less prone to misunderstanding and confusion) when ESG(E) has first prepared the ground.

Preparing the ground does not, in this instance, mean compromising or concealing differences. On the contrary, the ESG(E) style is to distinguish the views of the two sides clearly when analysis and discussion have established that they are indeed opposed (as during several years, for instance, over the rate of closure of surplus school places that might be considered practicable).

But in the main their reports (incorporating their joint assessments, presented to both sides of the consultative council, without political direction from either) have been agreed ones, and correspondingly authoritative. Some have been stark; for example, the analysis in the ESG(E)'s July 1980 report (subsequently published) of the gaps between the levels of teaching costs and non-teaching costs proposed in the March 1980 public expenditure White Paper on the one hand, and what would be needed to maintain 1978/9 standards on the other; and of the scale of compulsory redundancies that the plans implied. None of this could diminish the deep disagreements between the secretary of state and the LEA leaders over the rate of contraction of the local education service that the government sought, nor make the resulting friction less inevitable. But the ability to continue to work jointly, in the

ESG(E) in this contentious context helped to sustain confidence in the partnership when other factors were eroding it, and both sides have made clear the importance they attach to it.

Much erosion has been caused by leaks. In the government of education where so many parties have legitimate interests, much of the business consists in the striking of balances and bargains. Often the government's role is to act on behalf of the very wide but inactive majority ('the public interest') in making bargains with directly interested minority groups. Experience shows that the best, and most enduring, bargains are those reached by responsible representatives with knowledge of and respect for all sides' real and legitimate interests, but free from the distortions caused by playing to various galleries – or by barracking from them. In other words, in privacy.

It may be that this whole process – the leaks themselves, the publicity given to them and the changes in working practice adopted to counter their prevalence – has done more than anything else to undermine the mutual confidence and trust on which the central–local partnership has been, and requires to be, founded.

It is unprofitable to debate whether the partnership is now at its lowest ebb, for there is no scale on which to compare its present state with, say, that of 1963 when the secretary of state overthrew a Burnham agreement on the grounds not of its cost, but of the educational rationale of its distribution, and imposed by statute a different distribution of the money on the teachers and their employing authorities alike. On that occasion the way out of the pit lay through the tough three-cornered negotiation by the leaders of the respective interests (in privacy) of an agreed new balance of influence and powers. The crucial question now is not whether the partnership finds itself in worse repair than then, but whether the means still exist, following the changes that this chapter has sketched, of re-establishing it in an agreed, respected and durable form.

3

The Local Authority Associations

JACK SPRINGETT

There have been local authority associations concerned with the interests of metropolitan and rural local education authorities for a very long time. The Association of Municipal Corporations (AMC) was founded in 1873 and included in its scope the former county boroughs. A hundred years later it was dissolved when the Association of Metropolitan Authorities (AMA) was formed. The County Councils Association (CCA) would have celebrated its centenary in 1989 but was dissolved on the formation of the Association of County Councils (ACC) in 1973. A third association, the Council of Local Education Authorities (CLEA), is a creature of the ACC and the AMA, and provides a forum in which representatives of all LEAs meet and on occasion speak effectively for the education service as a whole.

No account of the present role of the associations can ignore the history of the rise and fall of the CLEA's predecessor, the Association of Education Committees (AEC). The AEC was founded in 1904 to fill a vacuum left when School Boards were dissolved under the 1902 Act and the School Boards Association was wound up. It rose to real significance after 1944, when the education committees of all the LEAs (now the county boroughs and the counties) joined in membership. For some thirty years it provided a strong, single voice for the education service. During the whole of this time Sir William (now Lord) Alexander was its powerful general secretary. It provided the secretariats for the management panels of the Burnham Committees and played a significant role in every major education development during that period. With the increased politicizing of the education service in the late 1960s, however, the internal strains set up by the desire to find a consensus in a single policy already were showing up. The AMC and CCA were jealous and resentful of its power, and particularly concerned that education alone among the local authority services was 'privileged' to enjoy a national body representative of service committees.

The creation of the CLEA was the price which the AMA and ACC paid to pursue their policy of bringing the AEC to an end. In November 1973 the two associations issued a joint statement. Significantly that statement made reference to education being seen as 'part of the totality of local government' and to the view that it was 'illogical for an authority to be in membership of two national organizations each concerned with the same function'. It referred, however, to the establishment of 'strong education committees' and the need for both associations to provide staff which would 'include officers of top ranking educational experience'. (Up to then the AMA, unlike the ACC, had not employed a professional education officer.) However, it also reserved to the AMA and ACC 'major educational policy' and 'parliamentary activities', together with 'discussions at ministerial level', except those 'arising from' association activities. A full reading of the document highlights the determination to keep the CLEA as a subservient body. It is not surprising that, at times, in recent years officers attending CLEA meetings have felt their members were constrained to extreme caution by the need to keep one eye looking over their shoulder on the policy committees of their parent associations.

The constitution of the CLEA however, whatever its inherent weaknesses, at least faces up to the reality (which the AEC did not face up to in its last years) that there can be, and often is, a deep conflict of interest between members of the AMA and ACC. Such a conflict often appears on political lines, but in fact it arises from the markedly different problems of the inner urban areas of social deprivation and the shire counties. When a genuine conflict of interests arises in this way, it is no use disguising the fact that there *is* no 'single voice' for the education service and the CLEA is both practically and constitutionally unable to act effectively. However, where the policy interests came together, the CLEA has played an effective and important role. Perhaps the most obvious in recent years was shown in the united opposition to central government's early proposals for control of the non-university sector of higher education which led to the establishment of the National Advisory Body (NAB). Also the CLEA's function in staging an annual conference at which representatives of all LEAs meet for public discussion of current issues – with the secretary of state attending as a guest speaker – is not to be lightly dismissed.

However, this question of the influence and power of the CLEA begs the question as to what in fact the parent bodies can themselves deliver. In truth they have no political power whatsoever – what they do is to exert great influence. They are essentially voluntary bodies, which as recent events have illustrated, the LEAs are free to join or not. However, it is significant that the LEAs have perceived the necessity for them for over a century – the one or two LEAs who have withdrawn membership in the last year or so might do well to study the lessons of history.

How do the associations exert their influence? They are essentially 'recognized' pressure groups, in the sense that they provide a means through which central government can formally and informally consult the LEAs as a whole and can secure representation of LEAs on both statutory and non-statutory bodies which have been set up by central government for the discharge of the process of managing the service at national level; for example, the Burnham Committees, the NAB, Youth Training Board and many others. The members – and officers – who act as the representatives of the associations can, however, only do so in so far as they retain the confidence of member LEAs. At times this sets up strains and certainly implies a need for members of the associations to keep in close touch with members of their constituent authorities.

The use of the associations as a means of consultation between central government and the LEAs is equally important. Consultation at member and officer level is frequent and few issues of national importance are settled without it. Nevertheless, the drift of central government from consensus politics is reflected in the education service, and there are several recent examples (see p. 34) of major decisions affecting education that have been taken without consultation with the associations in a way which would have been inconceivable a few years ago. However, the associations *have* been involved by central government in the national administrative bodies which have resulted from these decisions. It is significant that it is the teachers' associations which have lost out in this respect as the secretary of state deliberately has moved away from *representatives* nominated by the teachers' unions to *individuals* appointed by him after considering (and after rejecting) the names put forward by teachers' unions.

The consultative process operates at two levels. There are regular discussions between ministers and senior members of the associations. They are of great importance. They take place in an atmosphere of relative informality. There is no verbatim record and, on the whole, reality dominates over a party political attitudinization. In this respect they contrast sharply with the meetings of the Consultative Council on Local Government Finance (CCLGF), where the education voice at national or association level is seldom heard and which tend to comprise the delivery of politically founded set speeches of a general nature having little or no effect on the predictable outcome of the meeting. It was, for example, at a meeting with education ministers and members of the associations that the NAB structure was born, the secretary of state tabling a paper which on examination the association members found close to the CLEA's own proposals for the management of that sector. Paradoxically the fact that these discussions are often effective sometimes poses real problems for some members of the associations. The ultimate legislative power rests with central government, and for 'Opposition' association members in particular, their involvement at the consultative level more especially as representatives on national bodies can present a political dilemma. Thus members could have taken the view that they did not wish to be compromised by involvement in the NAB's difficult decisions, given central government's financial policies. But that would have removed their chance of influencing national policy – and they can in the case of the NAB point, for example, to the secretary of state's decision to add £20 million to the 'capped' pool for 1984/5 in the light of representations from the NAB committee. The political pressure on Opposition members to withdraw from NAB particularly from LEAs affected by the closure of some colleges was, however, considerable.

The shift of power to the centre which we are experiencing sharpens up this dilemma. Hitherto central government's intervention in the management at school level has been by exhortation and persuasion. Events since James Callaghan's Ruskin College speech – the 'great debate' followed by a wave of papers from the DES and HM Inspectors on the curriculum – have, however, now taken a new turn as central government takes new financial and controlling powers. Financial initiative was at first necessarily through other agencies – for instance, the massive education and training programmes for young people and adults funded through the Manpower Services Commission (MSC), the Technical and Vocational Education Initiative (TVEI) and subventions through the Department of Trade and Industry. More recently, the decision of the secretary of state to take into his own control 0.5 per cent of the education 'share' of block grant (as encapsulated in the Education (Grants and Awards) Act 1984) and the decision of the government to appropriate to the MSC a very substantial part of non-advanced further education (NAFE) spending as announced in the White Paper, *Training for Jobs*, mark the most significant changes in central–local relationships this century.

How can the associations react to these developments? Up to the Grants and Awards Act, they had even taken the view that it is better to influence such developments than to opt out on principle; hence participation in the Youth Training Board, presence on the Area Manpower Boards and discussions about the allocation of funds under the 1984 Act. They are aware that the secretary of state has created a powerful force for the central direction of the curriculum. The tripartite Schools Council is replaced by a force with very much greater resources under sole government control. Those resources far exceed the margin available to LEAs for curricular developments. It is perhaps not surprising that the secretary of state seems willingly to accept discussions with the associations as to their use. He is, after all, assuming a new accountability which he might otherwise eventually regret handing over to a successor government. However, *Training for Jobs* has strained relationships virtually to breaking point. By July 1984, months after its presentation in Parliament, there was still an adamant refusal on the part of the AMA at least to discuss its implementation, though the ACC appeared to be seeking ways of opening up discussions without abandoning its strongest opposition to the principle involved.

Both the story of the demise of the Schools Council and the method of announcement of the government's intentions with respect to what is now the 1984 Act and the White Paper, *Training for Jobs*, illustrate clearly central government abandonment of consultation and consensus and the decision to drop the principle of representation in favour of central government nomination.

After reluctantly co-operating with the Trenaman review of the Schools Council the associations broadly welcomed the ensuing report and registered with the DES their assumption that the secretary of state would, after considering the responses, consult further about whatever decision he had in mind. It was a vivid illustration of the changed central government view of the 'partnership' that his decision to withdraw support from the council was taken unilaterally and without prior warning for either of the other two partners involved – the associations and the teachers' unions. This was all the more extraordinary since the DES and the associations were equal funding partners in the Council. But the dilemma which faces the associations is illustrated by their decision to accept membership in the new curriculum and examination bodies which the secretary of state established.

So far we have concentrated on the consultation and representation effected by the associations at member level; they do, however, exert very considerable influence at officer level. Each association has a small professional officer team. Their effort is inevitably reactive rather than initiatory; but in addition, they are able to call on officers of their member authorities who have traditionally given their time generously to the associations. The DES welcome the interaction with officers of the associations and their advisers, including treasurers and solicitors and chief executives. It enables them to get the reactions at an early stage of 'practitioners' working in the field. The consultations at this level extend over the widest possible range of matters of which perhaps the most important is the Expenditure Steering Group (Education) ESG(E) (see pp. 36–9). The range covers proposed primary legislation draft statutory regulations and circulars but much of the consultation takes place at early 'formative' stages, and while the underlying central government policy drive may well be predetermined, there are many practical matters which can be shaped and amended by reasoned argument. For example, during the passage of the Education Act 1981 pressure from back-bench members caused ministers to consider amendments affording access by parents to professionals who had been involved in assessments of children's special educational needs. The original amendments were judged by officers in the association to be quite unworkable and subsequent changes make them less objectionable.

The officer-level consultations may serve as preparation for member meetings with ministers. At best they will result in an agreed paper setting out the issues and pointing up the potential areas of agreement and difference of view between the DES and the associations. Occasionally the views of the AMA and ACC will differ, and here again as with the preparation of papers leading up to (abortive) discussions concerning amendment or repeal of the Remuneration of Teachers Act in 1980, these areas can be identified in such a discussion document.

There is another underlying change in the relationship of government to the LEAs which has been illustrated by the flow of legislation and statutory instruments in recent years. Neither the member nor the officer discussion has diminished the zeal displayed by Parliament in legislating for the minutiae of the administrative process. Governments of both parties appear convinced that little that is good will occur in local government unless it is prescribed by them in great detail. In fact the complexity of the resulting legislation is such that it has been difficult even for specialist lawyers to keep up to date. Certainly the 1980 and 1981 Education Acts were no exception to this rule. Their final form bears witness to the limitations of the associations' consultative process. Both associations indeed have a considerable number of 'vice-presidents' in the House of Commons and the House of Lords, who are invited to propose amendments in the interests of the LEAs and briefed as to the underlying reasons for them, but this procedure has only limited effect. The oppressively bureaucratic and prescriptive detail of the 1981 Act is especially to be deplored as illustrative of Parliament's grandmotherly surveillance of the LEAs. It is in sad contrast to the history of LEA initiatives over the past years before they were effectively strangled by severe limitations on their cash resources. The LEAs' record in the development of special education and the outstanding achievement of the development of the public sector higher education system owe little to Parliament's prescriptive powers. It is sad to see younger LEA officers, whose memories are necessarily shorter, giving a welcome to prescriptive legislation as a means of pressurizing LEAs to 'improve' standards for which cash resources are lacking.

The work of the Expenditure Steering Group (Education) (ESG(E)) has already been referred to. The steady and subtle change in the relationship between central and local government is illustrated by the changes in the working of this group and its subgroups. When the expenditure steering groups for the various services were established, their formal purpose was to service the CCLGF which had itself been established to provide a forum for consultation between ministers and members of the associations about the overall level of local authority expenditure. Procedurally the expenditure steering groups prepare a report which is intended to inform members of both sides of the CCLGF about the resources required to pursue alternative policies – and the policy consequences of alternative levels of expenditure. In practice, the ESG(E)'s considerable influence over the years has been effected through channels other than the formal CCLGF machinery. The ESG(E) is composed entirely of officers on the local government side and officials of the DES (it is chaired by the deputy secretary with responsibility for finance) with representatives of the Treasury and other departments (for example, the Department of Employment) concerned. The associations' teams include their education officers and advisers to the chief education officer and treasurer. The DES secretariat prepares virtually all the papers and sets the agenda. The associations fulfil their usual reactive role – this is not surprising since the DES commands the resources at the national level with access to statistics and data.

The ESG(E) is above all *professional*, its documents are, on the whole, rigorous, numerate and exhaustive. It begins its deliberations early in the 'bid cycle' for the ensuing fiscal year. By the time it presents its report to the CCLGF, in the autumn, government financial policies, especially in recent years, have been substantially determined and the scope for significant movement from a predetermined position at the CCLGF has been minimal. As government policies have become more overtly and rigidly 'expenditure led' this has become even more true and the nature of the ESG(E)'s work and influence on the policy-making process has changed.

Since its inception the DES has welcomed the ESG(E) as a machinery for involving local authorities in the expenditure survey cycle. Department officials and association officers do not, however, work in a vacuum, they are tuned in to the policy options likely to be acceptable to central government and the LEAs respectively and are in constant touch with ministers and members. The contact which it affords DES officials with 'practising' chief officers has helped them to guide ministers while government policy options were at the formative stage. In the earlier years before cash limits dominated the scene, the ESG(E)'s work fell broadly into two sections. The first – which it still retains – is the substantive task of 'costing present policies'. That was simply the task of calculating on a specified price base (that is, prices and wage and salary levels at a stated time) the likely out-turn of expenditure with the preceding and current year, and after allowing for predictable changes (for example, variations in pupil numbers), the forecast of expenditure on that price base for the following years. This was a sophisticated exercise and the ESG(E) developed techniques to discharge the task – notably, for example, in its model for the projection of non-teaching costs. Much of this technical work was carried out by a subgroup. The second stage of the exercise called for professional judgement – for example, the relationship between falling rolls and pupil–teacher ratios and the curriculum and their relationship with premises unit costs. The association representatives would also endeavour to ensure that adequate account was taken of the effect of all government legislation and other initiatives. For example, the effects of employment legislation, legislation relating to Health and Safety at work and, more recently, the cost of operating the 1980 and 1981 Education Acts. In short, the partnership operated well and the associations' representatives felt they had a genuine opportunity to strengthen the hand of DES officials and so influence government policy at its formative stage. The ESG(E) could not itself determine any of the options, but by focusing on real practical problems, for example, the curricular effects of reducing teacher numbers pro rata to pupil numbers and the need to maintain or improve student 'access' to further education colleges, it could set the agenda for the final government decisions taken after the formality of the meeting of the CCGLF.

The nature of the exercise undertaken by the ESG(E) has changed in recent years; the deteriorating economic position and the introduction of budgeting in 'cash' terms has meant that the question the ESG(E) is attending to is not so much what is required to maintain alternative policies, but what are the policy implications at that level of expenditure. Thus in 1983 the ESG(E) was required (1) to make, as hitherto, a projection of expenditure on the basis of present policies in 1984/5 and 1985/6 but to do so in *cash* terms (not on some predefined price base), and (2) to consider the implications of levels of cash expenditure 2 and 5 per cent below the levels thus assessed. This had to be done on the basis of clear assumptions as to pay and price movements (and estimates were required of the variation of the projections which would result from each 1 per cent variation in those assumed pay and price movements). As part of the process of making those projections the ESG(E) needed to compute as accurately as possible the out-turn for the previous year (1982/3).

Therefore, the ESG(E) does not any longer pretend to influence – through the CCLGF – the level of expenditure on the service by the consideration and build up of policy options. It *does*, however, influence ministerial argument and government decision by its vital job of keeping the record straight. For example, its review in 1983 of the provisional actual expenditure for 1982/3 and forecast out-turn for 1983/4 was realistic, being based substantially on known pay and price movements and related to known LEA budgets. A difference between the rate support grant (RSG) settlement figure and the estimated out-turn could be due either to LEAs having pursued policies different from those underlying the RSG settlement or to pay and price movements having differed from those assumed in the settlement. For example, the LEAs had been unable to run down teacher numbers at the rate assumed and had maintained 'student access' to NAFE and advanced further education (AFE) colleges. What is essential where estimates are framed in cash terms is that the reality of what is happening in the LEAs shall be reflected in the ESG(E)'s arithmetic; otherwise cash-limited national expenditure could prove unable to support the policies they purport to sustain. When the RSG settlement is announced, it should be clear what changes have been taken into account and what are the underlying pay and price assumptions. For example, in 1983 with a public pay sector limit of 3 per cent, the settlement was some £150 million below the ESG(E) forecast based on 5 per cent. If the pay increase exceeds 3 per cent, LEA finances will be squeezed but it is the job of the ESG(E) exercise for the following year to bring back reality in relating estimates to policy. It was as a result of such an exercise in 1982 that central government added an 'unallocated margin' of over £900 million in the final stages of reaching a settlement for 1983/4.

The second part of the ESG(E) exercise in 1983 – the illustration of the implications of a 2 or 5 per cent cut in the 1984/5 estimates – provides ministers and members of the CCLGF with arguments to be used in central government discussions and within the associations which are important to the process of heading off damaging cuts. The ESG(E)'s report must inevitably be in general terms, referring to areas where the axe would inevitably fall such as expenditure on the maintenance of buildings and on books and equipment, discretionary awards, educational support staff and capital expenditure with revenue implications. It also, however, illustrates that if curriculum imbalance and mismatch of teachers are to be avoided, the consequent reduction in the number of teachers could not be managed by natural wastage and many thousands of teacher redundancies would be necessary. In short, the change that has occurred in the ESG(E)'s role is that it is now essentially defensive rather than constructive, but the opportunity for co-operation which it affords the DES and association officers in ensuring a sound numerate basis for the development of national policy is in no way diminished.

No account of the work of the associations would be complete without reference to grants working groups (GWGs) established by the Department of the Environment to develop formulae for calculating the grant-related expenditure assessments of the LEAs. This is no place to develop an exposition of the working of the block grant mechanism, but the level of an LEA's grant-related expenditure assessment is vital in the determination of the level of its government grant. Association officers – finance and education – and advisers attend meetings of the GWG education subgroup at which the DES is strongly represented. The interests of the AMA and ACC are often in conflict; for example, in respect of the weight given to social deprivation factors. No purpose is served by attempting to disguise such a conflict of interests. Officers of both associations do their best to 'hold their corner' and to see that the options put to ministers include those which they would wish to see used in the interests of the majority of their member authorities. The final decisions are taken by central government at the political level.

The work of the expenditure steering groups and the grants working groups underline the value and significance of the role of the associations. However, there is no doubt that when central government abandons consensus, strains are set up both within the associations and between them and central government. As consensus fades issues become increasingly politicized. Differences between member authorities within each association are sharpened and differences between the associations – usually controlled by different political parties – are more profound. *Training for Jobs* deeply offended both associations. Its unsubstantiated criticism of the past record of the LEAs was resented, its purposes abhorrent. For several months neither association would talk to central government about its implementation; but divisions inevitably began to appear. Central government holds all the legislative and virtually all of the financial powers and can look to its supporters within the associations for 'loyalty' justified on grounds of realism. So when the AMA still refused to talk, and the associations tried to patch up their differences, central government wielded its block grant muscle to rally its supportive LEAs and coerce the rest; the constitutional weakness of local authorities was exposed and political forces once again threatened to split the associations. The AEC in its final years lived on the myth that consensus was possible and political differences could be patched. The CLEA, created with clipped wings, has at least been more realistic in this respect. Confrontation with central government has now put strains on the AMA–ACC relationship which jeopardize its future. How will the associations survive the major constitutional change through which we are moving?

The overall budgets of local authorities are constrained by penalties and rate-capping. The distribution of the budget between and within services is more and more subject to central government influence. In the education service we have seen successively specific grants for teacher training, the TVEI, the Grant and Awards Act and the whole thrust of government intervention through the MSC – the Youth Training Programme, the Open Tech, PICK UP and other directly funded projects, and now *Training for Jobs*. Also we have seen partnerships replaced by nominated bodies in the field of curriculum and examinations, the publication of HMI reports not only on schools, but passing judgements on LEAs as a whole, and we have 'value-for-money' audits under the 1982 Finance Act.

It is difficult to avoid the conclusion that the LEAs are being steadily driven into an executive role and that the traditional partnership in policy-making is fading fast. How much the associations can do to stem this process is debatable. The obstacles are considerable if only because central government sees local government as an essential agent in the fulfilment of its economic and social policies with which large elements of the local government sector profoundly disagree. Moreover, the rigid adherence of the local authorities to the principle of non-specific grant denies central government the facility to steer resources channelled through local government even between major services. Above all, neither central government nor local government displays trust and confidence in their former partners. At some stage the associations could set out on the arduous task of changing these attitudes. A joint declaration with central government on the principles governing their relationship and their respective roles would have been possible ten or more years ago. The opportunity may return but with left and right in both national and local politics moving further apart the time is not propitious. Meanwhile so long as the broad statutory division of responsibility remains the associations must continue their traditional role as the sole means of dialogue between ministers and the local authorities collectively.

4

The County LEA

GEOFFREY MORRIS

Those of us who started our professional careers in the 1950s and 1960s have been obliged to learn new skills and acquire new attitudes in the years that followed the general availability of the Pill in the late 1960s, and the oil crisis in the early 1970s. Having served our apprenticeships in the years of expansion (not without their problems we need perhaps to remind ourselves), we were faced, without much preparation, with the problems of contraction: a sharply reducing number of pupils and what is likely to be a permanent reduction in the financial resources available for the education service. Of course there will be relatively minor shifts of emphasis in public spending priorities as governments change, but no prospect of the massive switch in resources which took place during the growth years, when in the years 1951–73 education more than doubled its share of the national income and when defence expenditure's share fell by 40 per cent. To do that would need either unprecedented growth in gross national product (GNP) or very significant reductions in other sectors of public spending. Neither of these seems remotely possible; on the contrary, any increase in our expenditure on the social services will be needed by the ageing population, and education will be fortunate to retain its present real term resources pro rata for statutory client groups.

Moreover, it cannot be said that public confidence in the education service is high, notwithstanding its extraordinary achievements over the whole of the period since the 1944 Act. By contrast, the resourcing of the service during the 1950s and 1960s was motivated not simply by the need to cope with the postwar 'bulge', but by the general belief that spending on education was a sound investment, that there was a measurable and direct relationship between education expenditure and the general economic health of the nation and that, in any event, education *per se* was a 'good thing'. That this is no longer so is evident. The reasons are complex and their examination beyond the scope of this chapter, but the fact reinforces the view that any substantial real increase in the resourcing of education is so remotely distant as to be not worth considering at present.

A third significant feature of the post-1960s education scene which needs to be noted alongside the contraction both of clients and finance is our old friend accountability. This phenomenon is not of course peculiar to education. Representing a flowering of the earlier consumer movement, it has taken the form of public mistrust of professionals, bureaucracies, large institutions and grand designs and has produced a healthy sharpening of the public's wish to hold properly to account those responsible for delivering the goods – be they services, system, legislation, or whatever. The progress of the movement through the education world can be plotted quite clearly from the William Tyndale case, the Taylor Committee (1975–7) and James Callaghan's speech of 1976, to the 1980 Education Act, the publication of HM Inspectors' reports and the opening up of the 'secret garden' as a place too precious to be left to the exclusive cultivation of professionals. The emphasis on value for money and the establishment of the Audit Commission in a sense bring contraction and accountability together. Events seem to have confirmed my belief that these two phenomena will together produce not only an unhealthy defensiveness, but great pressure towards centralization; if the cuts become too savage, you ask the cutter how he would do it, and the cutter is by definition the 'centre'. Moreover, when the pressure is on, the urge to pull decision-making into the centre and try to control events from there becomes almost irresistible, and it is not in the least surprising that the trend towards centralization has increased so markedly in recent years.

This, then, was the background which heralded the new decade and against which Cambridgeshire (and no doubt other authorities) started shortly before 1980 to review its whole approach to the management of its services; and the aim of this chapter is to describe how this has affected the education service so far and our hopes for the future. Much of the story is about systems and management techniques, but we shall start with philosophy and simple belief.

There is, as is generally known, a long tradition of community education in Cambridgeshire – 1984 was the sixtieth anniversary of the publication of Henry Morris's *Memorandum on the Village College*; and the experience has left us in little doubt that institutions flourish healthily when they have a substantial measure of control over their affairs. Morris saw the village college as 'the training ground of a rural democracy'. My own belief is that the most effective way of resisting improper central government incursions into local affairs is not to try to bolster an abstraction called 'local government', but strengthen local institutions by putting responsibility for them as far as possible into the hands of those who use them and work in them.

Most people share a common interest in their own development and that of their children; they want to have a say in how they are organized and governed, and most are interested in their immediate locality and the fortunes of the country: neighbourhood and nationhood, seldom anything in between. Counties these days exist still for those interested in cricket but are of little concern for most people in local government (as the turn-out in local elections confirms). People will lobby and fight and march in defence of their local school; that is their unit of loyalty, not some distant bureaucracy known as 'the council'. So I believe in reinforcing that loyalty by delegating to the schools and their communities everything that the law and practical management will allow. Central and local government have vital roles of course but these should be concerned with establishing frameworks, distributing resources, monitoring standards and not with prescribing content or process or pace. That, paradoxically, seems to me to be the more effective way of ensuring that education remains local; at the very time when all the pressures are towards centralization, we should resist and delegate. But it is a risk-taking formula and letting go can test the nerves.

However, the motivation for wishing to enhance the power of the institution is not primarily defensive, and the policy is driven by the conviction that it represents sound management principles and practice. In the process of thinking through its new approach to handling the problems of the 1980s and 1990s Cambridgeshire made extensive use of management consultants and their message was very much in tune with the emphasis on delegation for which the county's education service had been well prepared by its history and tradition. That is not to say that there were no new ideas; on the contrary, the consultants stimulated the development of attitudes and concepts which are quite foreign to the local government culture and have led to the breaking of many moulds and taboos. But their main message: 'be very clear about policy at a political level; equally clear about exactly the kinds of jobs needed to deliver those policies, and then nail the accountability for achieving those results firmly on to the holders of those jobs right down the line', sounded a distant but familiar echo to those of us brought up in the Morris belief that 'Good government and self-government might at last be combined in the countryside'. Though their ideas were expressed in language which would have made him wince, the simple message: 'delegate to the lowest level compatible with effective management', or simply 'delegate and trust', would have struck a chord with the founding father.

Against this background we began to think of the implications for schools at a time when the curriculum would need to change significantly if it was going to meet the needs of the country during the rest of the century; when economy, efficiency and effectiveness were going to be the watchwords and when public scrutiny and demands for value and money were likely to intensify. We recognized that whereas responsibility for curriculum is delegated to school level under the articles of government, real financial management was not. Was there any reason why responsibility for real decisions about spending should not be held at the same level as responsibility for the results of that spending? Such a union would accord with the tenets of good management practice and promote good housekeeping through financial incentives and thus achieve better value for money. The idea was attractive managerially and politically (there was broad consensus among the parties), while for the educationists there was the prospect that the power to manage their financial resources would give schools the ability to change direction in curriculum terms, even though in practice this was unlikely to be more than a touch on the tiller. If we could devise a workable system for delegating financial management to schools and to develop the right attitudes and skills among their heads, it might allow them to bring a greater degree of accuracy to their academic planning and to respond quickly to the need for curriculum change.

There was a sound base on which to build. Heads of all schools in Cambridgeshire already had delegated to them financial powers and responsibilities which were wide (though by no means uniquely so). They had complete powers of virement over items falling within capitation, which was itself a broad group, since further widened, so that it now includes such things as examination fees, telephone charges and other administrative costs in secondary schools, freedom to appoint and deploy numbers and grades of non-teaching staff to suit their particular needs in accordance with a points scheme related to the size of the school and various responsibilities relating to the maintenance of buildings. There had already been pilot schemes for increased financial responsibility (IFR) which added to the budgetary control vested in schools (cutting out functions previously carried out in area offices), gave them control of income from sales and lettings, the power to determine their own charges for lettings and to retain 60 per cent of net income above a set target, and facilitated the carry-over of unspent money into a new financial year.

There had been a good deal of committee interest in these early developments and much informal discussion with officers about how to progress to the next stage. Some members were enthusiastic supporters on the grounds of conviction about the soundness of the management principle; others wished to push on because, at a time of severe reductions, they had listened to heads telling them how they would have been able to make less painful cuts in their own schools given the freedom to decide; others were suspicious of a further cost-cutting exercise. It is significant that two almost identical proposals were made at a meeting of the education committee to introduce a fully developed pilot scheme – one by a prominent Conservative (a successful businessman), the other by a Liberal (the retired warden of a village college).

The pilot scheme for local financial management (LFM) started in April 1982. It consists of six secondary schools varying in size and organization: 11–16 and 11–18; from 816 to 1,820 pupils; and a single primary school of 360 pupils. They were all volunteers. We thought about selecting a carefully balanced group which included sceptics as well as enthusiasts, but after a series of meetings with all the secondary heads in the county, we concluded that the balance of advantage lay in taking the volunteers first. There are of course many reasons why heads should have hesitated before wanting to add to their burdens in this way: lack of training, lack of relevant back-up expertise in the schools, and, above all at times of great financial difficulty, a disinclination to be associated directly with specific reductions and thus perhaps to incur some of the odium. So the doubters greatly outnumbered the believers, though it is interesting that one or two additional volunteers have come forwad since the pilot scheme started and are waiting in the wings for their chance to join the company.

It was encouraging that there was one primary school prepared to volunteer, even though the scheme may have limited scope for application in the primary sector other than in large schools. Also it was important that the governing bodies of these schools should be behind the scheme since the powers and responsibilities are formally vested in them at school level. The study was to last for three years, but this has since been extended to four.

The bare bones of the scheme when it started were these: the LEA sets the overall budget for the individual school, the school accepts it (if it does not, it can leave the scheme) and manages it by having virement across virtually all headings, including staffing in every category. The LEA provides monthly computerized accounting data and particular costs as requested. (One of the schools is experimentally on-line to the computer mainframe in the shire hall.) The area education officer (AEO) has to be satisfied of the reasonableness of virement that concerns staffing. The education committee retain their general responsibilities, policies and liabilities for the service provided in the schools, and the schools must operate within overall policies of which the conditions of service of all staff is in this context clearly one of the most sensitive. The governing body and head must keep expenditure within the total budget agreed at the beginning of the year; in their planning they need to take acount of, and make provision for, the costs implicit in subsequent years, and while being aware of the authority's general policies, they should make no assumptions about additional funds for inflation! They should, therefore, be aware of the prudence of retaining some unallocated funds. The education committee, for their part, expect not to reduce a school's budget during the financial year; but if circumstances outside their control force such a measure, the reduction will be of the same proportion as that affecting the whole service and will be notified as a single sum for their head and governors to apportion in whatever way suits their particular school. Financial credits and debits will be carried from one financial year to the next.

The detail is of course more complex than this simple outline is able to convey and space does not permit a full account of the technicalities. But to give one illustration: the head/governing body has discretion over the teacher staffing budget, but the additional costs of maternity leave are added; so too is the additional cost of illness in excess of six weeks. Account is taken of 'protected' posts in drawing up the budget. The supply teacher budget, although calculated separately, can be managed together with the main teacher budget, with virement between the two. Most budget headings are included in the scheme (for example, rent and rates) but some are still outside: the main maintenance and repairs budget and the school meals service. It is hoped that some of these will be added as the scheme progresses and various technical problems are solved. In April 1982 the budgets approved and notified to the schools ranged from £165,000 (a primary school with 367 on roll) to £1,310,000 (an 11–18 comprehensive school, 1,821 on roll).

Thus far the scheme has operated essentially as freedom of virement within a budget drawn up on the basis of historical data and practice of particular schools, together with freedom to carry over savings into the following year. The stage we are now about to enter will involve each school drawing up its own budget, using a single figure calculated by the authority. This figure will derive from a formula which will resemble that used in the Burnham Report for calculating a school's group – numbers and ages of pupils on roll – and thus will contain an element of rough justice. Establishing the base line of the budget is a key factor in the scheme. To this extent the exercise is uncannily like the distribution of grant by central government to local authorities with all the same questions and answers about the fairness of the starting-point, the relative efficiency of the institutions and their previous track record for good management. But all were agreed that simplicity was important, and we therefore eschewed sophisticated formulae which might have given a more accurate distribution but which would be over-complex and doubtless lead to lengthy argument. Thus one of the most critical and sensitive features of the scheme has been resolved in a way which is wholly consistent with its underlying philosophy: schools are more likely to accept the 'ownership' of a budget they themselves have created rather than one devised by the LEA, more likely to use the budget-making process itself as a creative policy and management instrument, and then more likely to manage it effectively.

The scheme is currently developing and evolving, the detail soon out of date; but the principle will not change and we should learn more about its application since the scheme is a pilot and evaluation has been an important feature from the outset. The steering group (three members of the education committee) established at an early stage a Review and Evaluation Group which consisted simply of the seven heads in the scheme and the chairmen of their governing bodies. Additionally, the services were secured of an outside consultant who is an eminent academic specialist in the field and has wide local government and education experience. The approach of the Review and Evaluation Group was to formulate problems to which the scheme could be regarded as a solution and then to judge the success of the solution. Unintended consequences were looked for and an evaluation made of the cost of the scheme in terms of the additional burdens placed on those responsible for running it. The group then attended to the question of what would decide for them whether the scheme had failed; clearly this included that it *had not* proved a solution to identified problems or that it *had* produced undesirable consequences or that the burden on those running the scheme was unacceptably high.

Space does not allow a detailed description of the evaluation so far; moreover, it is by definition a continuing process. But after two years, there is little doubt that the scheme is worth pursuing, that experience in the schools is transforming attitudes as well as improving knowledge and that too there are technical problems still to be solved. Although no training was provided and no additional staffing resources allocated to the pilot schools, it is evident that the weight of the burden has fallen less on them than on the authority's officers responsible for providing information and responding to requests for clarification and advice. What is important is that the learning process has been mutual – for officers the detailed effects of financial policies at the point of service delivery, and for the schools recognizing the link between an input of cash and the outcome and, not least, understanding that the LEAs' problems and achievements are mutual to their own.

And this last point is perhaps the critical one in the context of the changing relations between the partners in the government of education, and in considering other models for the future. Although we speak of partnership at local level between the LEA and the school, and rightly value the professional relationships between teachers and education officers, few heads and virtually no teachers identify themselves with the LEA in the same way that their officer colleagues do. Might a policy of maximum delegation to schools, paradoxically, serve to strengthen that relationship? Certainly a fully developed LFM system working across all schools in LEA, or even including just the secondary sector, would profoundly change the relationships between the two. If an authority is prepared to delegate to that extent, it will undoubtedly wish to secure or clarify the mechanism by which the institution renders an account of its stewardship and is unlikely to rely simply on the articles of government as presently written.

One model being piloted in Cambridgeshire (though not in the LFM schools – they have enough on their plates as it is!) is performance management based on the traditional line-management approach. There is nothing new about this system, although it is very new to local government and rare in education. Its introduction in Cambridgeshire was achieved with the help of the consultants mentioned earlier and has now been fully operational for two years for chief officers, deputies and other senior managers, and for one year with the next tier of managers. Founded on the principles outlined at the beginning of the chapter, the system is based on clear job descriptions within which an agreed list of 'principal accountabilities' is the key. These describe the purpose of a job in terms of outputs and achievements, unlike the traditional job description which typically lists activities to be performed, so that there is very little about the 'how' of a job but much about the 'what'. Performance measures are then agreed for each accountability (a difficult exercise for most jobs in the education service), and against these performance is measured on a systematic, regular basis from year to year with the additional aid of a number of agreed short-term goals. The system has been successful in making clear and explicit the links between the policy and aims of the authority and the jobs through which those policies are delivered. The expectations the authority has of its officers are, as a consequence, much better understood and this has undoubtedly improved performance, produced a more confident approach in people and made them feel sharply the accountability they have in achieving results. Although the actual appraisal is carried out by superiors, the flavour of the system is very much self-evaluative.

Would this be transferable to schools? After floating the idea with half a dozen secondary schools, a small pilot involving just three of them has now started. Less than half a cycle has been completed, so that it is far too early to assess the likely outcomes, but already a number of lessons have been learned and problems identified. Not surprisingly, one of the most difficult questions to be resolved is who appraises the headteacher? Ask a head the question 'to whom are you accountable?' and the response is likely to list the pupils, the parents, the governing body, the wider community outside the school and perhaps also teaching colleagues on the school's staff. It will usually take some prompting before 'the local education authority' is added to the list. Moreover, even this begs the question to whom *exactly*? The CEO? – 'yes, but he's really too far from the action and in any event could not appraise more than a tiny handful of heads'. His deputy? – 'yes, but similar constraints apply'. The SEO or area officer or one of the inspectors/advisers? – 'well ... no, not sure that they have enough status to appraise me' tends to be the response from the established head of a large secondary school.

Of course, in a sense, they are correct in first identifying their accountability – a moral or professional accountability perhaps – to their client, and only secondly the formal one to their employers. Such a response is not only consonant with the English tradition, but also recognizes, properly, the immediate accountability to the governing body which makes simple line-management structures difficult in our system. It may be that performance management of the kind described is not the appropriate one in our deliberately diffused arrangements which so puzzle outside observers, and which make the pinning down of accountability so troublesome, but it is early yet to make that judgement. I do believe, however, that we cannot continue to manage the service in the kind of environment described at the beginning of this chapter with the degree of ambiguity which now exists, and we must patiently try to tease out, clarify and then make explicit the management relationships which are at present opaque and understood only by experienced insiders. Certainly if the way forward is to be towards the self-managing institution, this is essential.

In this chapter I have attempted to describe the response of one LEA to the uncertainties and strains caused by the dramatic changes of context – economic, demographic, political and educational. In devoting more management responsibility to school level and being very sure about accountabilities we believe that the education service will be better equipped to handle these uncertainties and that a stronger and clearer role will emerge not only for institutions, but for the authorities themselves. The LEAs have expended their energies prodigally on administrative detail which is inappropriate to that level of government. At the time of writing government proposals to change governing bodies into consumer groups represent a serious obstacle to the kind of structures that I have argued for since devolution to school level must assume a governing body composed of a balance of interests – providers as well as clients – within the local community. But provided common sense prevails on that issue, the way forward, I believe, must be to make sure as we can that our schools belong in a real sense to the people who pay for them, work in them and learn in them, and in doing so establish a clearly understood and agreed relationship between national strategy (government), local provision, direction and monitoring (LEA), and day-to-day management and operations (schools). In that way education will remain responsive, vigorous and, above all, local.

5

The Metropolitan LEA

WILLIAM STUBBS

In 1885 the Local Government Auditor intervened to prevent the schoolkeeper at the Beethoven Street School in Paddington from teaching woodwork to senior pupils in the school. The auditor maintained that the law only allowed the London School Board to pay costs arising from education, and as far as the auditor and the law of the land were concerned, this was defined in a code issued by the education department of central government. Teaching woodwork was manual training, and manual training was not in the approved code, hence did not qualify for grant aid from central government and was not an appropriate cost to pass on to the ratepayers. The London School Board which had been endeavouring to extend the school curriculum beyond the limited range of activities on which grant was paid had to seek alternative sources of funds in order to keep this initiative going.

A hundred years later similar issues concern those responsible for the provision of education; the influence of central government on the curriculum of schools, the distinction made between education and training for young people and the consequence of legislation restricting expenditure on education. I should like to proceed and examine a few of these issues to show – illustrating from the Inner London Education Authority (ILEA) – the extent to which central government is increasingly involved in the administration of the local education service.

However, before examining the change in relationships, it might first be helpful to have a reference point, and that surely must be the Education Act of 1944. The Act laid responsibilities on each of the partners in the education service and gave powers to the main providers – general powers to the secretary of state and more specific ones to the local education authorities and schools. This approach reflected a long tradition prior to the '44 Act and was to influence ministry thinking thereafter.

> It is a decentralised service 'conducted by representatives of local bodies which are not the agents of the central authority'. (Sir Amherst Selby-Bigge, Permanent Secretary, 1911–25, Board of Education)

> It is a basic feature of the public service of education in England and Wales that, while it is a national service, it is locally administered ... The education service is operated as a partnership between the central authority and the LEAs. (Sir William Pile, Permanent Under Secretary of State, 1970–6, Department of Education and Science)

This diffusion of responsibility, however, was not straightforward and led to a complex interdependence between the various participants described by Eric Briault, a former education officer of the ILEA, as a 'distributed system of decision taking and responsibility so as to form essentially a triangle of tension, checks and balances'. It is within this system of checks and balances that the expansion took place of the education service throughout the 1950s and 1960s, and the early 1970s.[1]

A close scrutiny of events over the last five to ten years would reveal that this balance of responsibility has been changing. Falling school rolls, the recession and unemployment have provided a rationale for central action. A number of specific new pieces of legislation, together with a series of developments which have occurred within the existing legislative framework, have enabled central government to take the initiative and substantially weaken the position of the local education authorities (LEAs). This has happened without any widespread discussion or parliamentary debate on the proper distribution of powers and responsibilites and with no coordinated consultation between central government and its partners on the reasons for such a shift in the overall position. Instead developments have taken place, one in isolation from the other, with the argument confined to the pros and cons of the particular issue being discussed. This has put considerable strain on the partnership between central and local government.

The following sections of this chapter show how these influences have affected the curriculum and the capital building programmes. These are chosen to illustrate a general trend. It would not be difficult to extend the list.

THE CURRICULUM

For over a quarter of a century after the 1944 Act no government chose to express any substantial view on the school curriculum. There the matter rested until James Callaghan's major speech at Ruskin College 1976 signalled a new approach to public policy on the curriculum which would involve much more active intervention by the Department of Education and Science (DES) and the HM Inspectorate. Later, following the general election in 1979 the incoming Conservative government continued the initiative and made it clear that the government would endeavour to seek a consensus for a national curriculum framework. There followed the publication of a 'recommended approach' to what was seen as a broad and largely common curriculum for all pupils. The LEAs were clearly expected to have regard to this government guidance as six months later, in October 1981, they were asked to review their curriculum policies in the light of the government's views contained in *The School Curriculum.*

For a brief spell attention then shifted away from the local authority scene. A committee of inquiry had been set up in 1981 under Nancy Trenaman, Principal of St Anne's College, Oxford, to give advice on the future of the Schools Council, the national body set up to give advice on curriculum and examination matters and on which were represented the principal parties in the education service. The committee recommended that the Schools Council should remain. This conclusion met with general support from the teaching profession and from the LEAs. Nevertheless, the secretary of state in 1982 decided to disband the Schools Council; this was a unilateral decision by central government against the advice of the other partners with whom at that time consensus was being sought on a national curriculum framework. This decision was soon followed by the establishment in May 1982 of the Secondary Examination Council and the School Curriculum Development Committee and whereas local authorities and the teachers' unions were given the opportunity to 'advise' the secretary of state on the membership of these two bodies, the convention was abandoned that these partners had in any way a right to nominate representatives as had previously been the accepted practice. Central government influence had clearly increased to a significant degree.

The following year (1983) the momentum for change was maintained with the DES reminding local authorities in October that reports were expected on their individual reviews of school curriculum policy. The secretary of state returned to the theme again in his speech to the North of England Conference in January 1984, when he referred to the need to give explicit definition to 'the objectives of each phase and of each subject area of the curriculum, and what in each needs to be learned by all pupils and of what should additionally be attempted by some'. The theme was repeated again and developed further, when Sir Keith Joseph speaking to the Council of Local Education Authorities Conference in Newcastle in July 1984 gave notice that the government would soon be publishing policy statements on specific subjects within the curriculum and a new discussion paper on the curriculum for pupils aged 5–16. This latter paper was released in September 1984 to the local authority associations as 'a basis for discussion which will lead in due course to a broadly agreed statement on the organisation and content of the 5–16 curriculum as a whole'. As might be expected, much of the document reflected widespread practice in schools. The document, however, made clear that certain provisions were part of 'government policy'. It is here that difficulties could be anticipated if this central policy were to be substantially at variance with those of the others with responsibilities for the curriculum: local education authorities, governors and headteachers of schools.

It is clear from all this that central government is exercising its legitimate interest in the school curriculum in a powerful way. It is now for the other partners to ensure that they fulfil their own responsibilities in this area. However, the rate at which the secretary of state is determining policy is so rapid that it is difficult for the other partners to retain their position. To give an example: the ILEA decided in November 1982 to set up an independently chaired committee to examine the curriculum and organization of secondary schools in the authority. The committee was expected to take and examine evidence, investigate the current practice in schools and make their recommendations within a year; the formalities of getting the committee together took two months but it started work in February 1983. A year later as a result of hard work from all those involved the committee under the chairman, David Hargreaves, produced a report, *Improving Secondary Schools*, with 104 recommendations for action. This was presented to the Education Committee in the spring of 1984.

Given the importance of the topic and the widespread interest which the report generated, it was agreed to defer any action until the views of all interested parties in the Authority had been obtained. Copies of the report were immediately sent to governors and teachers in schools, both county and voluntary, parents and other organizations who had given evidence to the committee, asking for their views. Throughout the summer term of 1984 groups met to consider the recommendations and a series of public meetings took place in the autumn of 1984. The intention was to ensure that all of those involved in schools had an opportunity to comment before final decisions on the recommendations were taken by the Education Committee in the spring of 1985. Even with this fairly tight timetable, the whole exercise will have taken two and a half years. In the meantime the Authority is expected to react to government policy which continues to develop separately.

What has been lacking in the meantime is the publication by the DES of LEA responses to that distant circular of October 1981. It is this apparent separation of government policy determination from an appreciation of LEA practice that will put at risk the consensus that is being sought. There is understandably anxiety among the LEAs that the rate at which central government continues to develop its own policy is not allowing time for the exercise of the legitimate interests of the other partners in the education service. This is likely to attract increasing comment as the timetable continues to unfold although the industrial action by teachers throughout 1985 in support of their salary claim has markedly reduced the momentum of curriculum reforms.

CONTROLS ON CAPITAL EXPENDITURE

Now let me turn to changes in the control over building programmes. The present controls on the capital expenditure of local authorities were introduced in the Local Government Planning and Land Act 1980. The system was claimed as one designed to relax the detailed control over capital programmes that had been a feature of the previous decade by introducing overall limits of expenditure within which each authority could determine its own programmes. The reality has proved otherwise.

In the late 1960s and early 1970s there were rolling programmes of various kinds. Major building projects were listed under three phases of development; preliminary, design and starts:[2]

Preliminary was the first formal stage and listed projects to be started within 5 years. If a project was included in a preliminary programme it was then possible to start the preparatory work, e.g. site acquisition and obtaining outline planning permission, in the expectation that the project would soon be approved.

The design list was drawn from the preliminary list and any project listed needed to be capable of being started the following financial year. This enabled detailed design and planning to be undertaken.

Finally the starts list was drawn up from projects by the DES and included projects in the design list which had by now been accurately costed. These were projects which would have to be started but not necessarily completed within the programme year. The DES endeavoured when possible to announce the starts programme about 6 months before the beginning of the programme year. At that time central government control was also reinforced by retaining the rights to

(i) approve individual projects in the building programme
(ii) impose minimum standards of accommodation
(iii) set cost limits.

Small building works did not require specific approval but the total expenditure on such programmes had to be kept within a limit set by the DES.

This system was changed with effect from 1 April 1975, when the system was simplified somewhat with the introduction of lump-sum authorizations for LEAs schools projects to replace individual project approvals. Individual project approvals were still required for major further and higher education (FHE) and all special school projects.

The rolling programme system was still maintained, in theory if not always in practice, by three stages of programmes:

(1) provisional – 2½ years before the beginning of the starts year;
(2) planning – 1¼ years before the beginning of the starts year;
(3) final – 6 months before the beginning of the starts year.

Formal costs limits were discontinued, but the concept of 'value for money' was retained by the need to obtain DES approval to a major project at the stage when tenders were obtained.

Both these allocation systems, however, related only to the total cost of the building work involved in the project, even though this could be spread over more than one year. The costs approved by the DES did not include professional fees, the cost of furniture and equipment associated with the project, or any site acquisition costs, and were not subject to government control.

This revision was to be changed again by legislation in 1980, which introduced the concept of 'prescribed expenditure' limiting the amount of capital expenditure actually incurred by an authority in any one year, and also extended government control of capital expenditure by including in the allocation extra costs in addition to the costs of the buildings. Now included were architects' and other professional fees, cost of land acquisition and the cost of furniture and equipment.

Control was also taken over the use of capital receipts which LEAs obtained from the sale of redundant buildings, although a firm promise was given that local authorities could use all of those funds to supplement their programmes. This was important as authorities had increasingly been disposing of unwanted sites and buildings to finance urgently needed new buildings. For example, in inner London the creation of two new comprehensive secondary schools consequent upon reorganization had been financed from this source.

It was generally acknowledged that the new system could work, given long-term stability of funding and procedures, and that it could be a useful long-term planning mechanism. Unfortunately the experience since 1980 has been of the government changing the rules several times and applying short-term controls to this long-term mechanism in a highly disruptive manner.

The new system started in 1981/2. Most local authorities, unused to the system and with little experience of cash-flow planning, were cautious and underspent. In order to ensure it did not exceed its limit the ILEA was required to reduce its planned programme of work and some areas of expenditure, for example refurnishing of schools, were stopped completely. In the event, the ILEA spent 90 per cent of its capital allocation but only after mid-year action to increase spending. The result was that a smaller proportion than planned was spent on building work. A further problem for that year, and every subsequent year, has been that the annual allocation was announced only three months before the start of the financial year – far too short for planning of projects which can take over two years from start to finish.

In 1982/3 the underspending trend continued and, in October 1982, local authorities were asked to bid for additional allocations. The ILEA did so and its prescribed expenditure programme was increased from £13·2 million to £16·5 million. There was another 'mid-year' review to boost spending. In fact £17·3 million was spent and was largely met from the underspending of the previous year (the rules allowed a 10 per cent carry-over). The percentage of building work remained low and the increased target was achieved only by spending on furniture, computers, equipment purchases and other financial transfers. There was, therefore, little genuine increase in building work activity on mainstream projects by local authorities, a fact widely known and accepted by the Department of the Environment.

The government changed the rules again for 1983/4. Ominously by now only 50 per cent of accumulated and new capital receipts were to be used in any one year to supplement the programme. The government, in effect, masked a cut in national capital spending by taking for itself 50 per cent of the forecast capital receipts to be generated by local authorities. The resultant cut in the ILEA's allocation was substantial – from £12·4 million in 1982/3 to £9·6 million in 1983/4.

By this time improved planning, programming and project management meant that more money was being spent on building works, and in 1983/4 three-quarters of the allocation was spent in this way. It at last seemed possible to work a system with a roughly stable target expenditure, using both government allocations and 50 per cent of capital receipts, with the authority achieving its planned proportion of building work and without resort to emergency 'mid-year' action. The following year was once more to see this newly established pattern seriously disrupted.

Barely had the 1984/5 financial year started when the government indicated that legislation would be introduced to reduce the permitted level of capital-receipts spending from 50 to 25 per cent, and to remove the freedom to carry over funds from 1985/6. This had the effect of reducing the ILEA's permitted maximum spending from £20·5 million to £16 million. This caused a major reprogramming exercise. More government action was to follow.

On 17 July 1984 the Secretary of State for the Environment announced that he was asking local authorities to introduce a voluntary 'sophisticated restraint' or 'moratorium' and local authorities were asked not to spend accumulated capital receipts or use the 10 per cent virement provision. They should spend only the basic allocations (ILEA, £10·5 million) and 50 per cent of new receipts generated this year. The consequences for the ILEA's spending if it accepted such voluntary restraint was a cut from £16 million to just under £13 million. It seems that LEAs in responding to a personal appeal to local authorities by the Prime Minister in November 1982, which had expressed concern at the consequences for the construction industry of the failure of local authorities to meet their allocated capital programmes, have obviously increased spending. Unfortunately the Treasury had apparently not taken this into account in its projection of public sector spending for the following year. Hence the brake was applied. We are, therefore, not only a long way from seeing the implementation of an orderly and properly planned system of expenditure on education building, but also experiencing an increase in the intervention of central government in local authority considerations.

EDUCATION SUPPORT GRANTS

This new scheme typifies the shift to greater central government power and involvement in the detail of LEA affairs which is the theme of this chapter. The secretary of state has clearly felt for several years that he has had insufficient detailed power to promote particular developments in education spending. Hence the Education (Grants and Awards) Act of 1984, which gives him significant authority to influence how the LEAs allocate their resources. To use his own words in his statement to the House of Commons on 12 June 1984 his aim was: 'to encourage local education authorities to redeploy a limited amount of expenditure into activities which appear to the holder of my office to be of particular importance.'

The important thing to remember is that these grants (ESGs) do not bring a penny of extra money to the LEAs collectively. The scheme provides a mechanism for redistributing money which would in any case have been allocated to the LEAs through the rate support grant mechanism. Now it is withheld to finance the new scheme.

The sum of money may not appear enormous in relative national terms:

the £30 million expenditure in 1985/6 comprises under 0·3 per cent of the total local authority expenditure on the education service, and indeed by law the total expenditure is limited to under 0·5 per cent of total local education authority spending. Nevertheless, at a time when LEA budgets are subject to increasing pressures and the scope for new initiatives is minuscule, such central direction has a disproportionate influence on local education policies.

The 1985/6 categories, for grants settled after consultation with the local authority associations, cover a wide range across primary, secondary, special and further education and it is difficult to complain about them, though it would not be difficult to complain at the short period for the submission of bids. (The DES circular was dated 18 July 1984 and bids were required by 1 October 1984, needing preparation over the summer period when all the schools and colleges were in recess.) The point of principle, though, is that it is the secretary of state who decides the priorities for spending money which would not otherwise be subject to his control. That is the matter of concern to those who value local discretion.

It is interesting that in the middle of the teachers action in 1985 when the secretary of state wished to divert money to support midday supervision in schools, the response of the Department has been to bring forward still further legislation to allow the ESG mechanism to be used for this purpose. The lesson is clear: once central government has a power it inevitably seeks to use it to the full.

SUMMARY

During this decade we have, then, seen central authority increasingly taking initiatives in the area of education policy. This will be welcomed by those who are frustrated with what they perceive as a fragmented, inefficient and dispersed education service. There are others who take the view that the concept of partnership rooted in the Education Act 1944 is a vital feature of the public education service in this country and if weakened would have serious consequences. This applies equally to the relationships between teachers and their employers, between parents and schools, schools and their maintaining local education authorities, and local authorities and central government. Without doubt, local decision making is slow, often cumbersome and inefficient in the short term. In the long term – and it will be in the long term that judgements will be made about the effectiveness of the education service – it is more likely that local involvement in decisions will secure lasting improvements. An enforced diet of decisions taken by those who have no direct experience or understanding of local circumstances is not likely to prove to be healthy.

Finally, one may well ask, what happened to the Beethoven Street School in Paddington? It is still part of the education service in inner London which is provided now by the Inner London Education Authority. Proposals now agreed by Parliament will make the authority directly elected, thus returning in some respects to the School Board model of 1885; the premises form part of Paddington College, a major further education college in central London and the courses now on offer include a variety of courses financed by the Manpower Services Commission and Youth Training Scheme. It is still the case that much of the tuition in the building is not paid for through the main programme of education expenditure: *plus ça change, plus c'est la même chose.*

NOTES: CHAPTER 5

1 cf. E. Briault, 'A distributed system of educational administration', *International Review of Education*, vol. 22, no. 4 (1976), pp. 429–39.
2 cf. D. Regan, *Local Government of Education* (London: Allen & Unwin, 1977).

6

The Teachers

JOHN SAYER

INTRODUCTION

A teacher is, at the same time, a member of a profession, one of a school staff, an employee in the teaching force of a local authority and the product of a nationally regulated supply to the education service. In the official language these four elements may form a partnership. In reality, since the mid-1970s, they have been at cross-purposes – like four tug-of-war teams with their ropes so crossed that at any one heave it is unclear who is the contestant at the other end. Where the ropes are entangled is the teacher.

It will be the argument of this chapter that the interests of national government, local government and teachers in schools can best be resolved by a contribution of all three to create an embodiment of the fourth element, the professional one, and that this in turn will bring about a coherent education service. It will also be argued that national and local authorities as at present conceived will increasingly have to give way to educational and professional concerns, which are essentially international, are best serviced on a regional basis and can best be delivered in the future in a context of local community education.

The conflicts since the 1970s have been more about control than what it is that should be controlled. Crisis management of the emergent effects of demographic decline, debased priority and economic recession have exacerbated rather than caused the conflict. Central issues are either not being faced for the future or are finding a response through agencies other than those which formally constitute an education system. These issues relate to a rapidly changing society; to information technology which will have as profound an influence on schools as robotics are having on factories; to the future effects of biotechnology; and to the brawls in the main street and alleyways of the world village.

There are 400,000 teachers in schools, working to 30,000 headteachers in England and Wales. Both numbers will decline. Teachers in further and higher education, in local authority departments, in training, advisory, or other specialized services and in the professional arm of central government are not clearly identified by themselves, or others, as being teachers; and this semantic difficulty is reflected in the divided career structures of a disorganized profession and service. For the moment this chapter centres on the teacher in the school – this being the immediate image for the public, and the reality for the majority of teachers, however defined.

THE TEACHING CAREER

Initial Training

A future schoolteacher passes through one of a variety of initial courses of training in different kinds of higher education establishment, some independent though heavily funded by national grant, others voluntary and still others nominally maintained by a particular local authority though almost totally financed by central government grant. Up to 1984 there has been very little co-ordinating control of the nature and quality of training to teach; controls of numbers admitted have, on the other hand, been relatively tight. The desire to establish criteria for all such courses and make them a precondition of accreditation to be recommended by a national body is one shared across the education service; the fear that this could be turned into a further example of central political intervention is another matter.

Initial Appointment

There is no formal link between initial training and first employment as a teacher. Teachers are still normally recruited in a national market, and training institutions are not supplying the particular local authority by which some of them are nominally controlled, or the particular schools which have shared in students' teaching practice. The outmoded attempts by the HM Inspectorate and the Department of Education and Science (DES) to encourage age- and subject-specificity of training have been at least modified by the wishes of practitioners and employers to prepare future teachers for greater inter-disciplinary coverage and mobility across schools of different kinds. So there is no professional link between qualification and probationary service of teachers, and nothing corresponding to the second cycle proposed by the James Committee. Probation, although nominally retained as a responsibility of central government, is recommended by the employing authority, usually with some involvement of its advisers, but in practice largely on the report of the head. Teachers will usually have applied for appointment to a specific secondary school, and often to a specific primary school. Their appointment is determined in a variety of ways, always involving the head of a secondary school, formally recommended for contract with the local authority. That contract may well now not mention the school, or if it does so, it will be made clear that service in another part of the local authority may replace it. At best, the processes of appointment and probationary service are something of a muddle. There is no formal pattern of induction to the profession; good practice is to be found in some schools, and is sometimes supported by local authorities.

Remuneration and Promotion

Salaries are negotiated by the representative associations of teachers and employing authorities but largely within the controls of central government. They have been unrelated to conditions of service, for the most part, and they have been paid through the agency of local education authorities (LEAs), funded partly from central and partly from local taxation, for which education in general (and teachers' salaries in particular) is something of a cuckoo in the nest. Superannuation, unlike salary remuneration, although also controlled within the Burnham negotiating committee, is managed direct from central government. Teachers would not, on the whole, be sorry to see salary arrangements centralized.

Promotion in schools is within a school establishment of scaled post allowances, broadly determined in the national salary framework, with some latitude for local authorities, and usually with the school itself (by whatever reification of the compounded recommendations of head, senior staff and governors) delineating the responsibilities and deciding who should be promoted to carry them out. Opportunities for promotion, particularly in secondary schools, have been severely reduced whether from within the existing staff or from national advertisement, and the resulting frustration leads to closer scrutiny of criteria and procedures for promotion, to attempts to reform national structures still reflecting times of growth and opportunity, and to more open and systematic staff development systems in which teachers, local authority officers and advisers, and central government could gain ground in decision-making, and school governors stand to lose what influence they now have.

Conditions of Service

In schoolteaching conditions of service are minimal and largely open-ended. In so far as they exist at all, they are included in the contract of employment with a local authority, the essential element being to assist the head. It is largely in job descriptions for the school post that anything tangible is to be found rather than in the contract with the employer. This curious state of affairs is in marked contrast to conditions of service negotiated for teachers in further education, and for schoolteachers in Scotland, in both of which union representation has been more unified and effective. Even more curious is the spectacle of employers in England and Wales now trying to secure conditions of service and trade unions resisting.

Teachers are weakly represented by a diversity of unions, two of them in membership of the TUC, the others having been limited companies and forced to be unions in order to have the right to represent members, following the legislation of the mid-1970s. Politicians and the public see teachers collectively as teachers' unions, and confuse teachers' control of what happens in a school with trade union power in general. In fact the power of unions inside a school is small though increasing.

A major body governed by a majority of teachers' union representatives was the Schools Council for curriculum and examinations. It was set up reluctantly by a government which would have preferred to have a body closer to its own control. An unwieldy body with which teachers in schools could not easily identify whatever the lip-service to it, the Schools Council ran through a succession of failures to reform examinations, came out of the 'great debate' badly and was brought first more firmly under the employers' financial control, before being replaced altogether by a government which saw red if teacher control was associated with trade unions. The two committees which have been set up as a more modest replacement of the Schools Council are under the power of the secretary of state, and while including and reflecting teacher interests, do not represent them and are not dominated by them.

Again south of the border there are no agreed criteria for the staffing of schools. There are norms for pupil–staff ratios, and there are huge variations from the norm across and within the LEAs. Any attempt to staff according to a curriculum is limited to the timetabled subject curriculum of secondary schools, and merely adjusts an allocation of staffing governed by financial circumstance and previous habit. The only condition governing the classroom is that it should be warm enough. South of the border, and outside further education, there are no maximum class sizes.

General Position

Even without the circumstances of falling rolls, it is difficult to justify the confusions, crossed lines of management and inappropriate systems which tug at the teacher from different directions at all points of a career. Training, terms of appointment and salaries do not begin to match up to either the unlimited expectations upon teachers and schools or what teachers actually do. The funding and organization of their work is, moreover, founded on outmoded curricular fictions, which are themselves the object of struggles for control.

THE TEACHER AND WHAT IS TAUGHT

There is no definition in law of what constitutes the curriculum, and the word does not appear in the main text of the 1944 Act. Yet everything done in school is expressed as though curriculum were central, so the word has become largely synonymous with whatever the school intends to happen, or school education. In its more limited sense of the formal subject timetable the curriculum is weakly justified after the event by a view of breadth and balance of areas of learning experiences. Its major controlling determinant is a public examination system at 16 – itself divided and the scene of struggles for control.

The only instructional requirement in law is religious instruction, which is honoured either in the breach or in programmes which attempt to answer rapidly changing needs and have little resemblance to laboriously 'agreed syllabuses', to which parents, pupils and teachers have not agreed at all. The only other legal requirement beyond the general provision of appropriate teaching is the one which secures that local authorities should make provision for practical instruction in secondary schools. The 1977 DES survey showed 80 per cent of secondary schools to be inadequately provided with practical facilities. So much for the law.

Since 1976 the DES has bluffed its way towards a measure of control of the curriculum. Its memoranda to local authorities and its publications on the school curriculum have a legal aura, and appear to require local authorities to state *their* curricular aims and to ensure that these are implemented. There is, however, no requirement in law for local authorities to have curricular policies or aims. Indeed some have tried to respond by taking the opportunity to usurp the authority of governors and headteachers for the curriculum in each school; but others have reaffirmed the latter and interpret their duties as having to do with 'control' variously envisaged from monitoring to delegating. So teachers in schools are left to interpret the various pressures and demands upon them from all sources, not least the insistence on public examinations; and not surprisingly, there is a rather negative consensus on what should be taught, a very large measure of common practice which is merely reflected by government prescriptions rather than owing much to them as a source.

However, undoubtedly there has been a response to the most recent government homilies, not least because some of these have been accompanied by earmarked funding or rapid spending money from central initiatives, some of them routed through another central government agency altogether, in order to circumvent the partnership with LEAs by giving them no real choice. Indeed any one school has since 1979 been bombarded with direct effects of government legislation and initiative to an extent previously unknown. Whatever their own initiatives, teachers in schools have had to come to terms with the publication required in the 1980 Act of specific kinds of information, especially examination results, to assist parental choice of schooling; the 1981 Act has brought a bureaucratic approach to mainstreaming of responses to special educational needs; the lower-attaining initiative for 14–16-year-olds is as divisive as it is generously funded; there is another begging-bowl rush by local authorities for funds from the technical and vocational education initiative, with schools expected to propose and respond in no time; schools have had to expand their energies on two-way speculation and planning, while the tidal fortunes of a common examining system depended on an overdue and by now irrelevant decision by the secretary of state; the certificate of pre-vocational education; intermediate-level examinations slipped in to please nobody but the private sector; the assisted places and other signals to encourage a shift from support of comprehensive education; the attempted prescription of a prescribed percentage of the timetable for science; a funded ration of microcomputers; and so forth. There has been no means of measuring the cumulative effect of these largely unconnected thrusts on any one school, but they are bound to have caused congestion and to have lessened rather than encouraged scope for developments according to local needs and perceptions. Indeed the most significant development is for schools to be on the receiving end, and this is closer to line management than to partnership; and of partnership it could now be said as Hunter's *Waters of the Moon* had to say of postwar Austria: 'you can't see the peace for the troops.'

LINE MANAGEMENT

Line management is indeed the formula being applied to and transmitted through local authorities to schools, making them akin to what one misguided chief education officer described as 'a branch office of Curry's'. The real question is whether there is a better alternative to the previous muddle dignified by being called creative tension, at a time when teachers' responses are particularly weak and their negotiation position even weaker.

A major instrument of line management is a one-way form of accountability to replace responsibility, all along the line. Local authorities as a result of the most recent legislation are penalized financially if they make good from local taxation the inadequate block grants from the centre. Effectively they too become field offices of state, with little more than a local executive role.

As education authorities in particular, they are reminded that the national curricular pressures begun in 1976 and intensified by Circular 6/81 require a continuous rendering of account. Circular 8/83 on the school curriculum may begin with the usual patter about partnership and respective responsibilities, but it reiterates to the LEAs (it is not even addressed to maintained schools as partners) that the secretary of state continues to require reports of the steps taken by the LEAs to develop curricula and ensure their implementation in schools, in the light of the DES school curriculum document. The LEA is enjoined to have a curriculum policy for its schools and to report how far the aims adopted by individual schools are compatible with that policy. It draws the HM Inspectors into line as regular informants to the secretary of state of such local authority developments and policies (or, no doubt, of their absence).

At the same time, and with complete consistency, negotiations are being pursued which could extend staff appraisal schemes as a condition by the management side of adjustments which are in any event badly needed in the Burnham salary gradations. Appraisal tied to salary reinforces a line from employer to employee, and could change the notion of co-operative partnership, where it still exists as laid down in most articles of government, between school heads and local authority officers. Until now the headteacher has been the employer's line manager in only one legal sense: in the operation of the Health and Safety at Work Act 1974.

As part of the tightening of central contol the secretary of state has enabled himself to earmark priorities for teachers' in-service education and training, at the expense of grant to local authorities to respond to the identified needs of teachers in schools. One of these priority areas, in school management training, is now related to the inquiry funded by the DES into the selection of secondary heads. Again the inquiry was directed towards the LEA selection process rather than the needs or recommendations of existing or potential headteachers. The outcome could well be a requirement for intending heads (in contrast to other senior managers in the education service) to have been placed by the LEAs on a centrally accredited school management course before being considered for headship.

The lines of control extend to teacher training courses and therefore institutions of all kinds. Circular 8/83 justifies itself by a reminder of the secretary of state's intention to discharge his powers on the accreditation of initial training courses. The new advisory council to assist in this exercise is to be nominated by him and to act according to criteria determined by him after amending advice from the Advisory Council for the Supply and Education of Teachers (ACSET), and of course to expect to be overruled by him if its recommendations are at variance with his wishes. The HM Inspectors will continue to develop their inspectorial role in the same teacher training establishments and to report separately.

These processes are not caused by, but justified by, problems associated with contraction. A local authority forced by financial restriction to toe the line in reducing its workforce must in turn assert its right to deploy teachers from schools which are to close, amalgamate, or simply shrink; at best, this can be done for the LEA by heads and their colleagues without inducing the need for officer controls – but it is an example of a negotiation between employer and employee in which the school as such may be excluded. Again, if there are ways to economize by sharing resources, courses, teachers, or students across institutions, this may best be affected by the wish of the institutions concerned to share in finding a solution rather than cause a problem; but if necessary, officers and advisers may be involved in co-ordination and arbitration across schools and colleges, and whatever their style of management are then placed at a higher level of decision-making. Another example of line management to the local authority education department is to be found in the 'statement' procedure of the 1981 Act. Instead of the shared inter-professional process envisaged in one part of the ambivalent Warnock Committee report, the 1981 Act has incorporated the report's contrary recommendation on stages of assessment, by which schools are at the beginning and bottom of a line of assessments, to be concluded by a decision in the education department of a local authority on whether to make a statement. Moreover, once a statement is made, a 'statemented child' becomes the direct responsibility of the LEA as distinct from the school.

In general terms, there may be seen to be a shift of management towards the centre, and of administration out to the schools. This reversal of positions remains largely unfounded in law, and there are signs that the DES will wish to take the next step to amend the legal basis of responsibility in order to match its current pressures.

CONTRARY TRENDS

Despite the apparent inevitability of the drift towards central controls and mechanistic organization, there are contradictions and signs of changes in the other direction. First, it is questionable whether the gadfly actively described has actually resulted in a trend at all or has merely reflected what was happening anyway. Schools which have kept one move ahead have been largely unaffected, and teachers as a general body have been less aware of the shifts in pressure than have heads. Secondly, there is a growing awareness that cumbersome central drives just do not work very well. The French are ahead of us in recognizing this. They too have problems of social and economic change, but far from relying on their notoriously centralized system, from which there has been at least one direct borrowing here, they have been using precisely the same arguments and situations to shift the scope for experiment and change away from the centre to the delivery points where teaching and learning actually takes place; to encourage thinking schools, and to resource experiments proposed locally rather than offer schools a bonus for doing as they are told. Thirdly, there are significant moves in this country to strengthen and extend institutional and local community management. One of these is the move towards fuller institutional management of resources, with powers of virement (see Chapter 4) and the other is the appeal of community education (see Chapters 16 and 17).

What has been happening in England and Wales in the last decade has amounted to tinkering. It has done little good to teachers or their ability to respond to future needs. It has divided them from other parts of the education system at a time when they are most in need of professional unity. The rest of this chapter outlines the kind of unity which should be achieved, and the kind of framework within which it could work.

TOWARDS A COHERENT PROFESSION

Schoolteachers, education officers, trainers, advisers, inspectors, specialized services such as educational psychologists, educational researchers, heads, counsellors, organizers, youth and community education workers, and lecturers and professors are all part of a potential profession. No one of these groups is in a meaningful sense a profession on its own. Only if they are identified as a whole can they be considered to form an education service; jointly to fulfil the objectives formed by the community; to have their work founded on a systematic body of knowledge and research of which an essential part is common to all; to have a common background of academic and practical training and to be in a position to regulate it; to generate in-service growth and development; and to share a common professional code of ethics. Only then is it a reasonable expectation that this wider concept of a profession should have the high degree of autonomy needed to fulfil the objectives willed by a society.

Several of the advisory or specialist foundations and councils which have been set up separately in recent years belong together: the Advisory Council for the Supply and Education of Teachers (ACSET), the National Foundation for Educational Research (NFER), the Council for Education Technology (CET), the Council for the Accreditation of Teacher Education (CATE), the Schools Curriculum Development Committee and Secondary Examinations Committee are among the obvious examples. Functions at present spread across these and across the DES (recognition and registration as a qualified teacher, or removal from that status) and myriad associations set up to represent good practice in each facet of education should be seen to derive from a general council representing a whole profession of educators and the education service as a whole.

The Weaver Report reflected the anxiety of the time (1970) that a General Teaching Council as then conceived would set too high and stringent standards for entry to the profession at a time when the government had to supply more teachers. It recommended therefore a division between an advisory commitee for the supply and training of teachers under the wing of the DES, and a GTC confined to registration, codes of conduct, professional discipline and good practice, with a majority of schoolteachers to direct it. This was a mere shadow of a genuine professional council, and suffered first from the disagreement of teachers' unions about numbers to represent them and about modes of election, and then from the obvious dislike of the secretary of state for union power in any form and the misapprehension that a GTC would be about that, in a negotiating employee sense.

Now that the concern about standards for teacher training is common ground the new council for accreditation may be seen to perform a part of the work of a self-regulating profession. Furthermore, it is now evident that the existing machinery of central and local government and more or less free-standing training institutions cannot be effectively wedded to in-service aspects of schools themselves without a coherent training agency, to which would be transferred the public funds at present inefficiently distributed by the DES itself to local authorities which vary in their capacity to make good use of them. I have recently referred elsewhere to the parallel in the National Health Service, which has now developed a full-blown training authority, taking over the budgets previously managed by the DHSS, and to serve as a national development agency to promote coherence across local, regional and national training of all kinds as well as promoting research.

Such a general council would have the role also of considering the big issues for the future which at present cannot be faced as a whole by a whole profession. It would learn much from the Scottish GTC and extend beyond the functions of that body. Far from being an obstacle to necessary and desirable change, it would provide a forum through which such change could become part of the common will once its implications for all had been shared; and it would absorb the separate thrusts of special pleading which bedevil any moves in current educational politics. It would not be involved in matters relating to salary and condition of service negotiations; but it would have identified criteria for staffing appropriate to the intended developments and thereby remove much of the need for argument about unreasonable conditions.

In its capacity to establish good practice the General Council would bring together research and policy, and would disseminate a fuller understanding of what teachers actually do and how they can best be enabled to do it most effectively; again by teachers, we mean those qualified to work in any part of the education service. It would be able to recognize how inappropriate is the present basis for staffing schools, as just one example, and would develop staffing models derived from agreed expectations, and the most cost-effective means to fulfil them. This cannot be done in a context of separate employment agencies. How else can we reconcile research which shows classroom activity to be only one-fifth of a teacher's actual professional activity, and staffing and timetabling habits which take four-fifths to be the norm? That is the measure of the fantasy world which at present passes for educational management, and which is responsible for increasing stress upon teachers and misunderstanding of their work in society.

Finally, a professional framework needs to be developed at a number of levels.

(1) *For the local community* – in a community management model, bringing together education and social services, local industry and all who have an interest in contributing to an educative society. Such a community would be unlikely to exceed 100,000 population.

(2) *A regional dimension* – this is urgently needed, through which a training agency could fund consortia of training institutions, employing authorities and schools, none of which is capable on its own of providing a full training service. It would be anticipated that in a region there could be a closer link between initial and in-service education of teachers, and the same consortium would be able to promote curriculum development and appropriate assessment, as well as provide a full complement of advisory specialists, drawing on expertise wherever it is based.

(3) *Beyond the nation-state* – since the teaching profession extends across frontiers and teachers (again using the word to encompass a whole profession) are still no more effectively organized as an international profession than they were fifty years ago. There are modest programmes of interchange at senior levels. There needs to be an organization capable of meeting the minds of all educators. Neither the European Communities, still reluctant to tackle non-vocational education policies, nor the United Nations Organization, with its education arm amputated, have developed such capacities. Both are badly needed for the future.

7

The Inspectors

NORMAN THOMAS

The HM Inspectorate of Schools (HMI) was first established in 1839. The first two bodies were appointed by the Privy Council on the recommendation of the Home Secretary, for there was as yet no distinct department of government for education. The local education authorities (LEAs) were formed more than sixty years later.

In almost a century and a half the two main functions of the HMI have remained in operation:

> Inspectors, authorised by Her Majesty in Council, will be appointed from time to time to visit schools, will not interfere with the denominational religious instruction, or discipline or management of the school, it being their object to collect facts and information and to report the results of their inspection to the Committee of the Council. (Committee minute, 24 September 1839)

> The employment of Inspectors is therefore intended to advance this object by affording to the promoters of schools an opportunity of ascertaining, at the periodic visits of inspection, what improvements in the apparatus and internal arrangements of schools, in school management and discipline, and in the methods of teaching, have been sanctioned by the most extensive experience. (Instructions to Inspectors of Schools, August 1840, para. 3)

In 1982 the HMI suggested the following definition of their role:[1]

> (a) to assess standards and trends . . . and to advise central government on the state of the system nationally on the basis of its independent professional judgement. This is its first and overriding duty; and at the same time

> (b) to contribute to the maintenance and improvement of standards in the system by the identification and dissemination of good practice; by bringing to notice weaknesses which require attention; and by advice to

> those with a direct responsibility for the operation of the service including teachers, heads and principals, governing bodies and local education authorities.

Both statements were made at times when the central government was moving towards a more positive role than previously in the formal education of children, although also conscious of the importance of the contributions made locally.[2] In 1839 the main problem was to build up a country-wide and tolerably efficient system of elementary education, encouraging local initiative. Now the problem is to establish consensus on a curriculum suited to our condition.

The balance between central government and local responsibilities has not always been so delicately poised. John Blackie, formerly Chief Inspector, records two extremes:[3]

> Unfortunately, in 1860, the practices, if not the ideals [of the HMI], were blighted by the Newcastle Commission, which recommended the introduction of Payment by Results.
>
> The details of the Revised Code of 1862 and the workings of this system until its abolition in 1898 need not be described here. Its effect was to narrow the curriculum to the three Rs, i.e. to what was examined, and to poison the relationship between teachers and HMIs. The former could only regard the latter as their natural enemies, and the latter, preoccupied with an entirely formal and mechanical annual examination, could not, however hard they tried, find the time or feel free to comment or suggest in the way that their predecessors had done.

Nor, one suspects, were the teachers in a condition to hear and interpret. Some HMIs expressed their dislike of the system immediately; all did so by 1869.

The period from 1944 until the early 1970s was generally a period of growth and expansion of the education service. The central government's mind and energies were occupied with expanding provision of places and teachers. In sharp contrast to the period of 'payment by results', 'neither the Minister for Education nor the DES intervened in matters of the curriculum or method. What went on in schools and institutions was a matter for HMI.'[4]

THE HMI IN THE PERIOD OF GROWTH

The HMI during these years was, by comparison with the earlier period, self-motivating. Much was and could properly be left to the inclinations and judgement of experienced individuals in the field responding to what they saw and heard in classrooms and workshops. That is not to say that there were no guidelines. Each new inspector was pleased to be able to thumb through the 250 pages or so of the *HMI Handbook* and its Inspection Supplement; and to turn for advice to his mentor or divisional inspector. Membership of an inspection team and attendance at specialist panel meetings and divisional meetings and conferences also helped to ensure broad coherence to the principles by which the HMI worked. The programme for the inspection of grammar schools was arranged centrally and issued in list 55A. But any proposal for the reporting inspection of a school or other institution came almost without exception from the HMI who was acting as the general inspector for the establishment. Inspection, as it always must be, was the basis of views formed by individual inspectors and adopted by the Inspectorate. The views were honed in small working groups and specialist panels and expressed through a short-course programme for teachers and others and through publications.

During the first four decades of the twentieth century the most substantial publication was the *Handbook of Suggestions to Teachers* series, issued in the name of the Board of Education. The postwar equivalent was *Primary Education*, published in 1959 by HMSO, with a foreword by the minister, but for which even the dust-jacket made it plain that 'the ideas and practices are selected from the best of those known to HMI of Schools'. Indeed in case there should be any doubt about the change of tone, the foreword indicates that the ideas collected together 'have no other claim to authority' than that they are 'a new anthology of the ideas and practices which teachers are successfully developing in the schools' and that they 'are not now contained in a *Handbook of Suggestions*; the old title is no longer in tune with the status of the teaching profession, or with the broader view which we now take of what constitutes good education'.

Some, looking back, might suppose they could discern the golden age of the HMI. By the time of the report of the 1968 Select Committee on Education and Science there was even the proposal that the imposition of reporting inspections should, other than in exceptional circumstances, be abandoned. The HMIs would serve best as friends and advisers to teachers; it was not always clear on what evidence their advice should be based.

The progression appeared to be from instructions to the HMI by Lords Commissioners, through suggestions to teachers by secretaries to the board, to advice to teachers by the HMIs. On one reading it might seem that the Inspectorate would enjoy its heyday, in which it would be the friendly and wise counsellor of all in the education service working on its own volition and according to its own predilections. It is tempting to say that the report of the 1968 Select Committee represented the most forward point of the swing of the pendulum.

It was no outburst of exasperation that led John Blackie to write 'as late as 1950' when referring to the Rt Hon. George Tomlinson's disinclination to control the country's education system. A growing number of HMIs were, during the 1950s, becoming concerned with the lack of interest shown by the office (Department of Education and Science administrators) in the full inspection reports they supplied. And by 1962 at least one newcomer was surprised, at his first divisional conference, to be told by more than one experienced colleague that the Inspectorate might just about last her/his time out but not, by implication, the newcomer's. Doing good as HMIs go is not, in the long run, an activity that the central government will pay for if it has no conception of what good is.

Even so, the formation of the Curriculum Study Group in 1963 by the DES Schools Branch was met with suspicion by many HMIs. The subsequent hostility of the teachers was such that the group was discontinued, to be replaced by the Schools Council on which both HMIs and members of the office served alongside teachers, representatives of the associations and others.

The HMIs were not expected to act as advocates of Schools Council projects any more than government policies. Nevertheless, the influence of this work on their activities was considerable. Those acting as assessors grew to rely more and more on the flow of information and opinion from HMI committees and papers; this provided an important stimulus to bring HMIs' observations and judgements together in a comprehensible and usuable form.

There were others. The 1968 Select Committee had proposed an increase in the use and publication of surveys by the HMI as a means of establishing good practice. The reflections of HMIs on their experience in schools had led to many publications: the *Education of Backward Children* (1937) was no. 112 in the Board of Education's pamphlets. Before 1968, a series of *Education Surveys* was begun and, in 1973, seventeen were in print.

One other account by the HMIs from this period should be mentioned because of its connection with later work. The HMIs were invited to assess the state of primary education for the Plowden Committee. Their response[5] was based on the reports and notes that had been made following visits to the schools over recent years. The exercise was undertaken with some delicacy. The notion of grading schools, even in the form finally agreed, was not welcome to some HMIs; and notes of visits were close to being regarded as confidential by the writer and his successor as general inspector of a school. In fact, and only partly for reasons of practicality, it was left to individual HMIs to interpret the gradings of 'their' schools from their own notes after discussion with HMI specialists in primary education and in the light of notes written on unnamed schools by those specialists. An important difference from many other published HMI accounts was that this was not a description of successful practice that others might be persuaded to follow, but a serious attempt to identify weakness and strength and their proportions.

Even before the 1968 Select Committee met, the balance had begun to shift towards HMIs acting as a nationally co-ordinated force on interests of national concern, and from HMIs operating individually and separately as advisers to individual teachers, schools and LEAs. Of course neither extreme has ever been a practical or desirable possibility.

CHANGES IN THE 1970s AND THE RESPONSE OF THE HMI

Between the Select Committee report of 1968 and the 1981–2 study of the HMI in England and Wales there were a considerable number of developments that had a direct bearing on the education service including the HMI. In 1972 the White Paper, *Education: A Framework for Expansion*, led to considerable activity with regard to nursery education and teacher training, though subsequent events curtailed the action. The minimum school-leaving age was raised to 16. Local government was reorganized and there was a substantial increase in the number and range of inspectors and advisers employed by the LEAs. The sharp division between schools and further education began to be blurred. There was growing dissatisfaction with the dual system of examination at 16. The number of comprehensive schools increased and the selection examination at 11+ became less common. Parents became more closely involved with schools. The number of children in middle schools grew towards the anticipated proportion of about 20 per cent. The Houghton award raised the salaries of teachers substantially and increased the proportion being paid above the Burnham scale 1. There were growing expressions of dissatisfaction about the behaviour of some pupils in schools and about the suitability of schooling for young people going into industry and commerce. There was concern about the ways in which schools were meeting the needs of black children and especially of girls with regard to science and mathematics. The Assessment of Performance Unit began to produce reports of surveys. The Schools Council was substantially remodelled and then brought to the point of extinction.

Including both the 1963 Select Committee report and the 1981–2 study there were nine internal or external reviews of part or all of the HMI. There were also important changes in the deployment of HMIs arranged mainly so as to allow speedier response to the interests of the day.

National Surveys

When the Ruskin College speech of James Callaghan was delivered in 1976, the two major HMI surveys of primary and secondary education were well under way, and it was already possible to speak with some assurance on the extent to which expressed complaints against the system were valid.

That is not to say that these were the only sources of HMI information. They took up a lot of HMIs' time in the preparation, inspection and writing; but except for a handful of people, less than half the official time even of those most closely involved in the inspections.

Other exercises were in train. The 1981/2 study, already referred to, lists thirty-eight HMI publications, in addition to the two major surveys, issued between 1973 and 1981. Some – like the series of pamphlets on the subject of safety in schools and colleges – were part of a long-standing commitment, others – like *Modern Languages in Comprehensive Schools* – were the direct result of inspectorial identification of trends. These were issued under the series title *Matters for Discussion*, in the hope, not fully realized, that they would allow speculative expression of views for debate between the HMI and the rest of the educational world. At least to those outside, the views often looked like firm declarations of faith.

Another review, *Truancy and Behavioural Problems in Some Urban Schools*, issued by the DES in 1978, was the result of a survey promised by the Secretary of State for Education at a conference convened in June 1976. This direct ministerial involvement is a timely reminder of the legal basis of the HMI's work: 'the Inspectorate has no direct responsibility or powers (other than delegated powers for advanced course approval in higher and further education) except the right of access to institutions and the duty to inspect on behalf of the Secretary of State.'[6]

Significant Studies Focused on the Curriculum

The *Curriculum 11–16 Working Papers* are of special interest because they relate to an exercise in which HMIs, LEA advisers, heads and teachers worked closely together in a curriculum development project. It was highly unlikely that the outcome would be precisely what any of the parties expected, but each had (and has) some responsibility for the outcome. The implication for future inspection will be considered later.

A View of the Curriculum followed. This was a statement on the whole curriculum by HMIs as part of a package, the office contribution being a *Framework for the School Curriculum*; both were published in January 1980 and are particularly significant because they were produced as a direct result of the government's growing interest in the curriculum and standards of performance in schools. The period of consultation that followed the publication of these two documents was for the time being rounded off in March 1981 by the government statement, *The School Curriculum*.[7]

The need for some publications became apparent in the course of inspection and through discussion with teachers and lecturers. In other cases HMIs perceived the need in discussion with LEA officers, relevant associations and ministers and officers of the DES. In all cases the trigger for the action was pulled inside the Inspectorate. It would be a simple man who supposed that he could identify an individual anywhere who originally set the sights, but not all of the activities would have had the same priority if someone else's finger had been on the trigger.

One other kind of activity of note here is the work begun in 1974 on the effects of changes in public expenditure. It led to publications in later years but reference to it appears in the HMI study in appendix D, among fifteen other issues receiving attention across the board; and with thirty-three government policies and initiatives and related DES operations requiring inspection and advice from the HMI on determined time-scales. A third list in the appendix contains forty-eight issues arranged according to phase or aspect of the education service; these include under-5s, primary, secondary, 16–19, NAFE, AFE and teacher training, Special Education, multi-racial education and disadvantage. Together they make a formidable checklist, some part of which an HMI must have on his/her mind even on a half-day visit to a small primary school.

Programming Time for the Work

There have been a number of important consequences of this developing activity both for individual HMIs and for the Inspectorate. They are partly the result of the number of identified issues, partly the result of shorter time-scales and partly the result of changes in the intensity of interaction with different sections of the education system, particularly on a national level.

It has become necessary, on a larger scale than hitherto, to direct the efforts of a number of HMIs to specific tasks, and to organize those tasks so that they meet specific criteria. This required action on two fronts.

Inspections of grammar and comprehensive schools were arranged, when they were done, by a divisional or the chief inspector as a matter of individual negotiation so far as the inspection team was concerned. The demand for specialists in phases, subjects and aspects of education made it essential during the 1970s to construct the programme nationally. It gradually included more kinds of activity and came to be a means of protecting time for locally chosen as well as nationally chosen work. Those most heavily committed are almost invariably from a changing group who are, for the time being, expected to give first priority to activities selected centrally – though they may have originated locally – and are freed from divisional responsibilities.

An Increase in Reporting Inspection

The two major surveys, though not the later ones on first and middle schools, called for sampling within a school as well as sampling of schools. It was not appropriate to write individual reports on the schools inspected and that was a disappointment to some chief education officers. Leaving aside the years most affected by the two major primary and secondary surveys, the number of reporting inspections increased gradually between 1970 and 1980 from 33 to 154. The numbers of inspections of individual institutions and surveys of groups of institutions – groups which varied considerably in size – increased from 170 in 1975 to 228 in 1980, with falls in the numbers of surveys in the years of the major surveys, though not in the numbers of schools affected.

Standardizing Information and its Use

The task of putting together the information and judgements on a particular topic is obviously considerable. *Primary Education in England: A Survey by HM Inspectors of Schools* was based on something like a million bits of information. The task would have been impossible unless the returns had been made in standard ways, and this was not a practice familiar to most HMIs. It was important that the standardization of the form of return should not improperly constrain the observations and judgements that HMIs thought it right to make, for this survey like all HMI work rests upon the quality of observation.

The same difficulties arise with ordinary notes of visits to schools. They are not recognized as being valuable sources of information, and continuing efforts are made to get the best value out of them without restricting the individuality of the writers.

In another form of words: it is important that the professional independence of the Inspectorate is preserved; and that cannot hold unless the individual HMI retains his/her independence. Though that is not to say that either individual HMIs or the Inspectorate have a right to publish at the country's expense or to act in opposition to the government's policies. However, they do have not only a right but a duty to inform the government of the day what the results of its educational policies are, as seen by HMIs in the course of their work.

It is this last that makes it important that the HMI should spend much of its time looking broadly at the work of schools and colleges and following up trends that seem likely to become significant. To limit action only to the immediate interests of ministers and of senior officers of the DES would be, in the long run, to limit one's usefulness to them.

The same applies to the LEAs. A beginning has been made in drawing together what is known of the education service in local authority areas as a result of inspection by the HMI. The early reports must rely more than later ones will on HMIs' notes of visit and patterns of visiting undertaken without the prospect of the exercise in mind. It is highly unlikely that every authority will like everything that is said about it. But it is essential, if the exercises are to be worth anything, that the reports are written frankly as well as sympathetically.

The Publication of Reports

These reports, as well as reports on schools and colleges since January 1983, are made available to the general public. Like so many other things that have happened in the last decade this is reminiscent of the past. The inspectors of the 1840s also had their reports made public. One, on King's Somborne School, Hampshire, written in 1848, has been much quoted in recent years because of the high quality of the leadership of the head, Mr Dawes, then mentioned by name.

The initial reaction of many to the news that modern reports were to be made public was to think of the difficulties that would come for the schools, especially if the reports were used by newspapers in a sensational or biased way. There has been a little, but not much, justification for that fear. It is also the case that HMIs are much more under scrutiny because their reports are made public and my impression, looking on from outside, is that HMIs have suffered as much as schools from unbalanced reporting of what they have written. Overall the advantages of openness and the wider availability of balanced views of the work of schools and colleges outweigh the disadvantages.

There is one last reflection to be made in this chapter on possible effects on HMIs of the changes in which they have taken part. The work done in the Curriculum 11–16 exercise; or in the evaluation of criteria for the proposed 16+ examination; or in the development of governmental curricular policies, including what must follow Sir Keith Joseph's 1984 Sheffield speech, have all taken HMIs close to being participators in the processes they are inspecting. There is much to be said for this, and there is no doubt that the HMI has gained respect from the teaching profession and others as a result of such activities. As with most changes, there are pitfalls to be avoided; HMIs must not put themselves in the position of seeming to praise whatever they promote, nor automatically blaming practitioners when their (HMIs') expectations are not realized.

The years ahead must continue to be years of change for the HMI. Relationships with the local authority inspectorates are much closer than they were but still need development. The coming together of schools and further education must be consolidated and reflected in the organization and work of the Inspectorate as well as in the DES and local authorities. The work on the curriculum requires a careful balance between assertiveness and reflection. The closer involvement with teacher training, including that taking place in the universities, will call for establishment of new working relationships and skills. The closer relationship between schools and parents and the growing importance of governing bodies may require HMI to adjust their working patterns so as to acquire more direct experience of these aspects of school life.

NOTES: CHAPTER 7

1 Published by the Department of Education and Science and the Welsh Office (London: HMSO, 1982), p. 80.
2 Page 2 of *The School Curriculum* (London: HMSO, 1981) illustrates the recognition of local rights.
3 *Educational Studies: A Third Level Course, Curriculum Evaluation and Assessment in Educational Institutions; Part 3 Inspections, Reading 1* (Milton Keynes: Open University Press, 1982), p. 8.
4 ibid., p. 12.
5 Paragraphs 269–76 of *Children and their Primary Schools* (London: HMSO, 1967), Vol. 1.
6 *Study of HM Inspectorate, England and Wales* (London: HMSO, 1982).
7 DES, *The School Curriculum*, op. cit.

8

The Listening School: Parents and the Public

JOAN SALLIS

There was a time when people thought they knew what schools were doing and did not question how they did it. That will possibly never return.

The prevailing fear about a system not entirely responsive to consumer wishes is a phenomenon of the 1970s and 1980s. Schools had lost many of the features parents remembered and employers, often going further down the ability groups for unskilled labour than in the past, unfairly criticized what they found there. At the same time, consumerism was fashionable in all aspects of our lives, and education was not exempt. The parent–teacher (PTA) movement was growing, and organizations like the Advisory Centre for Education (ACE) and Confederation for the Advancement of State Education (CASE) gaining strength. Parent power was in the news, with CASE and the Conservative Party comically competing in their Parents' Charters.

The first experiments in reformed governing boards with parent representation and teachers which marked the late 1960s continued into the 1970s. Mr Callaghan's Ruskin College speech in 1976 was the climax of a lot of rumblings about schools' fitness to serve modern society, and this inaugurated the 'great debate' in which industrialists, educators and parents talked about the content of learning and the purposes of schools.

Meanwhile the Taylor Committee (1975–7) was looking at school–community relationships, especially as expressed in governing bodies, and the Warnock Committee, apart from its better-known recommendations, was quietly paving the way for expert judgements on children's needs to be questioned and supplemented by parents. The 1980 Act, besides providing for universal parent representation on governing bodies, purported to give parents more choice, and certainly provided, in the regulations made under the Act, for parents to have a great deal more information. The 1981 Act gave parents of children with special needs a new involvement in decisions about their education and special appeal rights. A steady stream of circulars from the Department of Education and Science (DES) has emphasized the desirability of schools articulating their aims and objectives with a view to securing the consent of governors and parents. There has been more emphasis on the local education authorities' (LEAs') responsibility for the curriculum, delegated to governors and explained to parents. Most recently the government is currently (1984) consulting on much more precise responsibilities for governors and a stronger voice for parents. (*Better Schools*, Cmnd 9469)

The unchallenged freedom of the professionals to experiment had overstepped the mark in the eyes of politicians and many parents. However imperfect the new structures of participation both as a means of giving the consumer more say and, even more important, safeguarding the rights of those children whose parents are not very adequate participators, they are here for a long time. But the best structures in the world will not work where human beings do not want them to work. As a parent who in small ways has striven to get better structures of partnership established, I know well now what a big job of persuasion has to be done to make partnership real.

It is over twenty years since I encountered the infants school which did not encourage parents to venture beyond the gate. In those days it was not uncommon. I did not do anything about it, which may seem a bit weak; but I don't believe you get anywhere by nagging about bad practice. The only way to improve things is to encourage good practice. It made me sad, not just because there were many children in the school whose parents needed help in supporting them, but also because we had just come to live in a beautiful and prosperous place where one would have thought the schools would have been magnificent (they are now, but that's another story), but this was a classic case of private affluence and public squalor. At the time there was not much interest in state education in an area where few influential people used it, and it didn't seem to have very high priority in hearts or pockets. That has all changed too, but all I thought about the infants school, and others like it, was how sad in a place where education didn't have many powerful friends to discourage even the unpowerful ones, who together might have made a difference.

Personally I have never had much time for participation as a hobby. The case for a better dialogue stands or falls on whether it makes for an enhancement of children's chances. I hope to identify some ways in which the structure and content of public education need to change, and cannot now change without better understanding between its providers and its users. First, it should be made clear that I, and many like me, have only ever been concerned to secure better and fairer provision, with public involvement as a means and not an end. Some of our tasks would be easier if we had moved rather faster towards a listening school and a listening education service. Some of our present difficulties would not seem so mountainous if there were more general understanding of what schools are trying to do, and if, in the now conspicuous absence of powerful friends, the unpowerful ones had developed more unity, more understanding and more clout.

It was in the late 1970s that I first had the opportunity to talk to teachers and administrators in an organized way. I found it frustrating since the education service, so drunk then with the heady scent of expansion, reminded me of Keats' bees, who 'thought warm days would never cease/For summer had o'erbrimmed their clammy cells'. I was, however, acutely aware of cold winds, sure that we must huddle together against winter and the dry coughs of contraction.

I ask myself now, with the public education service so beleaguered, what it was I was trying to communicate. Many things which have become platitudes as we have lived through them. No need to tell anyone now that all that lovely money was not going to be left in education without a fight when child numbers fell, and that it might be a bit naïve to plan for how we were going to use it to raise standards. No need to warn that the clamour for more central prescription would not go away, and that without more local accountability schools might find it hard to keep that freedom and variety which is the envy of countries which do not have it. And need, above all, to point out that we are rapidly establishing a two-tier system of state education. There still is one very good service for those who live in the right places, and who have parents who can get and use information, make wise choices, write a good note, fight a good campaign and dip into their pockets to fill the gaps. Then there is a basic service for the rest. This process is aided by cuts and abetted by falling rolls. Cuts add to the range of educational experiences which lucky parents will by some means or other provide themselves, and unlucky children will fail to get at school. Falling numbers work quietly to segregate the strong and supportive – and demanding – from those who will not complain however much the soup is watered down.

None of these terrible things could happen if parents and the public knew enough about their implications, which means understanding more about the aims and needs of schools than most have grasp of despite the efforts of the best schools and best LEAs.

In general, the education service has failed to communicate its purposes over the last twenty years or so – and is now paying a heavy price in the lack of effective public pressure to protect those purposes. The pace at which it is outgrowing its defensive and secretive traditions is impressive but still does not match the need for public understanding. In particular, people do not understand the case for the breadth of the primary school curriculum (no popular newspapers carried the message of the primary schools survey of 1978 that the basics were better taught in a rich curriculum than when too heavily concentrated on). Nor have they grasped the full implications of educating young adults of all abilities and backgrounds under the same roof since constantly they draw their comparisons from not so distant times when it was only children who were educated compulsorily, and secondary education was for volunteers. Above all, there is little understanding of the indivisibility of a good education system, the irrelevance in the end, of individual achievement alone. Most of what is said to parents by teachers and LEAs is still in terms of what they hope (and realistically may expect) for their own children. Rarely are they encouraged to think that among the things they want for their families a decent world to grow up in might be pretty high on the list – and the world consists of other people's children.

These failures to understand make parents easy game for doorstep salesmen, peddling 'you-add-the-egg' basic education mix, school yarns from the 1930s in which the irregular verbs and the theorems and the rivers of Africa are not wasted on those who are only going to stack shelves in Tesco and, above all, those bright but fragile baubles of choice and freedom whose edges are so sharp when they shatter. The roaring trade in these commodities makes one despair of ever getting public pressure behind the full curriculum for all, behind the necessary reforms in the values and priorities of secondary education, and a thoughtful and (in the short run) unselfish strategy to plan for contraction in such a way as to make choice more real for everyone. Difficult as it may be, the education providers have, in my view, no option but to expose the fraudulent dream pedlars and substitute a convincing prospectus based on understanding and consent.

Public understanding is needed to support three important propositions. First of all, that to reduce the curriculum to its 'essentials' robs all children, but robs some much more than others. Unless from the earliest years all children are given windows on a world beyond the mean streets, with schools equipped to offer more to those whom life has given less, the personal achievements of a minority who enjoy home support, parents who can add the egg to the mix and a life rich in educational experience, whether or not school provides it, will be hollow at best and provocative at worst. But the values based on educating the whole child (and all our whole children) cannot survive without enormous and broadly based public support – they have too many enemies and are too expensive. Even the best professional cannot in the end provide for the disadvantaged of all kinds (and all classes!) without the understanding and support of their parents. Ways must be found of broadening the base of this partnership.

Secondly, public understanding must be sought for the reform of secondary education to provide appropriate goals for all, to break the hold of minority interests on the curriculum, to think deeply about how to prepare young people for a world in which work must change its significance. I'm sorry to say that I believe we are in danger of taking a tragically wrong direction in the pursuit of what we call 'relevance', and could in the year 2000 be looking back on half a century in which we established a system of education based on the division of scholars, technicians and labourers, half-reformed it and then went scuttling back to it. Yes, of course we must seek a programme of learning which has value and meaning for all in relation to the experience they will have later, and if that is relevance, who can be against it? But an 'irrelevant' education has long been the privilege of a fortunate and confident minority and their life-chances have been not one whit impoverished, indeed they have been enhanced, by their acquaintance with theorems, irregular verbs and the rivers of Africa. This is the unassailable irrelevance which rests on the right to learn things which have nothing to do with the daily round and the common task; to learn about other places, other peoples; to marvel at the wonders of the natural world and the achievements of humankind; to have the imagination stirred and the curiosity engaged; to feel joy and pain in experience not one's own; to play with numbers and with words, and as an Anglo-Welsh poet put it, 'to grind them fine and patch them, for their sake, and other reasons which you may not guess'.

An irrelevant education, in the sense of an experience which enriches, ennobles and transcends the commonplace, should be the right of all and not the privilege of a few. I am also wanting to say that a relevant education, in the sense of an experience which substitutes something a bit more to the point than the rivers of Africa, one appropriate to the modern world, one which is alive to the technological possibilities of our time and one which, above all, is not ashamed to accept that wealth-producing activity must engage our best brains if we are to support the delights of irrelevance we all prize so much, ought to be offered to all too, not just to those who can't manage the irregular verbs. Public understanding must be sought for an appropriate curriculum for all and we must wrestle with our fundamental confusion about scholars, technicians and labourers, for our thinking is so destructively tripartite. There are in many people's minds, whether they admit it or not, such categories, those who can handle ideas and therefore lead, those who are good with their hands and those who are not much good at anything. And in our sick system of values those who are good with their hands are well over halfway to not being good at anything. I have O levels, you have CSEs, she has a personal profile. Managerial, technical, manual, administrative, executive and clerical. We are in danger of dividing responsibility for the older school population between the education service and manpower services, and we all think we know the lines on which it will be divided. Tragic, when the lives of most will be purposeless unless we can change the focus. We all need to revalue manual work – even if unpaid – as peaceful, satisfying and dignified, and to find the joy of making things, mending things and growing things; we all need to revalue personal service, especially to the disadvantaged and the casualties of change; we all need to revalue the environment, enjoy it more and improve it; and again we *all* need to value learning skills more than any skill learnt, and adaptability most of all. We may have to revalue fun.

Above all, however, we must find ways of engaging the very able in the technology which alone can provide the means thus to refashion our values. Alas, I do not see the way in which responsibility is being shared between education and manpower authorities helping much with that.

Thirdly, public understanding is needed to plan bravely and sensitively for contraction. The dream-pedlars I spoke of are very successfully confusing this issue with their emphasis on the market forces which they allege are so healthy for educational standards, so vital to the preservation of parental rights and so efficient a means of reshaping the service to its new slimmer size. This is in my view a dangerous proposition, whose acceptance will exacerbate the two-tier tendency already apparent, obstruct necessary curriculum reform and cruelly deprive generations of children.

I doubt whether I need to point out that the consumerism implicit in letting market forces do our planning is full of false analogies. Children can't be taken back to the shop like faulty merchandise – they have only one chance, and if for some that chance is to be in schools condemned to a slow and painful death by the operation of geography and demography, social prejudice and fashion, it is irresponsible to pretend that it is the false god of choice, and not we ourselves who have brought it about. Children are not the ones who exercise that precious choice, they merely suffer the limitations as choosers of those whom they have not themselves chosen – their parents. Children's chances should not depend so decisively as they already do on the capacity of their homes to choose, to push, to support and to supplement, and a *laissez-faire* attitude towards falling numbers only makes that worse. Children can't wait while market forces sort out the schools with survival quality. Children – even other people's – are the future, and their schooling is not a commodity bought and sold and concerning only those who buy and sell it. What impressed me most during my enforced study of the history of public participation in education through the centuries was that, even when it was such a minority pastime as almost to be a spectator sport, no simple consumerism was ever apparent in discussing it. It was accepted that it still concerned everybody, even when only a few were receiving it.

This unashamed advocacy of positive action to remove slack from the system, before it does its wicked job of segregating the strong and isolating the weak, implies hard decisions about school closures and admission limits, which, given the politically appealing doctrine of consumerism that prevails, *cannot be implemented* unless the public have understood and consented to the measures needed for the greater good. Such consent should not even be sought except on the basis that schools with confidence problems will be the subject of investigation, open debate, prompt remedies and extra support because a monopoly provider cannot expect people to trade in their freedom without trust and openness about the reasons. That is quite a mouthful, since all the traditions of the service provide little between two extremes, that of paternalism and that of consumerism. Either 'we decide what's good for you and enforce it' or 'you decide what's good for you by your actions and the devil take the hindmost'. I have tried to say that the former is unrealistic and the latter cruel and irresponsible, yet not only tradition but the whole trend of education law and the way it is interpreted makes a middle road very hard to find.

The way in which government, the LEAs and schools treat parents (I am trying to say) discourages any but selfish attitudes and comments. The way in which the public are involved in decisions about the size and shape of the service increasingly discourages any broad view of the needs of children. The 1944 Act in the early years of its operation put some emphasis on the publication of general plans for a local education service. These provisions were defunct long before the 1980 Act put change firmly on a school-by-school basis, and even when an LEA-wide package of change is put forward – for rationalization to meet falling numbers or comprehensive secondary reorganization – the DES deal with it school by school and respond to public comment only on that basis. Throughout the 1970s and 1980s this tradition has become stronger, and one's memory throws up many instances of an LEA trying to do something with a philosophy, a consistency and purpose going far beyond the case of one school or group of schools for survival – Birmingham, Manchester, Croydon and Liverpool spring to mind – only to risk fragmentation of those plans by the DES because the only voice of public opinion which came through was that of 'save our school'.

You cannot blame the save-our-school marchers since there is no tradition of telling parents any more than they need to know about the problems of schools or local services, nor are there many structures within which they can express more thoughtful reactions. There are honourable exceptions, the LEAs which use their governors properly (by which I mean asking them *all* about common problems, asking the nursery school about the tertiary college, asking not only the comprehensive that it is proposed to turn into a grammar school, but also the one which will be made into a secondary modern by that action) and LEAs which encourage parents and parents' organizations to join together to talk about all the children. All too often, however, school is set against school, all the consultation is with those whose reactions are predictable. All too often consultation isn't thinking aloud, but presenting already hard options or options deliberately reduced to curtail discussion, or deliberately increased so as to confuse the public. All too often the save-our-school emotions seem to be almost stirred up by the way consultation is handled.

I have, then, identified three areas of concern which I suggest suffer particularly from poor communication. Needless to say, the best schools will go on with the hard, often thankless daily job of involving parents better, explaining their purposes better, listening in a spirit of equality – not patronizing benevolence – to what people say. There are schools which are informing their governors properly and allowing them to help, and there are schools which have the confidence to be open about their problems. Some work very hard to overcome the diffidence of parents who find schools intimidating, constantly watching the structures of parental involvement and the techniques of communicating to make sure they do not exclude or diminish anyone. This is an area parent groups must watch too: nuts and bolts are very important, and so are unspoken messages. Those who see 100 per cent participation as a goal may unconsciously become a bit self-righteous. To expect 100 per cent participation is both unrealistic and a bit impertinent. The important thing is that the school should be the sort of place where parents feel comfortable if they *need* to come in. That is why seven members of the Taylor Committee attached such importance to *individual* rights to access and information, and put in a Note of Extension on the subject.

Although the standard of home–school relationships has improved so much over the past twenty years or so, there is still a wide gap between the best and the worst. Some schools still have invisible white lines denoting territory. Without knowing it, they set the limits of parental engagement and then complain about apathy. Often they boast about the practical help and support they get from parents, and boast also about the fact that parents have such confidence in the school that they are uninterested in curriculum issues. They have the same attitudes to their governors. They will unconsciously distinguish between those who have articulate aspirations for their children, responding to them positively, and those who seem to be intimidated by the whole aura of school, whose anxieties and sense of inadequacy they often increase. They may conceal from their more demanding parents that they have any problem pupils, or any resource problems. They miss many opportunities.

First, if they are to engage the sympathy of the confident and fortunate, they must be willing to bare their wounds, whether those wounds arise from lack of resources, the social problems of pupils, or even the limitations of their own professional skills. Pride and infallibility make few real friends. Secondly, they need constantly to seek new ways of illuminating their purposes, and especially the justification for the less obviously utilitarian things they do. Above all perhaps, they need to find ways of giving parents a sense of the value of the parenting role, so sadly devalued. The lesson of the Haringey and similar research is clear. Parents who were non-English speaking, illiterate, poor and timid, as many of them must have been, could not directly assist with their children's reading. If you had said that you would take photographs of their chimneys on alternate evenings, and had been able to persuade them that their permission for this might help their children's school work, then it probably would have done. It was not about reading, but about messages received by people who had previously assumed that they had no educational function or value. For the same reason I have known primary heads who have set great store by the personal interview early in a child's stay at the school, taking immense trouble to offer any time and place. The best account I heard of such an interview was from a head who said that on this occasion she told the parents nothing about the school. She merely emphasized what a lot of parents taught in the pre-school years, and how compared with these skills, those learnt at school were quite modest.

When I was in Australia looking at their arrangements for involving parents and citizens in schools, I visited one school where a very disadvantaged situation had attracted funds even from the federal government. Some of the money had been used to build and support a very well-used 'drop-in' centre, and in terms of social support it was working well, but despite a headteacher who wished to involve parents in decisions about learning, they would at first come no closer. In their own eyes, having merely(!) borne and brought up children, and done nothing else in their lives, they had nothing to offer. What changed things was using some of the money to teach them pottery, a skill which they were then going to share with children in the school. It was the possession of a skill which gave them the confidence to participate in professional activity. Perhaps one should look for solutions to some of schools' problems in adult education, or in the development of the full community school.

At secondary level there is a great need to open up a dialogue on living with teenagers. Tensions arise because schools expect homes to hand out the tablets of stone, and homes expect schools to do so. Both somewhat overestimate the influence of the other. There isn't any discussion about agreed policies, no drawing up of short (very short) lists of the really important things and distinguishing them from the long list of tiresome but passing manifestations of growing up. Even the recognition that both sides find it hard would be constructive.

What help could schools get in communicating with parents? Well, the omissions are so many and so serious that I hardly know where to begin. The DES doesn't have any section devoted to it. There is no nationally sponsored and organized research into what works, even though thousands of our best teachers are begging for advice on how to do it better. At the LEA level, even though this is the level at which responsibility for an efficient service rests, and even though all research emphasizes the part played by home effectiveness, there are few oganized structures to improve the job that schools do in involving homes. Again there is no organized research. There is very rarely an inspector or adviser for home–school links. There are few LEAs which provide resources for home-link teachers, mother and toddler clubs, drop-in centres, or parents' rooms. There are not even many which do something very easy, cheap and effective, which is to run a 'good ideas' news-sheet, constantly updated, spreading among schools the good practices developed by personal initiative. Teacher training, both initial and in-service, is sadly lacking in practical skills of communicating educational points to parents and developing the right sort of relationships. I suggest that anything which is done to remedy these omissions should have as its main focus the need to get away from the idea that parents may only legitimately be interested in their own children's needs and progress. This is an accusation often levelled at parents, as officers and teachers sigh despairingly over the hopelessness of getting support for more caring policies. But schools, teachers and LEAs encourage this selfishness. Most are kind and welcoming when a parent has an individual worry; but the curtain comes down at once if there is any attempt to relate that worry to school policy more generally. At the LEA level I have referred already to the school-by-school basis of most consultation about changes in the local system. At school levels also an assumption that people will react responsibly when given the facts and some encouragement to take a broad view might well have surprising results.

Most of what has been written about relates to the task of raising public awareness of the need to protect the breadth of the curriculum, extend the school's care for the least advantaged and thus create a climate in which discussion of necessary curriculum reappraisal could take place. In other words, an educational objective. I now begin to touch on the structural problems of the service and the need to win support for far-seeing and perhaps painful changes to protect the schools from the debilitating and divisive effects of unplanned contraction. The changes I would wish to see have become obvious: more broadly based consultation with governors and parents, frankness about the alternatives, vital information about how shrinkage threatens the school curriculum, about size and staffing and about the consequences of letting market forces do the planning; and willingness by the LEAs to inspect schools which may need artificial protection, and honest and generous approaches to the problems revealed. There is no point in having all the information which the 1980 Act required to be made public if we don't *do* anything with it. And, in addition, a bit more honesty about sixth form options, even if some teachers don't like it: there are places where the choice of subjects and subject combinations is just not good enough, or where adequate choice can only be provided at great inconvenience to everybody. Sometimes such things as the nostalgia attached to the old-style sixth form and the public unawareness that there could ever be anything wrong with small schools seems to be deliberately exploited. Parents must know the true cost of what they are asking for: for example, the cost to country *towns* of keeping village schools – desirable of course, but rarely realistically debated. They often don't understand about selection either, especially the younger generation who scarcely remember the old arguments. So it is easy to propagate the myth that in the old days everybody used to go to grammar schools, wear ties, got seven O levels and respect authority, and that we could have that back. If I, as a parent, who campaigned long ago against selection point out that we can indeed have schools something like that for percentages varying from 5 to 35 per cent, but that of course it is a system built around failure for the majority, I become in the instant a rabid 'lefty'. That is because nobody ever explains to people what the options are.

Finally, perhaps we should ask ourselves whether some day we could not have a better education law offering more support to the LEAs in maximizing the quality of opportunity in bad times as well as good? It is clear, and often said, that the 1944 Act affords very weak protection for the broad curriculum and the life-long entitlement, and that we need a more precise definition of duty. It is less often said that the 1980 Act offers little support for planned contraction, and indeed even encourages a market-place approach. I sometimes wonder whether the LEA's basic legal obligation should perhaps be expressed in terms of facilitating equal access by pupils to whatever quality of opportunity the law requires them to provide. This would give a target philosophy for planning and for admission policies. It would put other desiderata, like having regard to parental preference, in an important but still subordinate place. It would provide a framework for positive discrimination, a need we have never seriously faced. We only played with it in the good times, while in the bad ones a combination of financial stringency and falling rolls actually has the opposite effect and handicaps the disadvantaged more.

You would expect me to say that any good new law for me would establish the equality of participation in school government which the Taylor Committee asked for, not the tokenism of the 1980 Act, and it would also provide training and support for the new governors not of a kind to make them some new kind of professional, but such as to give their ordinariness a confident voice. It would restore the habit of consulting about, and submitting to the DES, plans based on general needs and not on a school-by-school model. It would give parents a right to form associations. It would make LEAs and governors responsible for promoting good habits of communication in schools, and make it clear indeed that their responsibility for an effective service included the better organization of home support for children. The same objective would be explicit in the sections on teacher training.

We hear a great deal about 'caring' schools, and of course we are glad schools think it important so to describe themselves. We hear less about 'listening' schools, which term implies a more equal relationship. I have suggested in this chapter some of the things which need to change if the messages which come through to the listening school, and the listening LEA, are soundly based on a knowledge of schools' purposes and needs and a concern for the well-being of all the children. This may sound idealistic, but I don't think it too difficult to get across to the public the message that the achievement of the individual in education is as never before hollow and meaningless if the society which is its setting is based on rejection, underachievement and unhappiness. Anyway, we have no option but to try. Without public support, the desperate need for a fairer, more responsive and more appropriate service can never be met.

9

The MSC

GEOFFREY HOLLAND

On 1 January 1984 the Manpower Services Commission (MSC) was ten years old. Most of those who were present at its birth thought they were witnessing the hiving off of a relatively neat, self-contained area of central government activities – the public employment and training services – and it is to be doubted whether any of the founding fathers of the MSC foresaw even remotely that within ten years the new organization would be a major public spender, in the centre of political controversy and debate and a major influence on the lives of many organizations far outside central government, not least in secondary and further education.

The MSC was a constitutional innovation. Rather too little attention has been paid to this aspect of its existence. For it was, and is, no advisory body, but a public board charged with executive responsibilities. In these matters the MSC is noticeably different from, say, the National Economic Development Council whose function is exclusively advisory. The members of the MSC do, however, have something in common with such advisory committees, namely, that they are *representative*. When a commissioner commits himself/herself to a particular programme, policy, or line of action, he/she is also committing many more people and organizations in the world outside. This commitment, often overlooked or undervalued by commentators, is the key reason why so many far-reaching developments have taken place so quickly under the commission's auspices and why, time and again, ambitious and difficult targets have been achieved in a remarkably short space of time.

It was not until the MSC embarked on its major study, *Young People and Work* (1976–7), that the shape of things to come began distantly to emerge. Up to that point the commission had, in essence, been continuing its inheritance, trying to introduce a new style of management into its agencies, trying to feel its way towards a broader manpower policy and seizing opportunities, as they arose, to do something useful to help those – particularly the young – who were most hit by rising unemployment. With *Young People and Work*, the MSC began to feel its way towards a more coherent approach to youth policy at least. Even so, the setting was still unemployment and it was youth unemployment which created the resources on which the commission could build.

From the MSC's study emerged the Youth Opportunities Programme (YOP), which swept up all the youth programmes that had gone before and introduced into every community the reality of a range of offerings, including training courses, work experience projects, workshops and much besides, from which unemployed young people could pick and choose according to their interests, motivation and needs. The Job Creation Programme Action Committees were superseded by the Special Programmes Area Boards. These covered the entirety of England, Wales and Scotland and, as had not been the case with their predecessors, their membership was representative, with employers, unions, local authorities and the education service, together with the voluntary sector, all finding a seat, as of right, around the table.

In retrospect, however, perhaps the greatest innovation was the introduction of the 'school-leaver undertaking'. This was a promise that every unemployed school-leaver would be offered a suitable place within the programme and that the offer would be made before the Easter after the young person left school. No other country in the Western world had introduced such a guarantee before (indeed none has yet followed). Yet this 'undertaking' focused the minds of all concerned wonderfully. For implementing the 'undertaking' meant that, in every locality, there had to be the right number of opportunities; moreover, they had to be opportunities of the right kind for the young people in each locality. And the 'undertaking' meant too that YOP, unlike its predecessors, whether in the world of education or the world of work, had to reach out to and engage the complete ability range of young people – those with A levels and those with no qualifications at all, those from ethnic minorities, those mentally and physically handicapped and young offenders, all had to be found a place. And they were. By Easter 1979 (the end of the first run of the 'undertaking') all the unemployed 1978 school-leavers had been offered a place in the programme and the same achievement was repeated each year throughout the life of the programme; moreover, in its last year the date by which the offer had to be made was brought forward from Easter to Christmas and the 'undertaking' still met.

It was with YOP that the education service began to take serious note of the MSC. Until the launch of that programme on 1 April 1978 such dealings as the education service had had with the MSC had been relatively marginal or distant. Suddenly here was something very different. In the first year of YOP under 200,000 young people took part. Very rapidly, however, that figure climbed until in the last two years that preceded its transformation into the Youth Training Scheme (YTS) half a million or more young people were entering YOP each year. At the lowest there was money to be had from the MSC and, apparently, plenty of it. At the highest, for all those in the education service (and there were many) who wanted to develop a whole range of post-16 provisions, not least for those who were not pursuing an academic stream, there was a major opportunity at last to do something. Further, the education service had a seat at the table of the Area Boards and began through that to play an important part in local MSC planning and operations. And for more and more clients of the careers service MSC programmes were the only immediate destination.

There were, however, a number of serious problems about this closer linkage with the MSC. Some of these could be, and were, overcome; for example, the need in some colleges for additional physical capacity or for more and different in-service training for tutors and teachers. Some were to be viewed as healthy challenges; for example, finding ways and means of reaching out to many young people on work experience schemes or devising a curriculum and teaching materials and methods relevant and attractive enough to unemployed young people to bring them in. Others were dispiriting; for example, the falling post-programme placement rate as youth unemployment continued to rise dramatically. Still others led to tensions; for example, the yearly repeated apparent conflict of objectives in which the MSC seemed always to be chasing numbers and sponsors and the education service were more concerned with the individual and the quality of the opportunity provided. And finally, some were disturbing, particularly after 1979 when the MSC's financial resources continued to increase while the education service, face to face with falling rolls in the school and tighter and tighter control of local authority expenditure, began to see its resources diminish.

Yet for all that, an important corner had been turned. The world of work and the world of education were coming closer together through the creation of worlds or states which were neither one nor the other, but bridged the two. People began to talk more and more about a coherent policy for youth and, in particular, for young people up to age 18. People were growing more aware that in some of our competitor countries things are done differently and more systematically, and that much higher proportions of any age cohort have broad-based foundation training or vocational education. People started to feel the constraints of an outdated vocabulary in which 'training' was one thing and 'education' another.

And most important of all perhaps, 'out there' young people were demonstrating quite clearly that they could and would learn if their interest and attention were sufficiently engaged. For many young people the prime motivator for learning was seen to be work whether that be a real job, work experience with an employer, or participation in a training workshop or project. And many of those who for years had sat at the back of classrooms, disenchanted and disengaged, began to reveal talents and a potential unsuspected in traditional settings.

In short, the tragedy of unprecedented levels of youth unemployment was leading to a small and at first, stumbling revolution. The government was providing more and more funds for young people, and in particular their post-school vocational education and training. An education service which had drawn a line at age 16 for many of its clients was now providing increasingly for those beyond that age. Employers were being drawn into the act and their workplaces were being increasingly used as places of learning. Exciting new provision was developing at an unprecedented pace: less than five years saw training workshops, community service and community projects reaching out to whole new sectors of the population and the new information technology centres becoming rapidly established. First-line supervisors and managers found themsevles acting as tutors and teachers.

It is tempting to describe all this as a local premeditated progression. In fact it was something much more typically British: a combination of the force of events which could no longer be ignored; a great deal of initiative, enterprise and imagination especially in local communities; a few happy – almost chance – discoveries; good luck; and above all, a realization of a situation so serious that inactivity was unforgivable.

Even so, it is arguable that very little of all this could have begun to take place without the unique constitutional innovation which the MSC represented. Almost every facet of what had been done up to about 1980 (and even beyond) had involved some kind of threat to some body or organization; the struggle had been, and remained, constantly to open up more room at the margin in which to act. It is doubtful whether any government department could have been so well placed as the MSC to facilitate and underpin such developments. Certainly when it came to a more permanent strategy, the commitment and involvement of all the partners would be essential.

Towards the end of 1980 there first appeared within the circles of the commission and the bodies represented on it a draft of a document entitled *A New Training Initiative*. It was subjected to intensive scrutiny and much working and reworking. It eventually saw the light of day in the form of a consultative document published in May 1981. It was a turning-point, perhaps an historic one.

Those who composed the text of the document had a variety of reasons for doing so. First, they were convinced that the time had come to give coherence to what, at that point, had been separate initiatives and developments on the training and vocational education front. Secondly, they were impressed by the fact that the deepest recession since the Second World War was not a recession like the others. It marked profound structural changes in the composition of the workforce, in the skills and knowledge required of that workforce, and in technologies and the organization of work. Thirdly, the recession had been marked, as had all its predecessors, by a dramatic collapse in the amount of training being undertaken by industry and commerce. Particularly dramatic was the collapse of the apprenticeship system. In the 1960s a third or more of the young people leaving school entered an apprenticeship training or something similar. By 1980 that proportion was down to one in fifteen young people.

There were other reasons too. The authors of the document were convinced that without the fundamental reshaping of vocational education and training Britain would be left increasingly far behind the skills, competence and productivity of its competitors. They were impressed by the contrast in both the volume and quality of training and vocational education undertaken in North America, in Japan and in Western Europe. In West Germany, for example, some 90 per cent of young people undertake some form of vocational education and 'apprenticeship' lasting two years or more. In both North America and Japan the investments in adult training and retraining, whether in the form of community facilities such as community colleges, or by firms, is ahead of most practice in this country.

And finally, the timing from the political point of view was right. A relatively recently elected government set on the regeneration of the British economy was keen to emphasize and back the importance of vocational education, initial training and retraining throughout working life. Moreover, if the truth were told, its policy on training had, up to that point, been looking rather negative with the review of their number, faith being pinned on the promise of non-statutory arrangements to take their place.

The *New Training Initiative* set out a programme for the rest of the decade. It proposed three major and interlinked objectives:

(1) The development of skill training, including apprenticeship, in such a way as to enable young people entering at different ages and with different educational attainments to acquire agreed standards of skill appropriate to the job available and to provide them with a basis for progression through further learning.
(2) A move towards a position where all young people under 18 have the opportunity either of continuing in full-time education or of entering training, or a period of planned work experience combining work-related training and education.
(3) Opening up widespread opportunities for adults – whether employed, unemployed, or returning to work – to acquire, increase, or update their skills and knowledge during the course of their working lives.

Wide consultations led to an agenda for action which was firmly based on widespread support from all partners for the three objectives and the general analysis of the *New Training Initiative* document.

Just before Christmas 1981, two documents were simultaneously published. The first was a government White Paper, the second an MSC document setting out an *Agenda for Action*. There was much in common between the two documents, particularly the endorsement of the three basic objectives and the clear determination that each should be pursued. The government for its part announced that it was prepared to put very large resources behind initial youth training. Indeed the figure of £1 billion per annum hit the newspaper headlines as the government announced that it was prepared to make this sum available for a new Youth Training Scheme (YTS) to begin the march towards achievement of the second objective of the Initiative.

Here, however, the initiative hit the first rocks of controversy. For the government White Paper described a Youth Training Scheme which would be open only to unemployed school-leavers and which would pay them an allowance of £15 per week. The young school-leavers would have a year's good-quality training and would obtain a certificate at the end. The MSC's own consultations had, however, suggested that a bigger prize might be within the country's grasp. Both the government White Paper and the commission's *Agenda for Action* announced that that possibility existed. The commission proposed to establish a Task Group to attempt to design such a programme. The government for its part indicated a willingness to reconsider the framework of its own proposed Youth Training Scheme should that Task Group design a scheme which would cover more young people, provide initial training of no less quality and keep within the government's expenditure plans.

The early months of 1982 were consumed in this heroic endeavour. Eventually, early in April, the MSC's Youth Task Group agreed the outline of just such a scheme. It was an historic moment. During several tense weeks the possibility seemed unlikely as the points of view of employers, trade unions, the education service and others differed. But the will to succeed was there. The report of the Youth Task Group was unanimous and the stage was set for the biggest single advance in post-school initial training for young people that this country has yet seen.

The YTS was to offer a year-long programme of good-quality training to school-leavers, both employed and unemployed. Opportunities for young people would build on trainees' existing experience and attainments and provide a foundation both for work and for further education and training as appropriate.

To qualify under the scheme a programme of training must satisfy criteria to be established by the MSC. From the outset these criteria were to require any training under the YTS to provide an integrated programme of training, experience and relevant education. In particular, opportunities were to provide for the trainee to

(1) be properly inducted into the programme and each element of it with assessment of the individual young person's attained skills, achievements and needs;
(2) receive a minimum of three months off-the-job training and/or relevant further education;
(3) acquire defined core skills;
(4) learn about and have direct experience of the world of work;
(5) receive an introductory programme of training and skills related to a broad group or family of related occupations;
(6) increase his/her effectiveness in defined 'process' skills such as planning or diagnostic skills;
(7) develop personal and life skills;
(8) receive advice and support throughout the programme;
(9) be able, at the completion of the programme, to transfer his/her acquired skills, knowledge and experience to other employment contexts, including further skills training or education.

In a significant departure from earlier programmes the scheme was to be launched and run through managing agencies. No organization was to be admitted to this company unless it could satisfy certain criteria, chief among them being capacity to contribute to the objectives of the new scheme and conformity to overall guidelines and policies established by the MSC. Any kind of organization, including a national organization, might apply to be a managing agency, but in practice the aim was to secure that the majority should be major employers, whether private or public. The responsibilities of a managing agent would include:

(a) design and management of programmes and opportunities;
(b) recruitment;

(c) supervision of young people;
(d) maintenance of quality and standards;
(e) recording and certifying progress of young people;
(f) ensuring access for trainees to support and advice during and on completion of their year's training.

The scheme was to be supervised by a national-level board under the MSC. Membership of the board was to be representative of employers, trade unions, local authorities, local education authorities, voluntary and youth organizations and the careers service.

Quality was to be a key objective of the YTS; the Youth Task Group made three recommendations:

(1) that at national level the MSC should establish a group of professionals with expertise in initial training, vocational preparation, standards and scheme design for young people who have left full-time education;
(2) that the MSC should develop its capacity to ensure the quality of the YTS generally, and more specifically to advise the new local boards which were to supersede the Special Programmes Area Boards;
(3) that the MSC should contract with other providers to develop and fund a network, preferably based on existing organizations and institutions, of accredited centres which would assume responsibility for in-service training, refresher training of supervisors, line managers and instructors, further education staff and other education and youth service tutors.

The proposals of the Youth Task Group were endorsed unanimously by the MSC at its meeting in April 1982. The government rapidly followed suit. The work of implementation began. The target was to secure sufficient opportunities for 460,000 entrants in the year commencing September 1983. It was, to say the least, a tall order.

Nevertheless, the target was met. Between May 1982 and the summer of 1983 over 400,000 training opportunities for young school-leavers were created, some three-quarters of them with employers. Major employers contributed about a third of the places, many of them taking in 16-year-old school-leavers for the first time for many years; 4,000 managing agents were identified throughout the country and appointed after close scrutiny and approval by the new Area Manpower Boards which had been established in late 1982; and 55 accredited centres for the training of staff, supervisors and tutors were identified and moved into operation on time. In the midst of all this turmoil the MSC's Training Services Division and Special Programmes Division had merged as one organization and had formed themselves into fifty-five area offices, each with trained teams of staff. It was a stupendous effort. The credit must go to everyone – to employers, trade unions (who supported the endeavour strongly from the outset), the education service, voluntary bodies and many others. The mobilization of so many people all over England, Wales and Scotland is possibly without parallel, certainly in peacetime. The commitment called for by the New Training Initiative (NTI) was indeed evident and the involvement of all the parties to the Initiative and the YTS from the outset had been triumphantly vindicated.

But the YTS was not the only development late in 1982. On 12 November of that year the Prime Minister announced the government's intention to launch an initiative to stimulate the provision of technical and vocational education for young people in schools. This was to be a pilot scheme of programmes of full-time general, technical and vocational education for 14–18-year-olds within the education system. The MSC, much to the surprise and certainly to the consternation of many in the education service, was invited to establish some ten pilot projects in various parts of England and one in Wales.

Each project was to be capable of providing a four-year course, commencing at 14 years of age, of full-time technical, vocational and general education, including appropriate work experience, and leading to recognized certification. The purpose of each project individually and of the pilot scheme as a whole was to explore and test methods of organizing, managing and resourcing replicable programmes of general, technical and vocational education and to explore and test the kinds of programme, curricula and learning methods required for success.

In approaching its new task the MSC set out five principles. It would work through the local education authorities (LEAs). Individual projects would adopt different forms according to different local circumstances. Projects based on existing facilities would be considered as well as new ones. Young people's participation in the scheme would be voluntary. The precise curriculum would be a matter for local determination within certain general criteria or guidelines which would apply nationally.

To assist it in its task the commission appointed a National Steering Group. The membership of this group was drawn from different sections of education, from representatives of the local authority associations, from industry and from commerce. The trade unions (including the teachers) were represented. The task of the National Steering Group was to establish national guidelines for the Technical and Vocational Education Initiative (TVEI), as it became known, and to oversee the project; to advise on the selection of individual LEA projects; to monitor progress; to advise on arrangements for evaluation of the pilot scheme and at regular intervals to report progress to the MSC and the Secretaries of State for Education, Employment and Wales.

The immediate task was to draw up the national criteria and guidelines. These reflected the commission's first principles and made it clear that programmes of education must be broad. The objectives must include encouraging initiative, problem-solving and other aspects of personal development. General education was to be an essential component of all four years of the programme. The technical and vocational element was to be broadly related to employment trends. Programmes must cater for young people across the ability range and must offer equal opportunities to boys and girls. Programmes were to be voluntary for the young people concerned.

Once the criteria were agreed, all 104 LEAs in England and Wales were invited to submit proposals. At this stage the Initiative did not extend to education authorities in Scotland (though it was to do so within the year).

In the event sixty-six LEAs submitted proposals for a total of seventy projects. About half the proposals came from metropolitan authorities, half from non-metropolitan authorities. After a mammoth and detailed examination of all the proposals, the National Steering Group put forward twelve projects for the commission's approval. The commission itself expressed concern about the geographical distribution of the recommended projects (the north and London were unrepresented) and added a further two from the National Steering Group's short-list to redress this balance. So fourteen LEAs were given the go-ahead to start their projects in September 1983; all did so. At this point interest switched to the students.

Suggested numbers for funding purposes in each project were 800–1,000 in the project as a whole, that is, 200–250 in each year. These young people had to be drawn from across the ability range. In only two of the fourteen LEAs did the MSC contract to fund higher numbers. In spite of the speed of implementation and the late date of the go-ahead for the projects (in some cases this was after the normal options procedures), the pressure on places was very high. The number of young people entering projects was in fact 7 per cent higher than planned entry figures. Numbers of boys and girls were fairly even. In all cases the TVEI students were fully integrated into the schools and colleges they were attending – they are only identifiable from their peers in so far as they have opted, usually for a minority part of their education between the ages of 14 and 16, to take up a TVEI programme. A number of projects are being run in schools with high proportions of young people from ethnic minorities. Some LEAs are offering TVEI in schools which are especially equipped for physically handicapped young people and the programme is, therefore, available to any such students for whom it may be appropriate. Schools in the scheme have, in addition, groups of students designated as 'special students'. Others have links with special schools. In all, about 100 schools and over 30 colleges of further education were involved in the projects which started in September 1983.

All in all, as 1983 unfolded, it became apparent that the TVEI had struck a chord in the educational system. Once the selection of the original fourteen projects had been announced, many local education authorities made representations to the effect that further significant developments in technical and vocational education were not possible without further resources. The MSC was therefore anxious to maintain the momentum generated by the initial enthusiastic response.

As early as June 1983, in response to requests from the commission, the Secretary of State for Employment announced that the government had asked the MSC for proposals to extend the TVEI from September 1984. This led in due course to LEAs again being invited to submit proposals for a second round of projects, and sixty-eight authorities in England and Wales did so. Once again the National Steering Group had the job of recommending to the commission which proposals should receive support. By early 1984 a further forty-six projects had been given the go-ahead.

Moreover, by the end of 1983 Scotland, which had initially foreseen difficulties over the introduction there of the TVEI, decided that the aims and criteria of the initiative were sufficiently flexible to permit experiments within Scottish education authorities which were at the same time consistent with the existing development plan. As a result, early in 1984 the chairman of the MSC invited proposals from Scotland for projects to start in the 1984/5 academic year.

The new Initiative is, then, well and truly launched, but the real task begins. Lessons have to be learned. Replication is the objective. Thus in the next few years an intensive programme of monitoring and evaluation of all kinds will be underway and its results will be of far-reaching significance for the whole education and training system.

The White Paper, *Training for Jobs* (Cmnd 9135), which was published on 31 January 1984 reaffirmed the government's commitment to national objectives to secure the development of the vocational education and training system, rehearsed the achievements of the previous two years and set directions for moving forward. So far as the MSC was concerned, the main features were the endorsement of the achievements of the TVEI; the continued strong support of the government for the development of the YTS and quality improvement within that scheme; and the endorsement of nearly every proposal of the commission for adult training.

The White Paper did, however, have a totally unexpected addition, namely, the announcement that the government had decided to give the MSC important new responsibilities by enabling it to purchase a more significant proportion of work-related non-advanced further education provided by the local education authorities. The government stated that it had decided that the amount to be devoted by the commission for such provision in England and Wales should increase from the current £90 million to £155 million in the financial year 1985/6 and to £200 million in 1986/7. The government's intention was that the commission should, by 1986/7, account for about a quarter of the total provision in this area.

The MSC was asked as a matter of urgency to consider, consult and report to the government on appropriate machinery at both national and local level for carrying out its enhanced responsibilities. The White Paper also conferred on the Secretary of State for Education an important new role in the consideration and approval of the commission's Corporate Plan and particularly in proposals substantially affecting non-advanced further education provision in England.

Whatever may be the outcome of the debate about this latest government decision, there is no doubt that, as we reach the halfway mark in the debate, the stage is set for significant progress towards the original New Training Initiative objectives. The government's White Paper itself alluded to the commission as a body which it was now asking to extend its range of operations so as to be able to discharge the function of 'a national training authority'. In carrying out such a role the commission, barely ten years after its first meeting, will find itself with six major concerns.

The first is to establish the paramount importance of the customer in vocational education and training provision. Vocational education and training are not ends in themselves, they are intermediate products. And what goes on in the vocational education and training system is a process which must have an outcome. That outcome must be satisfaction of the customer, whether the employer or the individual.

Secondly, any relevant vocational education and training system must have a secure and reliable system for designing and marketing products that the customer needs and wants, offering them in an attractive and cost-effective way.

Thirdly, the system must be concerned to open up access to learning on a scale which we have not attempted before. This will imply taking learning to the customer as well as opening up places of learning to the customer. It can only be achieved by exploiting to the full the potential of the new technologies. No less important will be to put a premium on use of technology of the work place as an entry point to learning.

The fourth major concern must be a new approach to standards and to assessment and testing. The country badly needs a system of standards based on the competency and ability of the individual or the employer-customer to secure access to local testing of standards by accredited agents.

None of the progress we seek can be achieved without securing a reliable system for providing an adequate flow of competent, up-to-date, well-equipped teachers, tutors and instructors. This must imply *both* initial training and regular updating. It must be about industry and commerce as well as the education service. It must be about the line manager as well as the specialist.

And the sixth concern will be to shift the focus of attention in vocational education and training away from processes and towards outcomes. This is not to say that the process does not matter – far from it; but for too long debate has centred around institutions, around the process of education and training and around the curriculum when what matters at the end of the day is the quantity, quality and relevance of the result.

It has been a heady first decade for the Manpower Services Commission. There may well be some in the world of education who wish that the commission would somehow go away. Like all statutory institutions, it can of course be abolished just as it was created by Parliament. But during the last decade even the MSC's sternest critics would have said it has been an important force for change and that its interventions, particularly in the youth field, have taken the country a long way forward a great deal more quickly than otherwise would have been the case.

The New Training Initiative was drawn up in the belief that time was not on our side; and with every year that passes, that becomes more and more evidently true. As a country we are competing in a world market-place, where technologies are readily transferable and where the speed of that transfer has accelerated. In that market-place what matters is the skill and competence of peoples.

For too long we have lagged behind our competitors both in the scale of what we attempt and in the quality of our results. Yet, paradoxically, because of these self-same new technologies which are transforming the industrial and commercial scene, it may yet be possible for this country to catch up and, unfettered from the shackles of decades of tradition, we may yet create a new tradition for ourselves.

Through the short but eventful history of the Manpower Services Commission that tradition has been in the making. Consistently it has sought to build on the best of the past, and to do so uninhibited. Ultimately others will judge, but in my view when future generations come to survey the history of vocational education and training, they will see the 1970s as a turning-point, when for the first time we began to face up to the real underlying tasks and make a ladder of opportunity for the whole of the working population, not just the lucky few.

PART TWO

Analysing Developments in Policy Sectors

10

Curriculum and Assessment

DENIS LAWTON

Curriculum and assessment are both key features of the changing government of education. Education cannot be 'controlled' without influence being exerted on the curriculum, and a major means of achieving that in England and Wales has been by controlling assessment, particularly the public examination system. Part of this account of the *changing* pattern of control will be to show how there has been a shift from indirect control of the curriculum by means of examining at 16+ and at 18+ to much more direct means.

A useful starting-point will be the Education Act 1944 and the events immediately preceding it, particularly the Norwood Report in 1943, which established the doctrine that assessment should be subordinate to curriculum. A practical application of this principle was that teachers should control and set their own examinations.

The 1944 Act did not include the word 'curriculum', and the only subject specified as necessary was religious education or religious instruction. It was left to the local education authorities (LEAs) to be more prescriptive about the general content of the curriculum – if they wished. But in the late 1940s and early 1950s they were very preoccupied with questions of buildings and reorganization, so that the responsibility tended to be delegated to school governing bodies who were generally pleased to leave these 'professional' questions to the headteacher and his/her assistants.

School examinations were the most important control over standards – initially for grammar schools alone, later for secondary moderns as well. The School Certificate examination was well established, and a degree of national control had been exerted from the centre since the establishment of the Secondary School Examination Council (SSEC) in 1917. The School Certificate influenced the curriculum of grammar schools in at least two ways: first, it established a 'standard' to be achieved by pupils at the age of 16 in the various subject areas; and secondly, because it was a group examination rather than a single-subject examination and because it was related to university entry requirements, particularly in the form of the London Matriculation, a minimum core curriculum was effectively prescribed.

In practice, nearly all grammar school pupils studied and were expected to pass, English, mathematics, Latin and/or a foreign language, a science subject and at least one other subject. Much of the pre-1939 debate about the secondary curriculum was that the examination imposed too difficult a task for many of the pupils in the secondary schools at the time. Hence the Norwood Report suggestion that the group examination pattern should be replaced by a single-subject system

In 1950 the School Certificate gave way to the General Certificate of Education ordinary level, and the Higher School Certificate was replaced by GCE advanced level. One of the consequences of this reform was to give much greater freedom to headteachers to permit hitherto unacceptable combinations of subjects. Although the 1950/1 change from the School Certificate to GCE had little immediate effect on the grammar schools, it was of enormous potential importance once the tripartite system began to give way to large comprehensive schools.

Another important development was that GCE was soon to become an examination taken by a growing number of 'more able' pupils in secondary modern schools. In the early days of secondary modern schools, to be free from examination pressures was regarded as an advantage. Throughout the 1950s, however, pressure built up, partly from parents and partly from employers, for schools to develop leaving examinations which would enable pupils to enter the job market with some kind of paper qualification. In 1954 5,000 pupils entered for secondary modern examinations of some kind such as Royal Society of Arts or City and Guilds. In 1955 half of the secondary modern schools were preparing pupils for external examinations of some kind. Many educationists became alarmed at the proliferation of examinations, some of them manifestly unsuitable for use as a school-leaving certificate.

The official reaction to this situation was to set up the Beloe Committee in 1958. The Beloe Report (1960) recommended an examination for secondary modern pupils which would be clearly different in style from the GCE. By now some kind of examination for a proportion of the population at the top end of secondary modern schools was regarded not only as inevitable, but desirable, even by many teachers.

An indirect effect of the CSE on curriculum planning was also very important: being a single-subject examination, CSE intensified the tendency of the schools to plan the curriculum in terms of 'pupil choice' rather than carefully planned balance. The drift towards a very small core and a wide range of option choices became the norm for comprehensive schools.

The postwar policy of 'decentralized teacher control' continued without any serious challenge throughout the 1950s and into the early 1960s. This period was characterized by harmony and near-consensus in education; there was an optimistic feeling that if only we could spend enough money, train enough teachers and get reorganization right, then education would solve many social and economic problems. By the 1960s, however, public criticism of schools and teachers became common. Moreover, in 1960 the 'teacher monopoly' was challenged by David Eccles, the Conservative Minister of Education. During the House of Commons debate on the

Crowther Report he announced his intention to 'make the Ministry's voice heard rather more often and positively and, no doubt, controversially'.[1] He used the phrase 'secret garden of the curriculum' as an indication of his concern that an important area of education seemed to be closed to public discussion. Soon afterwards the Curriculum Study Group was established, but teachers' unions and the LEAs became so hostile to it that in 1963 Eccles's successor, Sir Edward Boyle, declared that the Curriculum Study Group would be replaced by another organization acceptable to the profession and the LEAs. The Lockwood Committee was set up and recommended that there should be a Schools Council for Curriculum and Examinations.

The establishment of the Schools Council seemed to be a victory for the teachers (and the LEAs) but it antagonized a number of civil servants at the ministry. Nevertheless, the Schools Council appeared to get off to a good start: not only were money and resources made available, but in accordance with the Lockwood recommendations, the influence of teachers was strong. The centralist tendencies of the Curriculum Study group had apparently been shaken off and decentralized teacher control appeared to be stronger than ever. The Schools Council also took over from the SSEC the advisory functions on school examinations. The Norwood policy of combining curriculum and assessment seemed to be settled once and for all. Much was achieved by the Schools Council, but perhaps the most important problem of all was neglected – planning the curriculum as a whole. Instead teachers were offered a variety of curriculum packages on various aspects of the curriculum, some of them very useful, but they did not add up to a plan.

In defence of the Schools Council it must also be said, however, that the Norwood policy of linking curriculum and assessment, which appeared to be such an advantage, was in fact a serious handicap. The first list of priorities established by the council included 16+ examinations and the sixth form curriculum; but the problem of reforming proved to be enormous and the repeated failures of the council in the examination area gave ammunition to those who wished to criticize and discredit the entire operation of the council.

The Schools Council took up this challenge apparently intent upon more dramatic changes, and by 1969 after co-operation with the Committee of Vice-Chancellors and Principals Standing Committee on University Entrance (SCUE), it produced a report which accepted the general criticism of overspecialization in the sixth form, and recommended that the A-level examination at 18+ should be replaced by a two-tier system: at the end of one year's study qualifying examinations (Q) should be taken on a much broader curriculum of five subjects (with balance built in by subject grouping rules), and a year later up to three subjects would be examined (F). There were many criticisms of these Q + F proposals both in schools and in universities, so much so that the governing council of the Schools Council rejected the recommendations of its own working parties rather than risk public hostility.

Q and F was followed by N and F: three normal (N) and two further (F) level examinations would be taken at the end of the sixth form course. An N level would be roughly half the work of an A level, and F would be about 75 per cent – thus three N and two F-level courses would not have entailed any more work than three A levels. In March 1979 Mrs Shirley Williams, as secretary of state, declared that A level examinations would not be abolished because there was insufficient agreement on alternatives. The Department of Education and Science (DES) demonstrated that universities and the Schools Council might have views, but final decisions about the pattern of school examinations was a part of central authority. Recent discussions about reform at 18+ take the form of candidates taking a mixture of A levels and intermediate or I level examinations (about 50 per cent of an A-level syllabus). However, it is difficult to see how two conflicting demands can ever be completely reconciled: the need for a much broader sixth form curriculum, and the tradition in British universities of a three-year honours degree which requires first-year students to be highly specialized before they embark upon a degree course.

The Schools Council encountered very similar problems in attempting to reform 16+ examinations, except that pressure from universities was much less important than a general concern for maintaining standards. During the 1960s discussions about raising the school-leaving age and the general move towards comprehensive secondary education made educationists more critical of the segregated system of two examinations at 16+, GCE for the top 20 per cent and CSE for the 40 per cent below that. By the early 1970s schools were demonstrating that they were not closely bound by these percentage guides; by 1975 nearly half of school-leavers had achieved at least one O level, and only 20 per cent had failed to achieve any CSE grades.

One problem about a common 16+ examination was whether it should accommodate this new flexibility or stick to the original guidelines. Bulletin no. 23 in 1971 recommended that the proposed common examination at 16+ should cater for those in the top 40 per cent of the ability range, with individuals in the 20 per cent below that range taking isolated subjects only. This limiting of the system to the top 60 per cent of the ability range, with the consequent neglect of the 'bottom 40', was a deliberate tactic designed to win over those who doubted whether a common examination system was possible without lowering standards.

In 1973 the trials between consortia of CSE and GCE boards were encouraging to those who wished to develop a common system. In July 1976 the Schools Council submited to Shirley Williams, Secretary of State for Education, a recommendation that GCE and CSE should be replaced by a common system, but Mrs Williams informed the council that there were still major uncertainties. It was suspected that these major uncertainties existed particularly in the minds of DES officials. The DES answer was to set up a further study group to be undertaken by the DES and HM Inspectorate, chaired by Sir James Waddell. The Waddell Report was published in July 1978 and made recommendations very similar to those of the original Schools Council proposals. New syllabuses should be introduced by the autumn of 1983, and the first examinations taken in 1985.

In 1979 there was a change of government and the new Conservative administration was less convinced about 16+ reform than Mrs Williams had been. In November 1982 a policy document was published, *Examinations at*

16+: A Statement of Policy. It described the steps necessary before a decision could be taken on a single system of examinations at 16+. By now the Schools Council had been replaced by the Secondary Examinations Council (SEC) and the document laid down the part to be played by this new council. A common 16+ system would depend on the development on national criteria for syllabuses and assessment procedures. By December 1983 the Joint Council of GCE and CSE Boards had completed its work in producing draft national criteria in twenty subjects as well as general criteria which would apply to all subjects.

Making national criteria a condition for the acceptance of a common system at 16+ was a very important move. Not only was the DES firmly in control of the new examination system, but by controlling the national criteria, there would be indirect control of the curriculum itself. It also became clear that the Conservative Secretary of State for Education, Sir Keith Joseph, was taking a personal interest in national criteria. But it was difficult to disentangle educational comment on the national criteria from political intervention. For example, the secretary of state said that he would not approve national criteria for physics examinations if they contained political and social implications. Despite such difficulties, Sir Wilfred Cockcroft, chairman of the Secondary Examinations Council, announced in December 1983 that the common system should go ahead.

Increasing central control was not, however, confined to indirect pressure on the schools by means of the examination system. During 1976 DES officials had been stung by rebukes in two public documents: an OECD report highly critical of the lack of DES policy-making, and the House of Commons Expenditure Committee which accused the DES of reducing policy-making to resource allocation. In the previous year the Prime Minister had asked Fred Mulley, then Secretary of State for Education, to report on four issues: the basic curriculum of primary schools; the comprehensive curriculum; examinations; and the 16–19 age-group.

The DES prepared a secret Yellow Book, which was deliberately leaked to the press before the Prime Minister's Ruskin College speech. It contained some sharp criticisms of teachers and the Schools Council. It appeared that the DES was aiming to take a much stronger role in policy-making in the curriculum, and would need to cut the Schools Council down to size in order to achieve that aim. Mr Callaghan's speech was an anticlimax because the public airing of the Yellow Book had enabled teachers and the Schools Council to counter some of the criticisms made within it, but it did launch the 'great debate' on education – a series of regional conferences on 'Educating our children' during February and March 1977.

In July 1977 the Green Paper, *Education in Schools: A Consultative Document*, made some general statements about educational standards, the core curriculum and the need for schools to have some concern for the preparation of pupils for the adult world, but a key statement was that it was not possible for secretaries of state to 'abdicate from leadership on educational issues which have become a matter of lively public concern'. The next sentence refers to the desirability for broad agreement on a framework for the curriculum.

The Green Paper was followed after the 1979 election and a change of government by *A Framework for the School Curriculum*[2] and then, in 1981, in the amended form of *The School Curiculum*.[3] But even more important was the centralist effect on local education authorities. Immediately following the Green Paper, the DES Circular 14/77, *LEA Arrangements for the School Curriculum*, was issued. The circular appeared to be seeking information about the curriculum rather than exerting strong centralist control. However, the agenda for a much more *dirigiste* attitude was clearly there. A follow-up report on the 14/77 review was much more demanding than the original circular: *The Local Authority Arrangements for the School Curriculum* stated that the DES was not satisfied with the kind of influence being exercised by the LEAs on the curriculum; some were not in possession of adequate information and had no satisfactory policy.

In 1981 after the publication of *The School Curriculum*, there followed another circular (Circular 6/81), reminding LEAs of their responsibilities on curriculum policy and curriculum control. There were two major thrusts to Circular 6/81: the first was to ask LEAs to review policy on the school curriculum and to plan future developments in accordance with *The School Curriculum*, and the second was to remind LEAs that governors should be concerned with the curriculum and that schools should set out in writing the aims which they pursue through the curriculum. Schools should also assess regularly how far the curriculum matched stated aims.

Finally, on 8 December 1983 Circular 8/83 was issued. In this the secretary of state asked authorities to inform him of the steps which had been taken since the issue of Circular 6/81, suggesting that HM Inspectors would also keep curriculum under review. The secretary of state asked for a response to this circular by 30 April 1984. It was also made clear that this would not be the end of the story – further reports and circulars were apparently to be expected.

Another aspect of increasing centralization was the interest shown in educational assessment and the accountability movement. In 1974 the Assessment of Performance Unit (APU) was launched. This aroused suspicion and hostility for three reasons: first, it seemed likely that the APU was really concerned with monitoring standards although presented as a means of diagnosing the problems of the disadvantaged; secondly, it could easily develop into another indirect method of controlling the curriculum (that is, teachers would teach to the test); and thirdly, it would encourage LEAs to indulge in testing programmes of their own even less desirable than the APU tests.

Although these suspicions were justified, the APU has not developed into an accountability monster. From 1974 to 1980 the tests did indeed become more and more openly associated with 'standards' and monitoring rather than diagnosis,[4] but the whole curriculum model envisaged by Kay[5] failed to gain acceptance and was replaced by a testing programme in English, mathematics and science. The LEAs have been encouraged to spend money on their own test programmes, sometimes very unsuitable ones, but the worst aspects of evaluation in the USA have been avoided and little backwash on the curriculum observed.[6] The work of the APU has also probably been overshadowed by the decision in 1983 to publish HMI reports on schools.

Another important development which can be traced back to the mid-1970s and James Callaghan's Ruskin College speech is the emphasis on linking the school curriculum to the world of work, for an examination of the proper relation between them was long overdue. A number of interrelated issues are involved. The first is that the English secondary curriculum has neglected 'the technical'. A second problem is the neglect of the 'bottom 40 per cent', while O levels dealt only with the top 20 per cent, and A levels were even more narrowly focused. The CSE examination attempted to cater for the next 40 per cent of the population, but did not reflect a curriculum which was noticeably less academic or more technical; similarly, those boys and girls who stayed on until the sixth form but were not 'A-level types' were regarded as a problem.

Finally, the majority of those in the 16–19 age-group, if they continued with any kind of formal education at all, did so in further education rather than the school system. Any connection between their job training and the school curriculum was purely coincidental. The doctrine that schools should not be concerned with vocational training was often interpreted to mean that the young need know nothing about the adult social, economic and political world.

All three issues – the neglect of the technical, the neglect of the less academic and of 'the world of work' – have been challenged since 1976. But the major thrust has come not from the DES, but from the Department of Employment's Manpower Services Commission (MSC).

The Schools Council's proposal to authorize a new examination for less academic 17-year-olds in the changing sixth form was not successful. In 1976 the Schools Council suggested that CSE boards should be allowed to organize a Certificate of Extended Education (CEE). Pilot schemes were worked out which appeared to meet with a good deal of approval and the committee chaired by Dr Keohane recommended, in 1979, that the CEE should be officially recognized and approved by the DES. But in 1979 the Mansell Report, *A Basis for Choice*, was published by the Department of Education, which included discussion of curriculum planning for 16–19-year-olds. The result was a range of pre-vocational courses which combined a basic core of general education with vocationally oriented instruction. The stronger vocational and industrial flavour were more in keeping with the new conservatism and the Keohane proposals were rejected. The Mansell recommendations now would be applied more widely. In 1982 plans were accepted for a new Certificate of Pre-Vocational Education (CPVE), which would start in 1984 for schools as well as in further education (or combinations of the two).

Meanwhile, earlier in 1982, the MSC had announced its plans for a new training initiative to begin in 1983, and a Youth Training Scheme (YTS) which would provide a full year's training, with pay, for jobless school-leavers. However, the MSC initiatives were not to be confined to the 16–19 age-group. In November 1982 a new Technical and Vocational Education Initiative (TVEI) was announced by the MSC. This was to be a five-year experimental pilot programme for about 10,000 14–18-year-olds in schools (or partly in schools). Schools were encouraged to plan a much more technical and vocational curriculum which would lead to qualifications not hitherto taken in schools. Local education authorities showed no reluctance at being included in this scheme, or to receive the cash that accompanied successful applications. In the first year fourteen LEA plans were to be taken on by the MSC from a much larger number of applications. Had the LEAs and the schools not been prepared to co-operate, the MSC was apparently prepared to set up technical schools outside the LEAs' control.

One interpretation of the TVEI was that it was a central plan to change the curriculum, deliberately excluding the DES because it had failed to deliver the curriculum goods quickly enough in the past. The advantages of channelling money away from the DES into the MSC was that LEAs would have to accept money under much more strictly controlled terms, including a very different view of the curriculum. For the DES to have taken such an initiative would, at that time, have been quite unthinkable. But an interesting by-product of the MSC initiative was that in 1983 a new Education Bill was introduced – the Education (Grants and Awards) Bill – to enable the DES to be able to play exactly the same game with the LEAs, that is, to invite them to bid for special grants which would be available for certain curricular priorities determined by the secretary of state.

This is not, of course, to suggest that the TVEI and other MSC initiatives are all to be condemned. Far from it: an overall shake-up of the curriculum might well be of some benefit. But what is disturbing is the way that such changes have come about, partly by central manipulation rather than genuine debate and partly by political pressures from DES ministers and others. The overall result is certainly greater central influence, and the precedents are by no means healthy. At just the time when the DES was busily engaged in changing its policy from non-intervention to more direction, it was outflanked by another government department unfettered by a tradition of having to consult LEAs and teachers.

On matters of curriculum and assessment the centralist tendencies of the DES go back at least as far as 1976, and possibly back to the 1960s. What has changed is the political flavour added to centralism since the general election in 1979. The accountability debate was becoming a serious influence by the early 1970s, but the monetarist ideology of the 1979 Conservative government gave a much sharper edge to such demands as 'value for money'; concern for standards was manifest in the 1960s and 1970s, but after 1979 the 'minimum state' idea tended to push curriculum planning in the direction of 'back to basics'.

One of the most interesting results of this increasing politicization of the curriculum is that it has become less and less satisfactory to talk of the 'central authority' of the DES as though there was a unified body of consensus. It is now necessary to subdivide the central authority into at least three major power groups: the politicians (the secretary of state, ministers and political advisers); the bureaucrats (DES civil servants); and the professionals (HM Inspectors). These three groups may occasionally agree on important educational issues, but are much more likely to disagree. The three

Table 10.1 *Interest Groups at the Centre and their Ideologies*

	Beliefs	*Values*	*Tastes*
Politicians	Market	Freedom of choice	Independent schools; fees
Bureaucrats (DES)	Good administration	Efficiency	Central control; examinations; and standard tests
Professionals (HMI)	Professionalism	Quality	Impressionistic evaluation

groups are different because they are operating with three different albeit overlapping ideologies which can be identified, to some extent, by careful analysis of the texts produced by each of them. I have suggested elsewhere[7] that it is useful to analyse the three ideologies by subdividing them in terms of beliefs, values and tastes. Table 10.1 may, then, be helpful in distinguishing between the three ideologies.

A further qualification of course is that the categories of ideology are not completely watertight. They do overlap considerably and individual members of the three groups may not be typical. For example, some DES civil servants may be much more like the politicians in terms of beliefs and values; similarly, some HMIs may be much more 'bureaucratic' than their colleagues, or even agree with the beliefs and values of the politicians. Nevertheless, such a distinction of groups with corresponding ideologies may help us to understand some of the tensions and misunderstandings at the centre.

Perhaps the most important feature of this lack of consensus is the fact that when the three groups appear to be talking about the same subject, they are often thinking very differently. For example, on curriculum the politicians appear to be obsessed with questions of standards, whereas the DES is looking for a neat solution to the problem of core plus options and HMIs have a professional concern for a common curriculum. Similarly, when discussing a topic such as the APU, the politicians' view might be something like a return to 'payment by results', whereas the DES would be concerned with the efficient monitoring of schools and HMIs see the APU as a means of improving the curriculum as a whole. In other words, we should regard the central authority not as a unified power base, but as a 'tension system'.

This should not encourage us, however, to underestimate the seriousness of the changes which have taken place in recent years concerning control and influence over curriculum and examinations as well as other kinds of assessment. Since 1979 a good deal more curriculum power has gone to the centre, and much to the political centre. Difficult independent bodies such as the Schools Council gave way in 1983 to non-representative councils and committees (School Examinations Council and Schools Curriculum Development Committee). The LEAs have been instructed by circulars, and schools have been directed by means of such documents as *The School Curriculum*. The partnership idea is now much less meaningful. The central control over examinations is as strong as ever; in addition, there is now considerable direct influence over the school curriculum, with much of the opposition neutralized. It remains to be seen how strongly the LEAs will react.

NOTES: CHAPTER 10

1 R. A. Manzer, *Teachers and Politics* (Manchester: Manchester University Press, 1970).
2 DES, *A Framework for the School Curriculum* (London: HMSO, January 1980).
3 DES, *The School Curriculum* (London: HMSO, 1981).
4 D. Lawton, *The Politics of the School Curriculum* (London: Routledge & Kegan Paul, 1980).
5 B. W. Kay, 'Monitoring pupils', in *Trends*, no. 2 (1975) (DES).
6 C. Gipps and H. Goldstein, *Monitoring Children* (London: Heinemann, 1983).
7 D. Lawton, *Curriculum Studies and Educational Planning* (London: Hodder & Stoughton, 1983).

11

Teacher Professionalism and Professionalization

JOHN EGGLESTON

This chapter will review the changing context of teaching professionalism and professionalization and show how the combination of changing appraisals of teaching and the changing market position of teachers have created a situation wherein a major governmental initiative on several fronts has been possible. This has involved both direct intervention and also a number of indirect challenges most notably through the work of the Manpower Services Commission (MSC). This wide range of initiatives may well diminish a number of traditional aspects of professionalism, notably autonomy and self-regulation. Yet it also opens up a number of areas of potential professional development, including an extended evaluative role, a fully professional involvement in the oversight of professional training and a more direct link with the public, both as parents and as employers.

The amorphous nature of teaching makes it difficult to answer whether or not teaching is a profession. Whether the profession has autonomy or control of recruitment, training and tenure requires an understanding of an immense network of subtleties and complexities, which determine how schools are run and how teachers are employed. In recent years this ambiguity has been presenting ever-increasing problems for teachers: first, because of the growing complexity of the teaching task; and secondly, because of the changing context of demand for and status of teachers.

AN INCREASINGLY COMPLEX TASK

Teachers have always assumed responsibility for what happens in classrooms. But this responsibility has always been exercised in a well-defined context. The public at large have had a general idea of what to expect in reading, mathematics, science, history and other subjects. They have known what, in general terms, to expect of children at different ages in different types of school This has often been expressed in terms of progress through well-known textbooks and syllabuses. But in the past twenty-five years this has changed. New subject-areas such as computer education, social studies and technology have emerged; new interpretations of existing subjects have joined them, such as the new mathematics and Nuffield science. Even more fundamental has been the insistence, through several decades of teacher training, that the needs of the child must determine the content and level of what is taught. This had led to a plethora of child-centred education with concepts such as 'reading readiness' and individual progress. It has also led to new administrative arrangements ranging through comprehensive secondary education, mixed ability teaching, integrated days and much more, all designed to protect both child and teacher from restrictions and expectations that are 'externally imposed'.

All this has resulted in a situation that has created severe difficulties for the administration and the assessment of schools. Within the system it is now very difficult indeed for the headteacher, local education authority (LEA) adviser or even the HM Inspectorate to appraise what is being achieved. No longer can a head have a detailed expectation of what should be being achieved by, say, a 14-year-old pupil in all subjects. A hundred development projects, special interest groupings, individual work and each teacher's own interpretation of the needs of individual pupils make this impossible. The professionalism of the teacher may have been increased, but at the cost of the professionalism of the head or the general inspector.

The increase in teacher 'autonomy' has seldom been matched by an ability to identify and comment on what has been achieved. The public examination system offers little help; only a small proportion of what is taught is examined and by no means all pupils take the public examinations at the end of their school career. Moreover, there is widespread doubt about the reliability and validity of public examinations and meanwhile the 11+ examination and all other intermediary 'public' tests of achievement have virtually disappeared. For the most part the world at large has to rely upon teacher appraisals of what is happening. These are not always highly informative as most parents who have waited in the line at school 'parents' evenings' know. A study undertaken by Sharp and Green[1] attempted to explore how teachers appraise progress in their classrooms. Their reported interview with a Mrs Carpenter, an apparently successful teacher of 'new mathematics', demonstrated the difficulties being experienced by even a qualified and competent teacher in reporting on what was being achieved:[2]

> When you've got a set plan ... everything in its place ... you taught length immediately after you taught so and so, and it was taught, you know, it was not a matter of children learning really, not in the way we'd been thinking that they should be learning ...
>
> *Interviewer*: How do you mean?
>
> *Teacher*: I mean we all, well, I have a little plan but I don't really ... I just sort of ... try and work out what stages each child is at and take it from there.
>
> *Interviewer*: How do you do this? How does one notice what stage a child is at?

Teacher: Oh we don't really know, you can only say the stage he isn't at really, because you know when a child doesn't know but you don't really know when he knows. Do you see what I mean? You can usually tell when they don't know ... [There was a distraction in the interview at this point.] What was I talking about?

Interviewer: Certain stages, knowing when they know.

Teacher: And when they don't know. But even so, you still don't know when they really don't [pause] you can't really say they don't know, can you? ... That's why really that plan they wanted wouldn't have worked, I wouldn't have been able to stick to it, because you just don't ... you know when they don't know, you don't know when they know.

Sharp and Green argue that Mrs Carpenter, along with other teachers in her school, however effective in the classroom, lack an 'accounting language' – a deficiency that calls for urgent rectification.

The problem is widespread. Many activities in the classroom go unappraised and unrecorded. The project, a popular form of teaching in primary schools, is a good example. Though all children participate in class projects, achievements vary widely. Many children fail to win the accolade of having their finished work displayed (even though this in itself is a somewhat unsure method of appraisal!). Even more seriously, many children fail to complete a significant proportion of work in the project and proceed through school via a series of uncompleted tasks, their work unappraised and unfinished and their readiness to proceed to the next level unachieved.

A CHANGED CONTEXT FOR TEACHERS

The collapse of *demand* for teachers has been reported extensively and is so well known that it is unnecessary to describe it in detail here.

From the specific viewpoint of professionalism and professionalization three problems exist:

(1) There is, in absolute terms, an excessive supply of teachers. As two of the central features of professionalism are scarcity value and secure employment, this alone has severe consequences for professionalism.

(2) It has led to a diminution of the teachers' salary position; since the Clegg award the real position of teachers' remuneration has worsened *vis-à-vis* other professions. Annual statistics published by the Union Bank of Switzerland[3] based upon a sample of cities of the world show that British primary school teachers now have an annual income markedly below that which obtains in North America, Australia and most of Western Europe, including Sweden, Norway, Denmark, Switzerland, Holland and West Germany.

(3) The reallocation of teachers following falling rolls and closures have obliged many specialist teachers to teach subjects other than their specialism. In medicine it is improbable that specialist gynaecologists would be required to become a specialist cardiologist or even to become a general practitioner. (One only has to reflect upon this

comparison to see something of the marginality of teaching as a profession.)

All this has not only direct but also indirect consequences for professionalism and professionalization that are even more powerful. *Professional status* is not made, it is given by non-professionals. There is frequent evidence in the popular press that the problems of curriculum and achievement and of teacher supply are leading to an articulate critique of teachers.

A typical example is:

> There are thousands of teachers who simply do not know what they are talking about. It is an alarming situation, and it confirms what many parents have often suspected – that little Willie's teacher is often only one step ahead of little Willie. That is why the Department's plans for more rigorous selection and training of teachers must be enforced as soon as possible ... before more children are thrown undeservedly on the dole scrap heap. (*Daily Star*, 22 March 1983)

> Military cannon may get mown down in time, but in education teachers who find that they have too little training and less aptitude for the task often stay put, being still less equipped for earning a living in any other way. (*The Times*, 22 March 1983)

Comments such as these probably have one of the most fundamental impacts on the nature of professionalism and professionalization, in that they are seen to represent the views of many of the teachers' clients – the parents, the employers and the children themselves. The criticisms are not confined to the media and the general public, they are sometimes echoed by the teaching professions. A recent report from the Secondary Heads' Association[4] criticizes teaching styles. They 'tend to promote passive dependency and resourcelessness, rather than autonomy, independence, inter-dependence and resourcefulness'. Youngsters are given 'too little opportunity to manage their own learning'. Content, not process, takes priority in lessons which tend to overemphasize intellectual skills and pay too little attention to a child's physical and emotional development. Greater efforts should be made to develop 'pupils' creativity, coping skills and cooperation'; there should be more 'coherence in the curriculum' which is 'too often a ragbag of single subjects without any overall rationale'.

CHALLENGE AND INTERVENTION BY THE CENTRE

There have been a number of recent developments that are specifically changing teacher professionalism and the process of professionalization, particularly in initial and in-service training.

New Developments in Assessment

The demand for a more effective assessment of the standards of performance achieved by teachers has now become a major political issue. The Secretary of State for Education's speech at the North of England Conference in 1984 achieved a remarkable level of popular attention and approval; particularly noteworthy was the public support of many of the teachers' professional organizations.

But the most striking feature was that Sir Keith Joseph was able to signal that the new technology of assessment was ready for use. It marks the beginning of a move from the conventional norm-referenced school-leaving examinations which assess a narrow range of school achievement for a narrow range of pupils. The development of a viable alternative of criterion-referenced assessment has been the subject of intensive effort in recent years, most notably by the DES's own Assessment of Performance Unit (APU). The unit has through work contracted with the National Foundation for Educational Research, Chelsea College and Leeds University established item banks of performance in mathematics, science and languages, these areas of performance being defined considerably more widely than that which is taught under those subject labels. In each area a range of achievements have been identified in gradients of difficulty which span virtually all aspects of what is taught in schools.

The tests are applicable to the work of children at age 10 and 15 (also 13 in the case of science) but could of course be calculated for any age. The items have been used to test performance of a 'light' national sample of some 1·5 per cent of the total age-groups. Much care has been taken not to allow the identification of individual LEAs, schools, teachers and children. However, with appropriate safeguards, the technology to undertake all these things with a fair degree of accuracy exists. (As with most systems of assessment, there are technical arguments; in particular, the Rasch model of total comparability between item scales is now used with considerably more restraint than was originally the case.)

The prospect of criterion-referenced testing is to make available a far wider range of a child's achievement and of a teacher's work to assessment. It is even possible to contemplate developing item banking and criterion referencing to a wider range of school activity. Aesthetic, physical, social and moral development have already been explored by the APU; the decision not to proceed with all of these items has been taken largely on political and administrative grounds rather than on those of technical difficulty. Meanwhile plans to assess design and technology through the APU are being explored.

Such moves, along with other associated techniques such as pupil profiling, have been reviewed extensively. A particularly important aspect is that they involve the active participation of the profession itself, so extending professionalism. This is made clear in recent accounts.[5] Together the new techniques present a prospect of a far more effective appraisal of professional achievement than heretofore – an appraisal that can be made available to the clients.

It is not only in terms of assessment, but also in method, that the new strategies of assessment will influence the work of teachers. The APU reports so far published suggest many ways in which the technique of teaching may be inappropriate and how it could be improved with better information from test results. Some examples of the way in which this is demonstrated by the existing report on mathematics testing are to be found in Eggleston.[6] The implications of all this for professionalism and professionalization, especially the initial and in-service training of teachers, are immense and likely to transform course programmes in the immediate future, giving a more hard-edged, scientific approach than heretofore.

Teaching Quality

Closely linked to changes in assessment is the most direct initiative on professional standards yet attempted by any government. In its White Paper, *Teaching Quality*,[7] the present Conservative administration, largely inspired by members of the HMI holding responsibility for teacher training, made a range of points specifically directed to the practice of teaching and the process of professionalization, advocating such changes as:

(1) The amendment of the Education (Teacher) Regulations 1982 to require employers to have regard to the formal qualifications of teachers in ensuring that school teaching staffs are suitable for their duties, and requiring a better match between staff qualifications and teaching tasks including more teachers with mathematics and science qualifications in primary schools and better subject match between qualifications and specialist teaching in secondary schools.
(2) New critieria for approved teacher training courses to be set by the secretary of state in consultation with the Advisory Council for the Supply and Education of Teachers (ACSET), with all courses to be reviewed against these criteria.
(3) A more rigorous student selection, and more rigorous tests of competence and suitability on completion of training, together with an increase in the participation of practising teachers in training through professional committees, participation in courses and other means.
(4) Better staff management in schools and LEAs, the criteria for redeployment to be enhanced professional development, not just a response to falling rolls.
(5) A planned programme for premature retirement to run at 5,000–10,000 a year among the over-50s to be based on teaching requirements rather than random opportunism – if necessary, to be augmented 'through compulsory redundancy among teachers under the age of 50'.
(6) Employers to be ready to use procedures for dismissal for the small minority of teachers whose performance cannot be brought up to standard: 'Unsatisfactory performance can be sufficient reason for fair dismissal'.
(7) More in-service training, particularly for heads and newly qualified teachers, and better induction arrangements.
(8) Teachers' self-assessment to be encouraged, but the LEAs should carry out their own formal assessment of each teacher's performance.

In his comments to the press the Secretary of State for Education emphasized the necessity to 'shake out' the teaching force, and the opportunity be seized to weed out weak teachers, particularly those who had 'run out of steam'. He also commented that it had 'only been discovered recently that the Education Secretary had the power to approve or disapprove courses'. Acting upon this new knowledge, criteria for courses are to be drawn up by ACSET by the summer of 1984, with a view to implementation by September 1984. The White Paper makes it clear that one of the criteria will be that courses are closely related to school subjects (particularly at secondary level) and to specific age ranges. Although such specification will not prevent newly qualified teachers seeking work in other areas, they are unlikely to obtain it. This will come about by application of the 1982 Education (Teachers) Regulations, which require a local authority to staff a school with teachers 'suitable and sufficient in numbers for the purpose of securing the provision of education appropriate to the ages, abilities, aptitudes and needs of the pupils'. The regulations are being amended as indicated in point 1, above.

Since the publication of the report ACSET has recommended that, in the interests of consistency across the country, a single council should be established to advise on the accreditation of initial teacher training courses in the universities and in the public sector. This recommendation has been accepted by the secretaries of state, who have announced their decision by means of Circular 3/84 which sets out criteria drawn up in the light of advice from ACSET.

The criteria follow lines somewhat similar to, but rather more stringent than, those anticipated in the White Paper. They include extensive local professional and lay involvement in training, a requirement for recent professional experience by a high proportion of teacher trainers, extended courses to thirty-six weeks per year for the postgraduate Certificate in Education, with a minimum of fifteen weeks' teaching practice. For B.Ed. students a minimum of twenty weeks' teaching practice in a four-year course is to be required. Specific qualifications in teaching subjects are also required, especially for secondary-oriented teachers; this is associated with proposed requirements for a far clearer identification of the age-group to be taught. There are also requirements for a more stringent selection of candidates with particular reference to their personal qualities.

The consequences of the combined activities of the emergent Council for the Accreditation of Teachers Education (CATE), local professional committees and the more intensive surveillance of both public sector education and university training departments are likely to be considerable.[8] They are likely also to bring a new stringency and consistency to the work of the teaching profession far beyond that yet achieved by the validation activities exercised by the CNAA and the individual universities in conjunction with the professional organizations. But whatever may be achieved in the elevation of professional competence, it is likely to be at considerable cost even to present levels of professional autonomy.

The Alternative System of State Education within the Public Sector

The Manpower Services Commission (MSC) established itself in a very few years as a major provider of post compulsory school education for many thousands of young people through a multiplicity of schemes, notably the Youth Opportunities (YOP), Youth Training Scheme (YTS) and Work

Experience on Employers' Premises (WEEP). In all of these activities the commission has undertaken its responsibilities to create an enhanced work capacity in its predominantly unemployed and young clients and has devised a system of education involving not only specific work experience, but through a variety of providing agencies, public and private schemes of personal and social development and the acquisition of a wide range of basic skills. Such activities include, where appropriate, the achievement of basic literacy and numeracy and have been conducted in a manner more reminiscent of industrial training than secondary schooling. Combined with close surveillance and evaluation, many schemes have been claimed to have achieved impressive educational gains. An important feature is that, like many other aspects of further education, this work has been undertaken with a wide variety of adults acting as teachers, many of whom have no professional training or qualification to teach. Many teachers employed by MSC courses claim that their success demonstrates the lack of necessity, even the futility of professional training.

One recent move which has considerably strengthened the role of the MSC has been the introduction of the Technical and Vocational Education Initiative (TVEI) programme, in which the approaches and methods of the commission are being implemented – with MSC funding and supervision – within the secondary schools themselves. The scheme commenced, in September 1983, in small groups of schools in fourteen LEAs, and is being extended from September 1984 to schools in some sixty LEAs in England and Wales. Although most of the teaching in the TVEI programmes is likely to be undertaken by professionally qualified teachers, the strategies they will be required to adopt are similar to those of the MSC in its post-school operations. In most schools, if not all, other adults will be drawn in from outside the teaching profession (from industry and commerce and from administration) to undertake teaching duties alongside the 'professionals'.

Not only does the TVEI hold out the prospect of professional 'dilution' and diminished professional control, it may also lead to an erosion of many of the traditional 'strengths' of the teaching profession. This could include one of the remaining 'monoplies' of the schools, the obtaining of 'academic' qualifications. Janes suggested that:[9]

> The end of much of the full-time 16+ work in sixth forms and colleges of further education could be in sight if the latest recommendations of the Policy Services Unit find favour with the government. In a confidential report due to be sent to the Cabinet office today, the Unit urges that the principles underlying the Youth Training Scheme should be extended as far as possible to 16 year olds intending to enter the professions – medicine, dentistry, accountancy, law and teaching, are quoted as leading examples.

The same prospect was presented in a different way by the retiring head of the HMI, Sheila Browne. Speaking in September 1983 of the attraction of the TVEI scheme for bright pupils, she noted that their 'defection' may push up the unit costs of traditional academic courses and possibly force hard-pressed LEAs into cutting the number of subjects on offer. She also commented: 'Because this reduction in population will increase the cost of an academic education for the groups left on academic courses, we are going to have to watch very carefully that we don't reduce what we provide for them, as in many cases we have done already.' It is interesting that, in exploring this possible challenge to existing professional practice, there is also associated with it a potential challenge to the process of professionalization, in that the established path through A-level examinations normally followed by intending teachers is also being held up to scrutiny.

CONCLUSION: A FOCUS FOR PROFESSIONAL DEVELOPMENT

It must be emphasized, however, that this chapter has focused on change in its discussion of the flux of professionalism in which some aspects decline in importance while others ascend. Underlying these changes are the enduring core of teacher professionalism. This includes such factors as the care and concern for the education of young people and the continuing refinement of the techniques of teaching that are most appropriate and effective for their age, aptitude, ability and background. It is these techniques, gradually honed to their highest level, that are widely regarded as constituting mastery teaching, and it is this mastery that is still the ultimate goal of professionalization and of all true professionals.

However, there is one major area in which further consideration is required. This is the crucial role of the LEAs who are the direct employers of the vast majority of teachers, the providers of the schools and the resources with which they work, and the agents of democratic local control of the education service as a whole. There is a good deal of evidence of the work of enlightened individual LEAs and their policies for teachers.[10]

Some of the areas in which LEA officers, advisers and inspectors work with established teachers to enhance professionalism include:

(1) The encouragement of practising teachers, with appropriate advice and resources, to guide and help initial teacher training students in their schools and to work closely with college tutors to ensure the most effective development of professionalism in the location where it is most likely to flourish – the classroom. This would also include providing appropriate facilities for college tutors themselves to play a part in the teaching of the classroom.

(2) The development of similar initiatives in helping and supporting teachers in their probationary year. Most authority advisers and inspectors already see this as a crucial part of their work, but in some LEAs more is done to enhance the quality of the school itself as a crucial learning experience in the development of professionalism.

(3) A major effort, which is already being made by some authorities, to facilitate their own participation and that of their teachers in the enhanced responsibilities of the professional committees which are now playing a far more important part in the arrangements for initial and in-service training of the various training organizations.

(4) An all-round enhancement of in-service programmes such as being achieved by some authorities to ensure that in-service work at all levels from short courses through to diploma and higher degree programmes truly reflects the needs of the teachers and the schools. Such authorities recognize that enhanced professional qualifications are no longer simply to be seen as a passport for upward mobility both in and beyond the school, but must now be seen as an enhancement to the continued service of the teacher within his own authority if not within his own school. For this reason new strategies are being adopted where dissertations and other studies of teachers in the university or college are being focused on the issues of particular concern within his own authority or school. Such approaches are devised by the tutors of the training institution in conjunction with the teachers and advisers of the relevant local authority, and it is even possible for arrangements to be made whereby the senior teachers or advisers of the authority play a part in the supervision of the study itself.

(5) A range of less structured means by which the professionalism of teachers in the employ of LEAs is enhanced by closer involvement with policy formation in administration, examinations, the curriculum and other areas of development. This may be conducted through the teachers' professional organizations, who themselves play a significant part in the development of professionalism; through teachers' workshops in which inspectors, advisers, training establishment tutors and relevant lay personnel may play a part; through specially organized meetings for governors, parents and employers; and so on. In these and many other areas the opportunities for the LEA to enhance professionalism are abundant, and increasingly being explored and developed.

(For a more extended discussion of the policies of the LEAs and their teachers see the other chapters of this volume.)

Not all of these new approaches and policies of the LEAs are co-ordinated at national or even regional level. If the new approaches that have been explored in this chapter are to lead to an effective new professionalism and professionalization, the co-ordinated role of the LEAs is vital and its development urgent. No LEA can avoid a response to almost every issue that has been raised in this chapter. But it is not only quantity that is essential, although without this the potential advantages of the new developments may be lost within an LEA. However, without a co-ordinated response, in partnership with the professional organizations, the execution of the professional role and the conditions in which it is exercised and the results it achieves will be localized and uneven and the teaching profession will risk fragmentation, localization and even immobilization.

NOTES: CHAPTER 11

1 R. Sharp and A. Green, *Education and Social Control* (London: Routledge & Kegan Paul, 1976).

2 *Teacher Numbers: Looking Ahead to 1995*, Report on Education, No. 98 (1983) (DES), pp. 1–5.
3 R. Enz, *Prices and Earnings around the Globe* (Zurich: Union Bank of Switzerland, 1982).
4 'Heads tell how schools could do better', *Times Educational Supplement*, 27 January 1984.
5 See H. Black and P. Broadfoot, *Keeping Track of Teaching* (London: Routledge & Kegan Paul, 1982); and D. Satterley, *Assessment in Schools* (Oxford: Blackwell, 1981).
6 S. J. Eggleston, *Understanding Mathematics* (London: HMSO, 1983).
7 *Teaching Quality*, Cmnd 8836 (London: HMSO, 1983).
8 Eggleston, 'HMIs move in on teacher education', *Times Educational Supplement*, 14 January 1983.
9 A. Janes, 'MSC latest – YTS for the professions', *Times Educational Supplement*, 1 April 1983.
10 See for example the submissions of many LEAs to MSC for in-service programmes under the TRIST (Technical and vocational education Related In-Service Training) scheme in summer 1985.

12

Managing Contraction

KIERON WALSH

The notion of professionalism is inevitably bound up with concepts of the autonomy and self-control of occupational groups; in contrast, management involves dependence and control. Concepts of management and professionalism tend to contradict rather than complement each other. Occupational groups which are wholly or predominantly employed within organizations inevitably face conflicting pressures resulting from a clash between the desire for professional autonomy and the need for managerial control. In the case of schoolteachers the postwar growth in the education service served to lessen the conflict resulting from the contrasting logics of professionalism and management. Expansion created the opportunity for teachers to determine their own careers within the system of employing institutions.

The contraction of the education service that follows from declining pupil numbers and financial cuts brings the two logics into direct conflict with each other. The Secretary of State for Education has made it clear that he considers that there is a need for more positive management of the teaching force by local education authorities (LEAs); the LEAs will need[1]

> to manage it [contraction] in ways which improve the match between teacher expertise and subjects taught; minimise longer-term damage from the changing age structure of the teacher force; maintain a reasonable, if necessarily low, inflow of newly qualified teachers whose high calibre, standards of qualification and up-to-date subject knowledge are important to the quality of schools and who need to be recruited now to provide leadership in schools in the coming decades; and raise professional standards by retaining and encouraging the best and most committed teachers.

This is a daunting agenda for the LEAs and a disturbing one for teachers. The possibilities for tension and conflict are obvious, and are all the greater given a teaching force which has become accustomed to autonomy and self-control as a result of a long period of growth. In this chapter I examine the mechanisms available to the LEAs in managing teachers in a period of contraction and their implications for professionalism and careers.[2]

STAFFING SCHOOLS

The first question that arises is that of how many teachers are needed in any given school. Typically the mechanism for determining the appropriate staffing complement has been the pupil–teacher ratio, usually with additions, often large, for special needs and purposes. As Dennison[3] has pointed out, the allocation of teachers to schools on the basis of a pupil–teacher ratio allowed curricular and other development within the school since extra pupils could be accommodated in existing class groups freeing the extra teachers for new duties. With contracting numbers, the loss of teachers tends to reduce curricular opportunities especially as schools fall below six forms of entry. Consequently the LEAs have adopted mechanisms that protect the curriculum as numbers decline, notably curriculum-based staffing. Those LEAs which have introduced staffing approaches have typically argued that they are not intended to be prescriptive, that the curriculum used to calculate staffing entitlement is not the curriculum that the school should teach. None the less, the tendency is inevitably one of control. As one chief education officer (CEO) said when interviewed, 'The teachers responding to the commitment shown [to improved staffing] should accept that the authority, in my person in particular, will wish to be involved much more closely than previously in all matters concerning the secondary curriculum and its outcome'. The autonomy of the teacher and the school in determining not only the extent, but the character, of the curriculum will be limited.

Within the school declining numbers and resources will tend to threaten the career prospects of teachers through the actual loss of subjects and through teachers being required to teach outside their subject specialisms. There is a danger of fragmentation of the teaching experience:

> Teachers who accept this more general role must not be handicapped in career terms in comparison with colleagues who remain with one specialism. Nor must they be asked to teach a timetable made up of 'remnants' left over when specialist colleagues have been allocated to more favoured tasks. There should be adequate recognition of the demands that are likely to be made on heads of department in these circumstances; non-specialist teachers may well need extra support when their knowledge is comparatively limited, particularly when work is being planned and prepared.

Contraction tends to reduce the degree of differentiation and specialization within the school. Pastoral structures are particularly likely to be reduced through the elimination of house or school divisions and the combination of pastoral, academic and administrative responsibilities. A lower degree of subject specialization is reflected in moves from departmental to faculty patterns of organization. The reduction in the number and size of schools reduces the number of administrative posts. The results of academic, pastoral and administrative changes is a decline in the variety of posts available to teachers in planning their careers.

RECRUITMENT AND APPOINTMENT

The most obvious impact of decline is the reduction of the number of entrants to the teaching profession and the consequent increase in teacher unemployment. Between 1975/6 and 1982/3 first appointments in teaching declined from 34,739 to 11,583 and they will continue at this low ebb until the late 1980s. Recorded unemployment rose from 9,236 in 1975 to 23,091 in 1982. Employment prospects are worse for those trained in public sector institutions as against universities and for those trained in history, art, English and geography. The teaching labour-market is now a buyer's market. When decline is anticipated, authorities are likely to appoint on a fixed-term basis, often for periods of less than a year. More teachers are now appointed on a peripatetic basis moving from school to school to cope with variations in need. Both these developments mean that the individual school is less likely to be seen by the teacher as the focus of his/her professional life. Control over teacher deployment is more centralized in the hands of the authority.

The continuity of teachers' careers is lessened by the decline in part-time work. As Trown and Needham[4] argued in 1980, the cuts of the late 1970s led to a disproportionate decline in the availability of part-time teaching, although since then the ratio of part-time to full-time staff has stayed constant. Between 1974 and 1982 there was a 29 per cent decrease in the ratio of part-time to full-time staff. The paradoxical result is that women teachers, who would prefer a part-time post, stay on full time for fear of not being able to find a job at all. The process of appointment itself is becoming more centralized as authorities seek to ensure that staffing levels are cut. In a small number of authorities the teacher's contract of employment itself has changed from appointment to the school to appointment to the authority, a move encouraged by the recent White Paper because it is thought to aid redeployment.

REDEPLOYMENT AND MOBILITY

In a time of growth and teacher shortage teachers will be more or less free to determine where they wish to work and to move from school to school, and authority to authority, as they see fit. As studies of teachers' careers have shown, mobility was a key factor in promotion and advance in the 1960s and 1970s.[5] Contraction brings with it declining mobility. Teacher turnover, which was viewed with concern by the Houghton Committee, has declined rapidly. A DES study of turnover in 1972/3 found annual turnover rates of 19·8 per cent in primary and 17·7 per cent in secondary schools. In the Inner London Education Authority (ILEA) the rates were 32·8 and 24·5 per cent for primary and secondary schools respectively. In 1979/80 the Association of Metropolitan Authorities (AMA) reported a turnover rate of 12·6 per cent for the ILEA as a whole. Rates of 9–13 per cent were reported by authorities in the Expenditure Steering Group (Education) (ESG(E)) negotiations. Lack of turnover is now viewed with concern by both the LEAs and headteachers, especially in secondary schools.

The LEAs have adopted a number of approaches in the attempt to increase turnover and mobility. All but one authority now have premature retirement schemes, although Hereford and Worcester are reported to be abandoning their scheme. Between April 1980 and March 1982 a total of 10,525 teachers retired prematurely.

Redeployment is widely used. In a survey of eighty-five authorities we found that 0·87 per cent of the total teaching force was redeployed in 1979/80, and 1·13 per cent in 1980/1. The majority of redeployment is voluntary but ninety-four of the 104 English and Welsh LEAs have agreements specifying compulsory redeployment where they feel it necessary. Redeployment has major impacts upon the school as a professional community of teachers. There is pressure on the relationship between headteachers and teachers. The Secondary Heads' Association (SHA) has advised its members that they should 'resist any attempt to delegate the responsibility for personal identification to themselves' but, inevitably, headteachers will play a major role in the redeployment process. The result may well be a worsening of relations between headteachers and the rest of the staff. Redeployment may also worsen relations between the staff themselves. Older teachers may put pressure on their younger colleagues to volunteer to move. Generally there is the tendency to attempt to pass on those teachers who are seen as weak and to keep the better teachers. Inevitably the LEAs play a major role in the redeployment process, partly because of the need for co-ordination across schools and partly because of the unwillingness of teachers to move, and schools to accept those redeployed. There is always a suspicion that the redeployed teacher is less able, which again serves to limit the willingness to move. Redeployment is particularly difficult at the secondary level, where it is more difficult to match the redeployed teachers to the places available. The rapid deceleration of the global decline in teacher numbers between 1982 and 1983 may be seen as evidence of this difficulty.

The more that movement between schools can be effected on a voluntary basis, the fewer difficulties there will be between LEAs, teachers and schools. The ILEA, in consequence, changed its redeployment procedures in 1982. Previously vacant posts had been reserved for those designated for compulsory redeployment, but from 1982, 'although teachers can still be designated as being at risk of movement, it is proposed that all scale 1 teachers assigned to divisional staff (and including those who have been designated) should be free to apply for any vacancies which exist at the end of May'.[6] In another authority all redeployment was seen as temporary and treated as a form of secondment between schools. In practice, a small number of authorities have adopted schemes for exchanging teachers between schools, and although they have had some success, they involve a considerable administrative burden.

RING-FENCES

A number of authorities, particularly in metropolitan areas, have adopted 'ring-fences' on the appointment of teachers, whereby the right to apply for vacant posts is limited to teachers already in the employ of the authority. Ring-fences are viewed equivocally both by teachers and authorities. Teachers see them as valuable in preserving jobs and enhancing career prospects within authorities but at the expense of reducing mobility and the quality of teachers appointed. The LEA officers see the greater ability to control teachers as being bought at the expense of risk to the curriculum. Small authorities and their teachers are likely to be particularly disadvantaged by the operation of ring-fences because their choices will be more limited. Ring-fences enhance the promotion prospects of teachers in authorities with higher turnover and reduce those of teachers in authorities with lower turnover. The decline in the mobility of teachers that has, in any case, been occurring because of the falling number of vacancies is enhanced by ring-fence procedures. It would seem plausible to argue that the mobility of teachers between schools and authorities, which was characteristic of the period of growth, resulted in a dissemination of experience and innovation. Mobility created a capacity for institutional learning. Without that capacity for automatic learning through mobility, there is a need for authorities deliberately to create alternative means for maintaining innovation and development.

AN AGEING PROFESSION

Despite the increasing use of premature retirement, the average age of the teaching force will inevitably increase over the next decades. The effects will be particularly marked because growth created a very young profession. In 1979/80 51 per cent of primary and 63·7 per cent of secondary teachers were under 40. Whereas, on the Department of Education and Science (DES) projections, in 1994/5 only 31·7 per cent of primary and 35·6 per cent of secondary teachers will be in this age-group.[7] Few in the education service can view this development with equanimity, especially if older teachers are less able to cope with the stress of teaching. The strong interest in premature retirement expressed by teachers in all authorities is, perhaps, an indicator of the potential for dissatisfaction in an ageing teaching force.

The lack of recruitment will also create problems for authorities as the ageing process works itself out. They are likely to find that there are discontinuities in the promotion process as whole generations of senior teachers holding promoted posts retire at once. A number of LEA officers have expressed the need for 'succession' planning if there are not to be difficulties of filling promoted posts.

PROMOTION, TRAINING AND APPRAISAL

Teachers' promotion prospects are presently governed by the Burnham system. The availability of promoted posts is dependent upon the number of

Table 12.1 *Proportion of Teachers at the Top of their Scale (Percentages)*

	1978	*1981*	*Change, 1978–81*
Scale 1	15·6	21·9	+ 6·3
Scale 2	35·9	44·3	+ 8·4
Scale 3	43·2	53·4	+10·2
Scale 4	62·8	74·7	+11·9
Scale 5	84·0	92·2	+ 8·2

points available in a school which is largely determined by pupil numbers. The system has been questioned by academics, educational administrators and teachers. Change in the system is being debated nationally and at the moment discussion centres upon the introduction of a career grade, an induction grade and promotion linked to appraisal of individual performance. The form of appraisal introduced for teachers – for example, whether it was by peers or by employer representatives – would be crucial in determining the independence of teachers as an occupational group.

Within the limitations of the Burnham system authorities have an impact on teachers' promotion prospects through their discretion on the allocating of Burnham points. The majority of authorities operate their discretionary powers in such a way as to allow schools less than the maximum possible number of points for promotion. Financial cuts have led authorities to execute their discretion more tightly than was previously the case.

Since 1978 there has been a rapid rise in the proportion of teachers at the top of their respective scales, as Table 12.1 shows. The rate of promotion over the next three years is expected to decline by about a quarter for scale 1 teachers, by about a third for scale 2 teachers and about half for those above scale 2. While their power is limited, authorities may well intervene in the way that schools use points in order to enhance the promotion prospects of one group of teachers as against another. The LEA as employer is thereby coming to influence the structure of the teaching profession more directly.

The mobility that characterized the period of growth allowed teachers to gain a variety of experience through movement between schools and the LEAs. Those who moved most were those who were promoted most, suggesting that mobility rated as an *ad hoc* training mechanism. The stagnation that may result from decline has been widely acknowledged. The need for in-service training as a means of countering stagnation is more talked about than acted upon. An increasing number of teachers is being seconded and the percentage of education expenditure spent on in-service training has risen slightly since the mid-1970s, but the levels of in-service training recommended in the James Report have not been attained.

More important for our immediate purposes is the approach to what in-service training is for. Whereas heads and teachers give low priority to management training, it is viewed as being of great importance by the LEAs and government. The LEAs and headteachers give a much higher priority to school-based in-service training than do teachers. As one authority reported:

> Courses for individual teachers may create 're-entry' problems and frustration. The effects of such courses are not often influential upon the institution as a whole. There should be a shift of emphasis from the isolated individual as the most useful recipient of in-service education towards the 'functioning unit' (the year team, the department, the faculty, the whole staff), as part of a co-ordinated and corporate approach to curriculum development and to evaluation of an institution's small performance.

The focus has shifted from the independent teacher to the institution and the concomitant shift from an emphasis on the teacher as independent professional contractor to skilled employee is clear.

MORALE

It is difficult to find unexceptional measures for the morale of teachers, but nevertheless it is widely acknowledged to be low and declining. Certainly there is evidence of increasing rates of absenteeism and the HMI has commented upon the dangers of decline for teacher morale. As well as difficulties involved in the teaching process itself, and there is evidence of increase in the difficulties of maintaining discipline, a major factor in determining the level of morale is the degree of certainty and uncertainty about the future. Closure and amalgamation places the future of institutions and consequently jobs in jeopardy. The vagaries of the local government financial system continually threatens pay and jobs. As teachers lose autonomous self-control the onus for maintaining morale passes to the LEA.

WOMEN AND DECLINE

The exigencies of falling rolls and financial cuts in their effects upon teachers as an occupational group bear disproportionately upon women. They are more likely to teach those subjects in which teacher unemployment is more prevalent, and they are more likely to be non-graduates for whom promotion and appointment is more difficult. The cutbacks in part-time and supply teaching and the declining opportunities for re-entrants to the profession limit the ability to maintain the momentum and continuity of their careers. The decline in teacher mobility that has accompanied the decline in available posts and the adoption of ring-fence appointment policies has affected women more than men. Given the importance of teaching as a profession to women in an economy where female opportunities are in any case limited, these effects are of particular significance.

CONCLUSION

The result of financial and demographic decline for teachers as a professional group is a move to a more managerialist stance by authorities and the development of more centralized control. As one authority's report on falling rolls stated:

> Especially in the context of contraction and falling rolls the authority has an obligation – both as an employer and as the provider of the education service – to 'manage' more effectively the careers of its teachers so as to help them maximise the satisfaction they get from their work and thus their contribution to that service.

But as John Sayer argues, 'Without the means for self-management, the more teachers are "managed" the less do they form a profession'.[8] Teachers have of course always been employed in organizations rather than acting as free-standing contractors like lawyers or, to a large degree, doctors. Growth allowed the profession to develop a series of characteristics that are now threatened by decline: these were high mobility; good career and promotion prospects; autonomy; and specialization.

Labour-market conditions gave the teacher a degree of dominance in the employer–employee relationship. While they had to work for an employer, teachers could to a large degree control and influence the conditions under which they worked. The conditions that created that control and influence are now being eroded by financial cuts and falling pupil numbers.

NOTES: CHAPTER 12

1 *Teaching Quality*, Cmnd 8836 (London: HMSO, 1983), p. 24.
2 K. Walsh, R. Dunne, J. D. Stewart and B. Stoten, *Falling Rolls and the Management of Teachers* (Windsor: NFER/Nelson, 1984).
3 W. F. Dennison, 'Teachers and shrinking schools', *Durham and Newcastle Research Review*, vol. 9, no. 43 (Autumn 1979), pp. 37–43.
4 A. Trown and G. Needham, *Reduction in Part-Time Teaching: Implications for Schools and Women Teachers* (London: Equal Opportunities Commission/AMMA, 1980).
5 S. Hilsum and K. R. Start, *Promotion and Careers in Teaching* (Slough: NFER, 1974).
6 See ILEA, *Contact*, 7 May 1982.
7 *Teacher Numbers: Looking Ahead to 1995*, Report on Education, No. 98 (1983), (DES), p. 10.
8 J. Sayer, 'Managing the teaching profession', *Local Government Studies*, vol. 6, no. 6 (November/December 1980), p. 47.

13

Finance of Education

TONY TRAVERS

PUBLIC SPENDING ON EDUCATION

In addition to the importance of education in the cultural and democratic life of the country, public spending on the service is a significant proportion of all national economic activity. In 1983/4, after several years of restraint, education spending in the United Kingdom represented some 13·3 per cent of all public spending (just under 6 per cent of gross domestic product).

Increases or reductions in expenditure on education, or changes in levels of provision, will thus have effects on overall government activity far greater than changes in other local authority services. Within local government education still represents about 47 per cent of all expenditure. Table 13.1 shows spending on various parts of the education service in 1983/4 compared with overall current and capital spending on all services; and on several other major areas of public expenditure. Spending on schools and on further education is for England only; that on universities, for the United Kingdom (the difference in treatment results from the presentation of the public expenditure White Paper).

Spending on education and science in the United Kingdom was just over £16 billion in 1983/4, which meant that about 13·3 per cent of all public spending was devoted to education. This proportion has fallen in recent years. Table 13.2 shows education and science current spending in England as a proportion of all public spending in each year from 1978/9 to 1983/4. The reduction has come about as the government has sought to achieve cuts in public spending.

The recent attempts by the government to reduce public spending have been concentrated on local authority services. These attempts to make economies have come at a time when there were already concerns with local government finance. Both the rating system and central grants have been increasingly criticized – this is because successive governments have cut the level of grant support (and have therefore transferred the cost of local services from taxpayers to ratepayers).

A more sophisticated attempt to discourage spending by progressive cuts

Table 13.1 *Education Expenditure, by Sector, 1983/4*

Sector	*Definition of spending*	£m. (*cash*)	*Percentage of UK public spending*
Under 5s	Current	305	0·25
Primary	Current	2,463	2·05
Secondary	Current	3,783	3·14
Special	Current	399	0·33
Universities	Current	1,305	1·08
Advanced further education	Current	600	0·50
Other	Current	3,468	2.88
Total	Current	12,323	10·23
Capital (all education)		516	0·43
Total education		12,839	10·66
Total education and science		13,356	(England)
Total health and social services		14,688	(UK)
Total defence		15,716	(UK)
Total social security		35,324	(UK)
Total public expenditure		120,328	(UK)

Source: *The Government's Expenditure Plans, 1984–85 to 1986–87*, Cmnd 9143, February 1984, tables 2.10 and 1.3.

Table 13.2 *Education and Science Current Spending in England as a Percentage of UK Public Spending from 1979/80 to 1983/4*

1978/9	*1979/80*	*1980/1*	*1981/2*	*1982/3*	*1983/4*
9·5	9·3	9·4	9·2	9·0	9·0

Source: As Table 13.1, tables 1.2 and 2.18.

in grant has occurred since the government introduced block grant in 1981/2. In the period since block grant was first outlined as a reform of local authority finance (in late 1979) a range of changes have taken place in the administration and finance of education.

Block grant offered central government greater scope to influence local authorities, which was the main reason for local authority opposition to it. As set out in the Local Government Planning and Land Bill 1979, the new grant would involve setting explicit spending needs assessments for every authority in England. These were to become known as grant-related expenditure assessments (GREs) and would be made separately for each service and then aggregated for each authority, and would give the power to reduce the grant paid to any authority which chose to spend above a specified margin over the needs assessment. Separate systems were to operate in England and in Wales, but Scotland was not affected by the change.

The Local Government, Planning and Land Act 1980 duly allowed the introduction of block grant. In addition, a new system of controls over capital spending was initiated, changing the basis of control over capital expenditure from loan sanction for projects to limits on cash spending. But it was block grant which encountered the greatest opposition from the local authorities and which was expected to have the most effect on education and other services. The first rate support grant (RSG) settlements to use the new grant were those for 1981/2.

Before the 1981/2 financial year had started, the government announced that each local authority was to be given an expenditure target for the year.

The basis for this target would be different from the GRE for the authority. Targets were also set on a different definition of spending and on a different price base for the GREs. In 1981/2 each authority was given a target 5·6 per cent in real terms below its 1978–9 current spending figure.

Later in 1981/2 the government decided that any authority spending over its target would be subjected to block grant penalties. This meant that in addition to the disincentive involved in the tapering off of grant increases for authorities which spent much over the GRE, there would also be great reductions for authorities spending over target (though the government exempted from penalties those authorities which were spending over target but below the GRE).

The arrangements established in 1981/2, of block grant backed up by targets and penalties, continued in 1982/3, 1983/4 and 1984/5. Alterations were made in the underlying factors used to assess the GRE, while targets for 1982/3 awards were set on the same definition and price base as was used for the GREs. Nevertheless, almost all authorities faced a different GRE and targets each year, often with considerable gaps between the two figures; penalties increased, particularly in 1984/5. The power to hold back block grant for authorities was enshrined in the Local Government Finance Act 1982, which also banned supplementary rates.

LOCAL AND CENTRAL GOVERNMENT REACTIONS

Opposition to the introduction of block grant and targets continued with their operation and intensified as the extent to which grant was being held back became obvious. The effect on overall expenditure was not what the government had hoped. In each year from 1981/2 to 1984 local authorities' budgets exceeded the government's plans. The figures in Table 13.3 show, for England, the plans and budgets (or estimated options) for education and for total current spending in each year.

These figures show how local authority spending in each year exceeded the government's plan by wide margins. In each year too education exceeded plans by less than the average. Local authorities asserted that the reason for the overspend was that 'the Government had set the plans unrealistically low. The Government did, in fact, revise upwards its earliest plans for 1982/3', and 1983/4 and 1984/5. An 'unallocated margin' of spending was

Table 13.3 *Local Government Current Expenditure, Plans and Out-turns, Education and All Services, from 1981/2 to 1984/5*

	Plan	*1981/2 Out-turn*	*Percentage difference*	*Plan*	*1982/3 Estimated out-turn*	*Percentage difference*
Education*	8086	8514	5·3	8865	9187	3·6
All services	16180	17472	8·0	18000	19054	5·9
	Plan†	*1983/4 Budgets*	*Percentage difference*	*Plan†*	*1984/5 Budgets*	*Percentage difference*
Education*	9155	9711	6·1	9532	10075	5·7
All services	18788	20550	9·4	19647	21439	9·1

* Excludes meals and milk.
† Does not include any part of the 'unallocated margin' which was added to current expenditure in 1983/4 and 1984/5.
Source: Department of the Environment, Rate Support Grant reports.

Table 13.4 *Cash Increase in Current Expenditure on Education, 1981/2 to 1983/4, Percentage*

Top 5		*Bottom 5*	
Hillingdon	+24·9	Coventry	+4·1
ILEA	+22·1	Salford	+6·5
Leicestershire	+20·4	Oxfordshire	+8·6
Brent	+20·3	Stockport	+8·7
Haringey	+20.2	Wiltshire	+8·7

Source: Hansard, 21 December 1983, cols 281–2.

added to the government's spending plan (which was the basis of the GREs) in England. The higher of the two planning figures (including the unallocated margin) was the basis of targets.

Although the overall level of spending did not fall in line with government plans, individual authorities did respond to the call for stringency. The percentage increase in cash expenditure on education between 1981/2 and 1983/4 varied from 24·9 per cent to 4·1 per cent. Table 13.4 lists the top and bottom five percentage changes in this period.

The fact that many education authorities were making considerable economies led the HM Inspectorate to comment unfavourably on provision in some of the lowest spenders during this period. Pressure on the government built up from sources including the House of Commons Select Committee on Education and Science and from interest groups. This intensified existing pressure within central government for greater national involvement in the provision of local education. Such pressure had long existed within the Department of Education and Science (DES). Mrs Shirley Williams, while

Education Secretary, had pressed for a specific grant for in-service teacher training. Local authority opposition to any movement away from 'general' (that is, unallocated) grants to those which had to be used for a specific purpose had managed to keep Mrs Williams at bay.

But the pressure for greater central attention to be given to protecting the curriculum and to ensuring that activities which the government felt to be of immediate national importance led Sir Keith Joseph to introduce a number of new specific grants. The first of these was for in-service teacher training, and was announced on 1 September 1982 in response to the Second Report for the Education, Science and Arts Select Committee for 1981/2. The report had called for, among other things, specific grants for in-service teacher training.

On 12 November 1982 the Prime Minister announced that there would be a new initiative for technical education. This initiative was to involve the local education authorities (LEAs) making proposals to the Manpower Services Commission (MSC) for particular schemes or modification of existing provision. If approved by the MSC, the commission would provide support to aid what authorities would themselves provide. The scheme would be for technical and vocational education for 14–18-year-olds and would operate, in the first instance, in a small number of authorities in England and Wales (it was extended to Scotland on 30 June 1983).

In March 1983 the DES wrote to the local authorities associations announcing their intention to introduce education support grants (ESGs). These would (according to the government) allow, first, the government to encourage LEAs to respond quickly to new demands on the education service; secondly, allow the targeting of resources towards particular initiatives; and thirdly, allow pilot projects to be financed.

When Sir Keith Joseph announced the proposed legislation to introduce the new support grants, he countered the complaints from the local authorities associations that the increased use of specific grants would erode local government's autonomy claiming that the education support grants would leave unchanged the fundamental relationship between central and local government. He claimed that the proposed grants would provide an incentive for LEAs to review their spending priorities in the light of national needs and that the scheme should help to improve standards and to introduce changes more quickly.

In November 1983 Sir Keith suggested eight possible initial activities to be funded by the ESGs; these were:

(1) schemes for developing records of achievement;
(2) consideration of changes in mathematics teaching following the Cockcroft Report;
(3) projects to assist curricular development in small rural primary schools;
(4) projects to improve performance of primary schools in the inner cities;
(5) developments in management of the teacher force;
(6) provision of microelectronics equipment for handicapped children;
(7) establishing resource centres for children with special needs;
(8) the promotion of information technology in further education.

The Education (Grants and Awards) Act received the royal assent in April

1984. Grants were paid out under the Act from 1985/6 onwards. The grants paid out under the Act would support expenditure equivalent to 0·5 per cent of planned education spending in any year. The proportion of education spending which could be supported by education support grants was increased from 0·5 to 1·0 per cent during 1986. Grants for in-service teacher training were paid out from 1983/4 onwards, under section 3(a) of the Education Act 1962.

A further major extension of central control over what had hitherto been local education was announced in January 1984. In the White Paper, *Training for Jobs* (Cmnd 9135, HMSO, January 1984, para. 55 (xi)), the government proposed that:

> To ensure that public sector provision for training and vocational education is more responsive to employment needs, the Manpower Services Commission's resources for purchasing non-related non-advanced further education in England and Wales will be increased to represent by 1986–87 about one quarter of the total public sector provision for this area, with a resultant reduction in local authority expenditure.

This meant that a further major part of non-advanced further education (the technical and vocational education initiative had already involved the MSC in parts of the education service) became centrally funded from 1985–6. The local authorities associations were opposed to the change, as they had been to earlier initiatives.

In addition to the reforms in funding local government education described above, there were other significant changes in the years from 1982 to 1984. For example, the control of advanced further education (that is, higher education outside the universities) was shifted from individual LEAs and a system of 'pooling' expenditure to a National Advisory Body for Local Authority Higher Education (NAB). This was set up in February 1982 to advise the secretary of state on the management and funding of local authority higher education. Although the body was, and remains, a local government-dominated institution (the NAB committee consists of eight members, six of whom are appointed by the local authorities associations), there was undoubtedly a shift of control from local to central institutions in its creation.

The gradual move towards greater central involvement in local education suggested evidence of increasing concern within central government (not only in the DES) about the provision of education. The Prime Minister expressed personal concern – for example, it was she who announced the new initiative for technical education in November 1982. The Departments of Employment (via the MSC), Trade and Industry each made inroads into what had hitherto been LEA provision. The DES, on the other hand, had to content itself with a few extra specific grants which between them came to total about 1 per cent of local authority education spending.

This was not for want of trying on the part of the DES. In 1981 the department proposed a radical new way of funding education which could have given it a far greater say in what each LEA spent. The proposal was made in an annex to the Green Paper, *Alternatives to Domestic Rates* (Cmnd 8449).

NEW WAYS OF FUNDING EDUCATION

The Green Paper was produced by the government as its response to growing discontent with rates as a local tax. The failure of successive governments to reform local taxation and grants was discussed earlier. But the Conservative Party had committed itself in the October 1974 general election to abolishing domestic rates. This commitment was somewhat weakened in 1979 to abolition of domestic rates after other direct taxes had been reduced. Nevertheless, many Conservatives (and others) both inside and outside Parliament were expecting action to remove or lessen the impact of rates.

Alternatives to Domestic Rates described several taxes which might be operated by local authorities; and in addition, a number of possible non-tax replacements for part or all of household rates. Local income tax, a sales tax, a poll tax and reformed domestic rates were examined as possible local taxes. The pros and cons of each were listed, though the tone of the document suggested that only rates were likely to be successful. Assigned revenues (that is, giving local government a part or all of one or more central government taxes) and additional grant were also discussed as possible ways of relieving the burden on domestic employers. Finally, annex B of the Green Paper expanded upon the possibility of reforming the grant system by discussing the reform of education funding.

One possible danger to the system of grants to local authorities would have been to pay a high specific grant in support of a particular service, leaving the rest of the Exchequer grant for equalization purposes. The 'natural candidate', according to annex B, for separate grant arrangements would have been the education service, which had had such a separate grant until 1958. Education accounted for about half of all expenditure by local government and was more than four times the size of any other single local service.

The Green Paper went on to discuss a specific grant which met the whole cost of education or one which met only 80 per cent of spending. It then mentioned the possibility of transferring education to central government. This, like a high specific grant, would have moved the cost of providing education from local to central taxation. However, taking the education service out of local government (or even increasing the preparation of local authority spending met out of specific grants) would have involved a radical change in central–local relations. Opposition would undoubtedly have come from both Conservative and other politicians. A less dramatic change which was also mentioned was the possibility of transferring teachers' salaries to the Exchequer.

Paragraph 7 of annex B outlined a further option. This was an 'education block grant' – which would have involved, in effect, two block grants. The first would have been for education only, while the second would have been for all the rest of local authority services which were currently supported by block grant. The existing block grant (which had replaced the needs and resources element from 1981/2 onwards) involved separate spending needs assessments for education and for other services, so that there would be no problem in developing an education grant-related expenditure assessment. There would, however, have to be quite separate grant-related poundages

(GRPs), schedules for variations in GRPs depending on spending in relation to the GRE, multipliers and all the rest of the block grant components.

Any move to an education block grant would in this instance have been designed to take the pressure off the rates. This, it was considered at the time, might have required £2 or £3 billion block grant in addition to that paid in 1982–3. (The figure widely discussed was 75 per cent of total education spending.) A similar scheme in Wales and Scotland would obviously have added to the extra cost grant. Although rates would fall because of the additional grant, national taxes would have had to be used. The 75 per cent education block grant would have added 3p to income tax.

Education block grant thus went the way of other alternatives to domestic rates. Nevertheless, the pressure exerted by use of the grant system, and the other changes in funding which were discussed earlier contributed to an overall move within central government for greater direction over local education.

THE CHANGING STATE OF LOCAL GOVERNMENT EDUCATION

The earlier sections of this chapter have examined the continuing pressures for reform of local government finance and the reaction of successive governments. Education and other local authority services were much expanded in the years following the Second World War and yet no parallel reforms took place in local authority finance.

The growth of a crisis in local government finance, brought about by the lack of reforming, was deepened by relatively unpopular structural reforms in 1974 and 1975; by a succession of economic crises; by changing attitudes towards the public sector; and by a reduction of the number of pupils and students involved in education. This led to pressure on and within the government to take action to change public education. Such actions have tended to involve accretions of power to Whitehall.

Central government has become increasingly involved with determining the level of total local government current and capital expenditure. The development of the Public Expenditure Survey system (and of the public expenditure White Papers) is evidence of this. Latterly this increase has spread to the control of individual local authority spending. This has been brought about, first, by block grant, and secondly by the introduction of rate limitation. Block grant brought with it the annual publication of an assessed spending need figure for education, and indeed for individual parts of the education system. Abolition of the Greater London Council will involve the government in control for three years over the Inner London Education Authority's expenditure and manpower levels.

In addition to such major shifts of power, there have been other, smaller developments which extended central control of influence over the LEAs. The MSC's move into further education is the most significant, though the increased use of specific grants may imply that further steps are to be taken in this direction.

THE CHANGING POSITION OF CENTRAL DEPARTMENTS

The changes which are described in the section above have had implications for departments of state. The Treasury, in its long campaign (since the mid 1970s) for cuts in public expenditure, has had considerable success in convincing successive governments to cut grants to local government and to take further steps to bring authorities under the same kind of control as central departments. The Department of the Environment, as the 'front-line' department for local government, has found itself pushing through a range of local authority legislation in attempts to fulfil government demands for reduced current spending. The Treasury's interest in cutting spending (which has involved cutting the real level of Exchequer grant) has to some extent conflicted with the DoE's interest in holding down rates.

The Department of Employment has, via the MSC, much increased its stake in education, while other departments (for example, Trade and Industry) have increased their spending in schools. The DES, on the other hand, has had a much less successful time. The attempt to introduce education block grant failed; meanwhile the government's expenditure plans for education have implied real and continuing reductions in spending. Only the introduction of new specific grants can be seen as successes for the DES in the field of local authority finance.

The DES remains notionally in charge of one of the major parts of public spending, though it has no direct control over local authority provision. This means that it can only have marginal influence over tiny areas of provision. If authorities choose to spend well below or above the average on, say, secondary education, there is little that can be done centrally (unless of course an authority can be shown to be failing to fulfil its statutory obligations). At a time when resources for local government are likely to continue to be constrained, the DES will probably continue to find itself under pressure to bring about changes in areas where its present powers will not allow action. This in turn will lead to further demands for central control. A Green Paper on Local Government Finance, published in January 1986 (Cmnd 9714), proposed the possibility of considerable extension of the use of education support grants.

THE FUTURE

Continuing pressure for greater central control could either lead to new legislation for general financial control over local government or to detailed control over services. If education is to continue to be provided by local government within a national legislation, then the finance and structure of local government itself will need reform.

Such reform would have to follow a period of research and consultation, and would need to consider questions of structure, functions and finance. Recent studies (from the government, in particular) have examined either structure or finance separately. Legislation to enact any changes would need to be given a decent amount of Parliamentary consideration rather than the over-rapid attempts at legislation which have been witnessed in the last few years.

If education is to remain a local service (surely the most plausible outcome), then local government finance will require reform. Education and other major local services would need to be funded from a robust and comprehensible local tax base. A local income tax (in addition to revalued rates) would probably give local authorities a plausible base from which to fund services. Grant could then be reduced. This ought to ensure that local services were funded from a strong and buoyant tax base and that central intervention was reduced. This in turn should strengthen the accountability of local councillors and officers for services provided. The January 1986 Green Paper considered a number of options for new taxation and grant arrangements for local government, though there was little likelihood of reform in the short term.

Strengthening and modernization of the finance of local government would be part of the solution to local government's problems. Structural reorganization which ensured that, as far as possible, all education authorities were in possession of a good tax base would also be important. Reduced central involvement in the day-to-day activities of the LEAs (for example, in capital spending programmes and school closures) would also be vital. Finally, it would be important that the public had open access to the information used in making decisions about education.

Unless changes are made, the degeneration of local government finance will continue. Pressures to take more decisions about educational provision at the centre would also increase. Local authority education is too important a part of our cultural, democratic and economic system to face centralization as a substitute for local accountability. Existing examples of centrally run local services (for example, health) make discouraging models. Reform is therefore urgent.

PART THREE

Scenarios for the Government of Education

14

A National Service: Strengthening the Centre I

MAURICE PESTON

There is one methodological point that needs to be made at the outset. During the past few years there have been strong moves towards centralization initiated by the Conservative government. Opposition to that has often come from Labour-controlled local authorities. Thus the debate on the structure of government has become highly politicized (or more highly politicized!). Each side is reacting against what it perceives to be the sins of the other. Not surprisingly, the result is not one of rational and dispassionate analysis of serious problems. It should be stressed therefore that those like the present writer who favour more centralization in education do not necessarily regard themselves as supporters of existing Conservative Party policies. Equally, Tory proponents of local government independence do not become socialists solely on that account.

A second methodological point that must be made is about size. Obviously the central government is larger than a local authority, but some local authorities are extremely large. The proponents of 'small is beautiful' will see little to admire in the West Midlands County Council or the Greater London Council (GLC).

The discussion of the relative roles of central and local government is usually based on the following considerations:

(1) *Tradition* – central and local government are both a part of our history and the (albeit unwritten) constitution. Each has traditionally had a role to play in education, and it would be a radical departure from that tradition to limit one or the other.

(2) *Democracy* – quite separate from their specific roles in education, both central and local government are part of our democratic political processes. For those processes to have much meaning each level must have its functions. While this does not necessitate a major educational function for local government, it is difficult to see what other functions it might have of a similar significance.

(3) *Efficiency* – the provision of education may be judged partly according to national criteria, and partly according to local criteria. Equally the adjustment for what actually happens with what ought to involves both national and local processes. To have only one level of decision-making and operations will lead to efficiency losses of a sort that economists, in particular, must object to.
(4) *Equity* – whatever the case for local involvement, there will always be a need for national concern with education which derives from a lack of congruence between local needs and local resources. This conclusion depends on it being accepted that educational provision should be more equally distributed than incomes and taxable capacity.
(5) *National needs* – again whatever the case for local involvement, education is so important to national welfare that central government can never afford or be allowed to ignore it. At the very least central government must concern itself with compulsion, the maintenance of standards, accreditation and similar matters.

Now in mentioning these areas of discourse several points stand out. First, it has been taken for granted that there must be some governmental involvement in education. This is prior to discussing the level at which it occurs. Secondly, there is the general acceptance of the special importance of education compared with most other goods and services which generate welfare. Thirdly, no distinction has yet been made between provision, control and finance.

In the United Kingdom at the present time education at all levels is largely state financed and largely state provided. (On the latter the universities are nominally independent institutions, and they certainly have a great deal more autonomy than the schools; none the less, in practice, especially in recent years, the provision of higher education has been dominated increasingly by government.) It is also true that education is state controlled in the sense of there being such things as a school-leaving age, publicly recognized examinations, legislation concerning parental rights and the activities of teachers, and so on.

Now it is usually argued that none of the actions of government logically entails the others. If that is so, there could be state provision, state control, or state finance each on its own. There could, for example, be state schools privately financed by user charges and subject to competition from private schools, with no legislative control of education at all. Alternatively, all schools could be privately owned and controlled but with fees met entirely by the state. Or again the state could limit itself to legislative and administrative control but refrain from any form of provision or finance.

In practice, matters are rather different. It is not merely that there have been independent reasons why the state has involved itself fully in education. In addition, provision, control and finance are seen as interrelated. This is partly for political and partly for economic reasons. If the state provides money, then it will see itself as having a duty to monitor how those funds are spent. (It is worth recalling in this connection the role of Parliament and of the comptroller and auditor-general in criticizing the use of public funds. It is a matter of regret, however, that this has become so limited at the present time. Members of Parliament appear to be more devoted to supporting the executive than criticizing its expenditure. Moreover, they have tended to confuse the discussion of the scale of expenditure with its form.)

While it may in principle be possible for government to offer finance without exercising some control or interfering in the educational process, in actuality it finds it impossible to exercise such restraint. Similarly, a decision to make education compulsory leads in practice to a decision to provide at least some schools, and in a highly unequal society, to pay for these by raising taxes. It may also be cheaper to see that standards are met by becoming directly involved in provision rather than monitoring from the outside.

Two conclusions should be noted here. One is that there is an enormous range and degree of state involvement in education. A second is that there is nothing sacrosanct about the precise way these affairs have been arranged in the United Kingdon in recent years. *A fortiori* there is nothing immutable about the existing structure of central and local governmental involvement in education; international comparisons alone suggest that there is nothing final or immutable about the situation in our own country. (The point may be emphasized by noting the difference in structure between Scotland and England and Wales.)

As examples both Germany and France exhibit in important ways a greater degree of centralization of the educational system than the United Kingdom. The extent of local heterogeneity is lower than in Britain, and it is not believed by most observers that this leads to poorer performance. What is, perhaps, more relevant is that it leads to *different* performance. Thus, the German system is academically selective at age 10–12, and is much more vocationally biased. There is a division of function between the federal government and the *Lände*. The latter have some power over the curriculum and in determining the methods of assessment of the school-leaving certificate. But the former concerns itself much more than British government does with the maintenance and equalization of standards. Similar comment on centralization of the curriculum and the setting of standards applies to France. Furthermore, in both cases the structure of the system is not left to local initiative.

Now it should be reiterated that none of this is intended to lead, at this stage of the argument, to the conclusion that other systems are superior to our own. Rather the point is to emphasize the logical and empirical possibility of alternative ways of doing things. Mrs Thatcher and Sir Keith Joseph have already shown this to be so, anyway; only those with more than usual British insularity would see something exceptionally original and daring in what they have done.

Let us now return to the examination of our five main themes. On tradition all that can or need be said is that there is more than one story that can be told about the history of both central and local government in education. There have always been tensions between the two, and it is impossible to believe that their present structural forms are final. However, what is surely apparent is that the trend since the Second World War, if not before, has been towards greater centralization, both of finance and structure.

On the former the problem has been overwhelmingly one of finding new sources of local revenue. To the extent that truly local income and sales taxes are rejected by central government, local authorities are limited by the rates which – although genuinely local taxes and easy to collect – are extremely unpopular. Surprisingly enough, despite their regressive character, this is true of the right as well as the left. Another possibility would be to introduce user charges for educational institutions, but those too would create more political problems than they would solve. The result of a failure to enhance local taxable capacity has been a high and growing degree of central government finance of local expenditure. In my view what is surprising about this is not how much it has led the central government to interfere in local affairs, but how little.

On structure the issues have been more political. Thirty-odd years ago the National Health Service was seen *as national*, and therefore requiring centralization. More important, the Labour Party's ideology of education, especially its desire to see the total abolition of the 11+ examination, caused it to favour central institutions. Of course the comprehensive movement is typical of how paradoxical this whole subject is. The abolition of the 11+ examination started very much at the local level, but the logical desire to make it universal led to legislation and growing pressure from central government to complete the job. Similarly, the training initiatives of the present government, despite some of their local origins, have become part of national policy (at least as much economic as educational). Attempts are being made to encourage local involvement, but these fall far short of allowing true diversity and the choice of separate paths of local development.

Turning to democracy, we have another paradox, namely, that it appears that democracy depends on both more and less central control of education. At the level of ordinary public comment parents, depending on circumstances, wish to be defended against the excesses of local politicians and central bureaucrats. If there is an 11+ examination, and their child fails to get into grammar school, they write to the secretary of state to do something about it. If central government provides places in public schools, and the local council does not use them, once again the parents turn to Whitehall. Equally, however, other parents expect a political change in Westminster to lead to universal comprehensivization of secondary education, the abolition of public schools, and so on.

Added to all this are the doctrines of the mandate, the decisive majority elected on a minority of votes, and growing politicization of all institutions. Suffice it to say that in this country over a very wide range of possibilities pretty well everything and nothing may be portrayed as democratic. In other words, likely variations in the degree of centralization of education *per se* have little or nothing to do with the enlargement or contraction of democratic processes. This is not to deny that in form local government is a democratic institution, but it is to reject the view that local government is somehow sanctified merely because councillors are elected. They must also be judged by what they achieve. If they make a mess of things, they must be subjected to criticism. If the mess persists, and a better alternative appears likely, to reject it on the grounds of defence of democracy is absurd. Of course municipal activities may be desirable in themselves, but it does not follow that that is the only criterion that should be applied. To put the matter in practical terms relevant to education, suppose a policy to deal with illiteracy required national intervention in local activities. Suppose, moreover, that the agencies of such a programme would be based locally. There is little or no reason why they should be placed within the ambit of the local education authorities (LEAs) solely on the grounds of local democracy. While it may be desirable to seek the assistance of local councillors and officials, the criterion must be primarily one of helping to achieve the objectives of the policy in the first place.

Thus, although it is important to recognize that local government is a breeding-ground for Members of Parliament, that too is insufficient to justify the persistence of local involvement with education, if that is not conducive to the efficiency of schools and colleges themselves. Thus my chief conclusion is precisely that the provision, control and finance of the education service, in terms of its governmental structure, must be assessed overwhelmingly according to criteria within education and not without. In other words, the efficiency and equity considerations must be the dominant ones.

This in itself is a methodological point, and does not imply either more or less local government in education. That is a matter of empirical study and judgement. It is also in some cases a matter of logic.

Consider, for example, the case for the comprehensive school. For a long while this was left to local initiative. Even when the central government started to press matters, it hesitated before it compelled the LEAs to act against their will. By the time the last Labour government summoned up the courage to act more vigorously, it was too late. Moreover, it is by no means clear that if it had been defied by a LEA, it would ever have retaliated in the destructive fashion exemplified by Mrs Thatcher.

None the less, if academic selection is to be abolished at 11+, both because of the damage it does to the individual child and to the education system as a whole, that applies to all LEAs, not some. Anything else is illogical. A similar point applies to the universality of examinations and school-leaving certificates. It is simply not a matter of local considerations, but of national ones in deciding the nature and form of such assessment procedures.

This relates to two quite basic matters of national concern at the present time, the extent of the vocational element in the curriculum and how it should be provided. These subjects are worthy of informed discussion at all levels. They give rise to various questions the answers to which are not all obvious. Thus it is reasonable to proceed cautiously, recognizing the experimental nature of what is happening. But the initiative, the overall responsibility and the monitoring of what happens must be national in character and rest ultimately with the central government.

On vocational training itself my personal judgement of the developments of the past decade or so lead me to two very strong conclusions. One is that if left to local government, little of great value would have occurred. The second is that while it is a pity that the Department of Education and Science

(DES) did not take the lead in promoting the cause of training, it is apparent that given their commitment to a traditional view of education, they could in fact have never moved in the right direction. Thus while growing LEA and DES interest in this area is to be welcomed, I for one would continue to give the dominant roles to the Department of Employment and the Manpower Services Commission. I would certainly not place the local arm of the latter under the control of the local authorities.

This leads me to the general conditions for determining the scope of central government intervention in education. The basis for that, as we have said, is decisions which have to be national in character. Questions of the school-leaving age and the structure of nursery, primary and secondary education come under this heading. Sometimes central government have involved themselves less than necessary in these areas. The reason for that has often been financial, namely, a desire to avoid the commitment to additional public expenditure that would result from equalization of provision.

The second ground for intervention arises when the activity itself is national in character and has nationwide consequences. The obvious example is higher education in all its forms. It has also been rightly recognized that the economic consequences of vocational training too are so broad that this requires central control and financing. A related area of national concern is the setting of teachers' salaries. While the local authorities are the nominal employers, their actions have national economic consequences which the central government is unable to ignore. There is an incomes policy for teachers no matter what the government pretends its overall economic doctrine to be.

Thirdly, intervention stems from a concern with the curriculum. The extent of central intervention has been debated, frequently with rancour, for several decades. It is mixed up rather less with local government and more with the professional position of teachers. On the compulsory or core curriculum the DES has erred until recently too far in the direction of local freedom. This could have been justifiable if it had proved possible to establish a central teaching body of great professional standing. The failure to move satisfactorily in that direction, and the general woolliness of the other bodies which have been set up to deal with the matter, leads inevitably to an increase in DES responsibility. The point holds, *a fortiori*, given the remarks made earlier on the extension of vocational studies.

The problem with this is the usual one of power without responsibility. If the DES is concerned with the curriculum and more generally with the standards that are achieved, it cannot ignore underachievement by particular schools with respect to particular groups of pupils. For many years now, however, it has done precisely that. Successive secretaries of state have been willing to accept the credit for success, while avoiding the blame for failure. Above all, parents dissatisfied with their local schools have been advised to address their complaints to the LEA. Indeed as far as our main theme is concerned, it might be said cynically that the chief role of the LEA is to protect the secretary of state from criticism, especially that to do with the actual performance of schools and teachers.

We are led, fourthly, on to the broad class of issues to do with finance and public expenditure. There has always been a central government interest here expressed via the various rather complex formulae of the rate support grant. The basic principle that lies behind all that is a desire to make more nearly equal the capacity to meet needs. In practice, expenditure per capita on education in general, and on specific items, vary enormously among LEAs. While some of this may be attributable to genuine differences in local requirements and the ways they are perceived, it is impossible to believe that there is not a residual variance caused by excessive meanness or profligacy on the part of some LEAs. Again my own opinion is that control in this area needs tightening up, especially where the source of the funds is the general taxpayer. But as is apparent from recent experience, that leads to major conflict with local authorities as presently constituted. There are those who believe that the problem can be dealt with by reform of the LEAs. The alternative is to strengthen the role of central government.

Let me add in regard to this that the present government's moves in this direction should not be regarded as all that need to be said in the matter. Because of the style that has been adopted, and because the relevant secretaries of state seem to be more interested in 'cuts' than in the provision of services, centralization has been given a bad name. My own view of the need for centralization is the reverse, the need to get mean authorities to spend more, and underperforming authorities to take their jobs more seriously.

15

A National Service: Strengthening the Centre II

BARRY TAYLOR

Recently I suggested to the newly appointed head of HM Inspectorate (HMI), Mr Eric Bolton, that the Inspectorate all too often seemed like football directors in their box complaining about the failings of the players on the field rather than the coach trying to improve matters between halves. On reflection I believe I had the wrong target (more about the role of the HMI later). It is the relative detachment of the Department of Education and Science (DES) and of ministers from the field of play which should be the real cause for concern. Admittedly the secretary of state and permanent secretary, and their immediate predecessors, have made sterling efforts, way beyond the call of duty, to spend time in schools and colleges, to meet the marginal groups who believe they have a stake in the education service and to respond carefully to pleas from parents and other complainants.

Yet it is all too easy for them to say – whether political or official – that it is for the local education authorities (LEA's) to determine priorities or to find the extra tender, student grant, or whatever. A recent secretary of state, Fred Mulley, put the position more graphically, constantly claiming to the increasing irritation of his listeners that he was only able to find money for the demolition of Second World War air-raid shelters. This was an evasion to put it politely, and certainly the present secretary of state is prepared to take a determined and positive stance in relation both to the quality and type of structural provision.

Yet, in general, the LEAs have to answer for the delivery or non-delivery of an effective service, in schools, in colleges and in community education; special educational needs; school meals; and the rest. In doing this they have the major handicap of being unable, of themselves, to will the means. Constitutionally the LEA is the district or county council and of course it can levy what rate it chooses (at least for a short while more) in order to fund the education service it believes desirable. In practice, the determination of education policy is delegated to the education committee, which with its officers must compete for local money with the other local government services. Because education is overwhelmingly the most expensive of them, the other services all too often act in concert to contain the ambitions of 'big brother'. It is less common now to meet local politicians, or even chief executives, who have a self-appointed mission to cut the education service down to size. Perhaps because they realize, belatedly, what a sorry figure local government would cut without it? The job has largely been done for them, in any case, by the operation of central targets and financial penalties.

The current means of financing local government services is incomprehensible to most of us, and indefensible to most of the rest. Those LEAs with the worst pupil–tender ratios or spending per capita find themselves labelled as 'overspenders' – be they Labour or Conservative controlled – and penalized accordingly. Not surprisingly, the gap between the best and worst providers is widening – and is, I believe, now unacceptable. For example, currently the Inner London Education Authority (ILEA) has an overall ratio of 1:12·6 and Hounslow 1:17·3, while Nottinghamshire affords a primary ratio of 1:20 and Oxfordshire struggles to maintain 1:24. Obviously an inner city area has pressures upon its schools unknown in a leafy suburb. But another recent survey shows that Newcastle and Birmingham have more oversized classes than almost any LEA in the country. Similarly, most LEAs with sparse population and thus a disproportionately large number of small schools which are expensive to staff have among the worst ratios in the country.

It is sometimes claimed that there is no correlation between quality of education, however judged, and class size. I am willing to accept that a class of, say, thirty may not have any marked advantage over one of twenty-six, but discrepancies of the kind which now exist in relation to staffing levels make a crucial difference to what curricula can be offered, how often teachers can be released for further training and how special needs of pupils can be met. In other words, to quality.

The simple answer is to establish a national education service on, say, either the National Health Service (NHS) or the Manpower Services Commission (MSC) model – but it would be wrong. I believe the case for an elective local government system is stronger than ever it was. If education, in particular, is too important to be left to the teachers, it is certainly too important to be left to the civil servants which, in practice, for most of the time, is the situation with both the MSC and NHS. It is in fact too important to be left to any one controlling organ – institutional governing body, parents, or LEAs – as central government. The concept of checks and balances – of partnering within the system – has a greater validity, not less, as popular aspirations become greater and resources to realize them more confined. A defence system undoubtedly, but a universal one runs the real danger of falling into universal error as the development of the Youth Training Scheme (YTS) may yet demonstrate. Maurice Peston (see Chapter 14) is right to assert that councillors are not sanctified by being elected, nor of course are MPs, and they must also be judged on what they achieve; but where is there encouragement to believe that a totally centralized system would actually be more effective, or even more equitable?

Let us consider briefly, and of course selectively, the track record of the LEAs in recent years. It is said that they have not displayed the speed, energy and thrust of the MSC. But nor have they been given vast quantities of new money to attend to a problem, be it vocational training or anything else. In any case, how much of the Youth Opportunities Programme (YOP) or YTS would have been delivered without the efforts of local educational administrations, careers advice staff and a substantial minority of committed elected members?

It will be instructive to see how effective are the LEAs in delivering the projects identified from 1985 onwards as attracting central government grant. The precedents are encouraging. Certainly those LEAs involved in the DES 'low-attainers' project announced by Sir Keith Joseph in Sheffield, in the summer of 1982, and 'up and running' a year later have displayed 'speed, energy and thrust' equal to that of the MSC – and a keen sensitivity to local needs as well.

The reorganization of secondary education has been carried forward generally in good order with the massive expansion of further education between 1955 and 1975, among other things, and the means for the New Training Initiative to become a reality as well as serving industry better than it has sometimes acknowledged. Largely unremarked has been the necessary rationalization of primary school stock in the postwar years, in one typical rural county involving the closure of a third of its 500 schools over twenty years, often in the teeth of opposition from local people or, at best, grudging acquiescence from successive governments. So let us pause before joining the fashionable denigration of the LEAs as ineffective and hidebound. Nevertheless, I believe the point of balance does need to be moved towards central government in important general respects.

But what is meant by central government? It is naïve to assume that the Secretary of State for Education has full delegated powers to carry out the will of Parliament in respect of all educational services. In fact government control of the education service, both in terms of direction and of detail, now comes from the DES and MSC, and the wonder is that the imposition of dual accountability has not created greater confusion which in large measure is due to the efforts of local education administrators. However, confusion there is – and the potential for much more. How, for example, will the department's Pick-Up programme and the MSC's Adult Training Strategy avoid tripping over each other in the confined world of adult retraining and skills enhancement? The CPVE is seen largely as the DES striking back, but whether it can carve out for itself a substantial clientele now that the YTS appears to have captured all those 16-year-olds who have neither a job nor a place on a full-time course remains to be seen. Much more fundamental is the creation of yet further confusion in the already confused rag-bag of offerings to the 16–19-year-olds. The BTEC and City and Guilds, and more recently the GCE and CSE examining boards, see commercial opportunities in the DES–MSC rivalling and often are developing similar course and examination/assessment patterns for both paymasters.

But it is at the school and college level that the divided responsibility is most damaging. Recently a senior DES official claimed that the MSC's perception of the education scene is 'LEAs – bad, colleges – good, college principals – wonderful'. Certainly the principals are having to live up to that assessment. They are expected to continue to answer to the LEAs for the majority of their work, to the local MSC officials for the YTS in its various modes as well as to the examination and validation bodies. They are now to be told – or asked – which quarter of their operation should henceforth be funded by the MSC. It almost seems as though a deliberate attempt has been made to create circumstances in which the delivery of a coherent pattern of education and training for 16–19-year-olds is impossible to achieve. Not the least damaging is the way in which the evolution of the YTS largely without reference to the conventional education system has widened the gulf between the further education providers, increasingly preoccupied with the new development, and the sixth-form colleagues still providing for the able A-level types and the 'returned empties' – that is, 16-year-olds trying to retrieve O-level failure. In many cases it can hardly be more than sheer chance where the 16-year-old finds himself, despite the best efforts of an overstretched careers service. Certainly the ability to wean more of the able away from A levels to vocationally targeted courses, commonly held to be highly desirable, is fatally handicapped by our divided and divisive system.

The introduction of the Technical and Vocational Education Initiative (TVEI) into schools compounds the felony. At the end of the second phase perhaps 1 per cent of the total school population will have participated; but what of the rest? Certainly replication will be enormously expensive on the basis of the models now developed. In the meantime the MSC seem determined to keep the TVEI cohorts separate and distinct from the mainstream, presumably to facilitate evaluation. Yet many TVEI-type initiatives also abound outside the pilot areas and they may well be more seminal in changing curricula generally. How much more sensible, then, if TVEI resources were part of the whole. My point is a simple one; we are developing two systems where there should be only one, whether for those under or over 16.

Nor is any attempt to define a precise boundary between education and training other than a considerable hindrance. So if individuals and society as a whole care to benefit from a more centralized service, first, we must make sense of the centre and that means the establishment of a Department of Education and Training to replace both the DES and MSC in relation, at least, to its youth training and adult training functions. There seems no reason, in principle, why such a department should be less responsive to employers' needs, and it may in fact result in the penetration by external influences much more deeply into the school system. The LEAs would then have the responsibility to deliver a comprehensive service, but with a firmer control of key objectives from the centre.

Even without a wholesale recasting at the centre, the mechanisms for delivering the service at the local level will need to be reviewed in one fundamental; that is, in relation to the intention to make the MSC responsible for 25 per cent of further education colleges' budgets. Even if this is not the fairly thick end of the wedge, it would seem sensible to create some kind of joint board consisting of LEA elected members and also members of the MSC area board to oversee the negotiations, and arbitrate in the inevitable disputes between the LEA officers, college principals and MSC staff. Such an arrangement would be easier if the MSC were to create an area board for each LEA. This would facilitate co-ordination not only in relation to the '25 per cent' issue, but the total provision of education and training.

More radically the transfer of the MSC area boards' responsibilities to the LEAs does not commend itself (only) to education committee chairmen and chief education officers hell-bent on aggrandizement – particularly if it were to complement a Department of Education and Training at national level. Obviously the current fashion to regard local democratic control with suspicion, in need of curbing rather than extending, does not make such a proposal any easier of realization. There are, in any case, substantial difficulties to be overcome. The spread of responsibility would be very wide; but the spread exists now, and at least there would be an enhanced possibility of a co-ordinated response to need at the local level. Government – any government – would be bound to take the view, perhaps rightly, that the more strictly vocational training could not be put at the mercy of the LEAs – as would both sides of industry no doubt; but there is no reason why a local education and training board should not have a much more substantial and influential minority of added members drawn from local employers and the trade unions than education committees currently do. Many would claim that the LEAs have conspicuously failed to respond readily and effectively to the training and retraining needs of industry. But given the vast sums of money currently channelled through the MSC, and *from central direction*, who knows what they might achieve?

A joint local board might still receive some instructions from the centre. Specific grants are now well established in the education service as well as in relation to training, and central government could quite properly place upon the board requirements as to the type and extent of provision and yet preserve the concept of local–central partnership. Certainly the mechanisms to ensure that government objectives are met locally already exist in embryo – a revitalized HMI attending to the quality control in schools and colleges, the MSC's monitoring staff to work in partnership with them at the work experience and employer-based end of the spectrum and provision, and the Audit Commission to ensure value for money. However, there is no gainsaying that such a local education and training board could be an even more threatening cuckoo in the local government nest. If local government could be brought to see such a creation and the consequential greater direction not only of objectives, but also of money from the centre, as an opportunity and not another attack, then a sensible relationship between education and the other local government services might be worked out. Alternatively, the boards might be free standing from the rest of local government but with a majority of members elected on the universal franchise.

Few causes can be inherently so lacking in popular appeal as local government reorganization; so those who wish to see an improvement of our present condition would be wise not to depend on such reorganization. Even without it, I believe the case for a closer working relationship between the LEA and the MSC at local level is overwhelming and the implementation of the White Paper, *Training for Jobs*, may very well be the means by which willy-nilly it is achieved.

But this still leaves a largely unco-ordinated effort in 104 LEAs to bring the curriculum – and the method – of our schools and colleges more in line with the needs, current and prospective, of our society. It is not that the system is solidified in aspic, just the reverse. In one LEA with more limited resources, and no more imaginative staff, than most the following initiatives are current. Their TVEI development is radically cast so as to result in the production of a modular curriculum with short-term objectives to be thoroughly assessed and certificated by one of the examining boards. Their participation in the Oxford Certificate of Educational Achievement is intended to produce a novel record of *all* the relevant qualities of every school-leaver – personality, characteristics and aspirations as well as skills acquired and examination successes. It is not clear, at least to me, how this compares with other current preoccupations such as the 16+ examination, the introduction of CPVE, or indeed TVEI. Also this LEA is a participant in the department's 'low-attainers' project, developments in relation to pupil profiles, rearrangements of the school-day, suggested self-study, and so on. These examples happen to be taken from secondary education; a similar point could be made for other sectors of the service. And the point is a simple one: many worthwhile initiatives are being seized but in relative isolation from one another and with many people in many LEAs covering very similar ground.

The virtues of allowing teachers with reason the freedom to plan their own curriculum and determine their own methods are so widely canvassed in this country that they do not need further justification here. But can it really make sense for, say, teachers in neighbouring primary schools to construct their own mathematics schemes without any collaboration? Does it make any more sense for an LEA to develop its common syllabuses in English or mathematics or PE without reference to the other 103 LEAs? Even if the only justification is economy of effort and effective use of resources, it must make more sense to plan more widely. But more important, even a workforce as large as that of the education service contains only so many innovators or pathfinders; we should be wise to maximize their impact, so that the rest of us can upgrade our peformance as the result of the dissemination of their work. Certainly when I was first teaching English, without any qualification in the subject, I would have been delighted to have received a model curriculum prepared by experienced practitioners; I am sure that there are still many teachers like me.

At least LEA-wide and regional planning is now more common; the South West Modern Languages Credit Scheme is one good example. But if the thesis is sound, then a more sharply defined national effort is required. Certainly we must decide on which of the many runners we are going to back and how they relate to one another. How will TVEI and 16+ live together, alongside the CPVE, YTS, I level, and so on? Are we serious about the development of the modular curriculum? Is the current shape of the school-day the right one? Do full-time students in further education receive too much teaching? What proportion of the population should we aim to cater for to 18+ as well as to graduate level? These are just some of the key questions which badly need answering, and which need an answer which is valid for – and accepted in – all parts of the country.

The DES, despite the valiant efforts of ministers and officers and the HMI, is simply not sufficiently involved in the 'chalk face' delivery of the service to produce, on its own, informed responses to these and other marginal questions. Those at the centre are spared the mind-concentrating need to justify the closure of its primary school to the village population or explain to a parent–teachers' association why their school must lose a teacher; hence the importance of the central–local relationship. Of course we could have a monolithic system, a caricature of what is commonly and erroneously believed to be the situation in France. That would undoubtedly stifle initiative and make it less, not more, responsive to our rapidly changing society.

There are signs that we are moving in the right direction. We now have a secretary of state who is prepared to devote a major speech to the teachers of history, a phenomenon which would have been unthinkable a decade ago when entry to the 'secret garden' of the curriculum was denied to virtually all except the teachers. It must make sense for ministers to be able and willing to set curricular objectives and also, with their officials and the HMI, to set the pace of development. This is precisely what they are now doing in a minor way via the 0·5 per cent specific grant mechanism. Indeed the defined objectives for that funding are very precise indeed (many at the local level would say too precise). Nevertheless, the principle is worthy of extension *provided* that there is a genuine central–local partnership in determining those areas which shall be developed. A couple of meetings with a handful of representatives of the Association of County Councils (ACC) and Association of Metropolitan Authorities (AMA) will not suffice. After all, the money is deducted from that which the LEAs might have expected to come their way and they are expected to contribute 25 per cent of the cost directly.

Despite the unwillingness of the government to question quangos, I believe the case for a national education council is overwhelming. It is the only mechanism which could apply itself effectively in answering the key questions outlined above, and many others. To be effective it would need to be chaired by the secretary of state or a ministerial colleague and to be kept as small as possible. This would be not at all easy as the main partners in education and training would have to be included: the LEAs, employers and trade unions, those maintaining voluntary schools, examining boards, the university sector and teachers' representatives. No doubt there would be many other claimants, but I believe the major element in the council, which should not number more than thirty, ought to be the LEAs, particularly if their responsibilities embrace training as well as education; in fact, in that context, local *education* authority becomes a misnomer. Such a national body would depend upon policy units to examine options and to propose. It may be argued that this will lead to the creation of yet another bureaucracy or extensions of existing ones, but if managed properly, it would mean that work now undertaken in a number of separate places in a largely unco-ordinated way would in the new examination and curricula councils, the ACC and AMA and the examining boards have a focus and a policy framework.

All this objective-setting, extension of partnership and co-ordination of effort will of course account for nothing unless money is available in roughly the right amounts and approximately the right places in the system. So we come almost full circle to the point where we began – to remark upon an existing system within which disparities from place to place, and not only in relation to pupil–teacher ratios, are considerable and appear not to have any logical basis. Furthermore, it is inconceivable that current initiatives – like the TVEI – can be replicated throughout the system without a massive amount of new money or, just possibly, a radical reallocation. Our current arrangements simply do not permit the latter to happen, tide-bound as we are by resource decisions taken in at least 104 different places, by committees of differing political persuasions.

On the other hand, a system in which all major resource decisions are taken by central government can in no real sense be seen as a partnership between local authorities and the government. Thus all responsiveness to local need and encouragement of local initiative, both considerable strengths of our current system, would be lost. This is not the place to become enmeshed in the proposal of alternatives to rates or the efficiency or otherwise of rate-capping, but central government could if it wished take direct responsibility for key elements of educational expenditure to permit it to regulate the flow of resources without destroying all local financial responsibilities. The element most often canvassed is teachers' salaries. It is certainly difficult to see how current inequalities in the teacher–pupil ratio could be overcome unless the government does assume responsibility. As well as meeting the salary bill, the secretary of state could – indeed would have to – determine the appropriate size of the teacher force for each LEA. The principles determining his decisions could be established by the national education boards, together with the weight to be given inner city areas, sparse populations, and so on. No doubt some of those decisions would be crude; but they could hardly result in the degree of inequality now experienced. The secretary of state would then have control of a key lever in achieving agreed objectives – to disseminate the TVEI, for example, to broaden curricula in small primary schools or introduce new courses (robotics is always the favourite example) into further education colleges. If these things can only be done with new money because the secretary of state and the board cannot identify functions in the service which can be curtailed, so be it. One of the essentials currently is to articulate the case for more education and training.

Fortuitously the Secretary of State for Health and Social Security has announced a review of welfare benefits. At the time of writing he has resisted suggestions that the review should embrace the provision of free school meals. If in fact government could be persuaded to substitute a cash benefit for the free meal, then LEAs could be freed from the straitjacket imposed by the current shape of the school-day. Without a long midday break and the considerable subsidy which, effectively, the school meal receives from other parts of the education budget in every LEA, a considerable sum could be available for, say, curricular innovation and staff development. Currently only a few schools are experimenting with a one-session day. It will take determined action nationally to secure for all what I believe to be on the evidence so far undoubted educational and financial benefits, and a necessary pre-requisite is to abandon the school meals service.

So we do need a service which is more truly national; which minimizes inequities; and which can determine priorities that must be pressed forward. Equally the delivery of the service and a key part of its funding must remain in local (and locally elected) hands. This is not the time, if there ever is a time, when responsibility (that is, education and training) should be more concentrated, our main thrust should be to enhance participation in discharging that responsibility at all levels – especially institutional. But the centre must be co-ordinated more effectively to allow for a clear definition of what we want from the education and training services, and that definition should itself be an exercise in partnership. The mechanisms to deliver in good order are equally important, hence the need to have unitary control of education and training at the local level. We do not have a national service locally administered at present; I believe we need one.

16

A Community Service: Strengthening the Institution I

DAVID HARGREAVES

In Britain the boundary between the education system and the community is still a strong one, no doubt for complex historical reasons. In many respects the nineteenth century was the battle-site between church and state for control over the nation's expanding schools. Those with great power fought among themselves, recognizing that control over the schools was a vital means of influencing the character of the nation and its social structure. The real losers in this battle were those who believed that people, especially working-class people, were able to organize their own education to meet their self-defined needs. In the late twentieth century the nature of the education battlefield is somewhat changed, though as we shall see there are resonances of the past. Discussion of the governance of education needs to differentiate between the various groups who strive for power and influence. In recent years attention has been focused on tensions between central and local government (for example, finance) and between central government and the professionals (for example, the secondary school curriculum). My focus is on the tensions between clients (parents and pupils) and the other major partners, and especially in relation to those forces which are working to weaken the boundary between the education system and the community.[1]

In a period when there is debate about the structure, content and purposes of secondary education we are soon led to ask two basic questions: What *is* the distribution of power and influence, and what *should* it be? Contested decisions are exposing and challenging the present distribution of powers. When it is planned to close a school in the light of falling rolls, or when it is proposed to amalgamate sixth forms into sixth form or tertiary colleges, for example, what are the rights of parents and teachers against administrators and politicians, both central and local? What kind and degree of influence should parents exercise on decision-making? How should the community be consulted? What weight should be assigned to parents' priorities against those adduced by central and local government? How do we balance the wishes and preferences of a community (here defined as the catchment area or clientele of a school) against the need for 'rational' and cost-effective planning by administrators and politicians? Exactly what does that fashionable concept, accountability, mean in terms of giving powers to parents? It is in the midst of this that community education has entered its period of most rapid growth. It is both part-cause and part-consequence of the current education disturbance.

A secondary school's links with the community are most naturally with the parents of the pupils. It is a good place to begin, though not all community educators would start from this point. Strictly speaking it is education, not schooling, which is compulsory in this country. If parents prefer to educate their children by appropriate alternative provision, they are free to do so; though, as Education Otherwise and similar groups have found, the state often seems reluctant to grant these legal rights to parents. The schools are chosen by parents and this means that the school acts *on behalf of* parents, which suggests that in principle parents should exercise considerable influence over the structure and content of schooling. Since in practice most parents send their children to school and the teachers are highly professionalized, parents are encouraged to *hand over* their children to the care of the school: it seems that teachers, like doctors and lawyers, are professionals who know best. The schools have thus fostered a deference to teachers, one which is maintained by holding parents at an appropriate distance: parents should trust the teachers rather than working in active co-operation with them. One of the most firmly established research findings of the last thirty years is that when parents are interested in and supportive of their children's education, the greater are the children's achievement at school, whatever the abilities or social origins of the children. It must be said that the implications of this fact have not been taken very seriously, for the practical consequences have not been acted upon. The reason is obvious: to do so would require a degree of parental involvement, a new conception of parent–teacher partnership which threatens the status quo. Many (but not all) teachers continue to think in terms of home–school *liaison* (that is, co-ordination and communication) rather than parent–teacher *partnership* (that is, active co-operation and collaboration). By keeping parents at arm's length, the teacher's traditional position is preserved and the barrier between home and school kept firmly in place. Teachers are forced to speak with a forked tongue: they know that parental involvement is desirable, but they also know, as those committed to the community have discovered, that this implies a shift in the balance of power between parents and teachers; so many teachers find excuses for taking no immediate action, while uttering the appropriate rhetoric.[2]

The attitudes of suspicion and caution persist and no doubt explain, in part, why the Taylor Report of 1977[3] has mostly met with a lukewarm reception. The great improvement in the attitudes of primary school teachers to parents has not yet been matched by a similar change in the secondary school sector.

On this issue the conservatism of secondary school teachers has been aided and abetted by local politicians on governing bodies, who see their own dominant position as threatened by parent governors. Both groups expect parents to trust them but remain reluctant to reciprocate that trust: partnership is sought, but not a partnership which entails a genuine sharing of power. Therefore, it is perhaps not surprising that so few parents are ready to accept this highly conditional offer of partnership. In Denmark, by contrast, the governing body or school board consists of five to seven parents elected by and from those who have custody of the children in the school. The headteacher, two teachers, two pupils and a member of the local authority participate in meetings of the school board, but they have no voting powers. (Moreover, six of the thirteen members of the local education committee are elected from among the members of the school boards.) It must be observed that the school board has considerable powers: it determines the school plan which, within the framework of Acts of Parliament, makes detailed decisions on the curriculum and timetable, optional subjects, streaming, and so on. The lack of conflict between the various partners arises from the real trust that characterizes the system. The parents have great power but the responsibility for exercising it leads them to trust professionals and officials. It is perhaps no coincidence that parent–teacher associations flourish in Denmark and in many schools three-quarters of the parents exercise the right to vote in the election of the governors. I find it difficult to resist the conclusion that if in Britain we gave more power to parents, we might then have the solid base on which the much-advocated parent–teacher partnership might be steadily built in the secondary sector. Our present stance, which is premissed on waiting for teachers and parents to be 'ready', induces apathy in parents and complacency in professionals and politicians who decline to take any initiative that entails a risk of power-sharing. There is thus an alliance of convenience between professionals and politicians against parents, and the Taylor Report was itself too weak to resist such an alliance.

There can be little increase in 'accountability' in the education system without a power shift, unless accountability means that those with power at present take into account the interests of those, such as parents, with little power; but such 'taking into account' will always be partial and selective. Community education is committed to a power shift but – and here is one of its central problems – its proponents have relatively little power to engineer the power shift. In the education system you can have power, but not the power to give it away; to have real power you must have both. Community educators, who are more numerous among teachers than among administrators and politicians, are thus restricted to sharing the trivia of power or to establishing machinery for consultation only. This brutal fact, in part, explains why so many community schools devote so much energy to *internal* power-sharing, to rethinking the nature of teacher–student relationships and to maximizing student autonomy. This 'liberal' attitude is inherent in community education, whose philosophy is founded on the principle of voluntary association and an education which gives people the capacity to organize their own voluntary associations to meet their needs. It is difficult to know how community schools can move towards greater *external* power-sharing but it must be said that too little thought has hitherto been given to devising strategies for changing the structure in which they are imprisoned. The more radical wing of the Educational Priority Area (EPA) projects was committed to preparing young people through the school for the reconstruction of their communities, but in retrospect these ideals look naïve for ignoring the need to accompany this with other structural changes. Midwinter[4] perceived the need for a much wider decentralization as a precondition for the success of community education, but strangely little attention has been paid to his ideas. Halsey[5] has recently suggested a less ambitious strategy, the abolition of the local authority. Influenced by Yugoslavia's market socialism and self-managing communities of interest, he proposes that we 'begin by making every school a direct grant school'. But there is a real danger that this might strengthen the power of central government quite considerably, especially if the HM Inspectorate were weakly led; and unless schools were deeply committed to the principles of community education, there is also a danger that the reform would strengthen the power of teachers. Halsey's proposals are curiously school-centred, ignoring the important developments in the most impressive community colleges, which are bringing together schools, adult education and the youth service on shared premises. In the light of growing youth unemployment, earlier retirement and shorter working hours there will be increased pressures for lifelong education, which may mean that the 'school' as we now understand it has not long to live.

Another issue is the *place of the community in the secondary school curriculum*. Despite comprehensive reorganization, many schools continue to make curriculum assumptions that derive from the tripartite system and the philosophy that underpinned it regarding pupil types. 'Able' pupils, particularly after the third year, are provided with an academic diet which reflects the curricular emphases of the former grammar schools and the demands of higher education. 'Less able' pupils, by contrast, come to constitute a 'problem' because these heavily academic courses are unsuited to them. It is still assumed in some quarters that these are more 'practical' pupils whose needs must be met by a practical curriculum that is relevant to their future lives. It is these pupils, then, who are most likely to be in receipt of not only vocational courses, but also various forms of personal and social education and community studies, including community service. Recent pressures from the Department of Education and Science (DES) and the HMI for a larger common curriculum for pupils in the fourth and fifth years are combining with the conviction of teachers and educationists committed to the principles of comprehensive education to promote a consensus that the curriculum must be more common and more applied/practical. While the motives may differ, with the political right seeking to make the schools more responsive to the needs of industry and commerce, and the political left seeking a curriculum and organization that is more egalitarian and more responsive to the needs of working-class pupils, the forces often combine in the same direction. Inevitably when the origins of these forces are so different, there are points on which a marked divergence is evident, political education in school being an example. In general, however, personal and social education is now one of the most significant curriculum growth points, and its progress is being accelerated rather than retarded by background political differences in motivation. Doubtless these forces might be resisted by the school were it not for internal forces pressing in the same direction. In their early days comprehensive schools tended to make a sharp divide between the academic and pastoral sides of the school, a division reinforced by the allocation of most of the ex-grammar school staff to academic departments and the ex-secondary modern school staff to posts with pastoral responsibility. In many parts of the country where comprehensive schools are well established, there is a new concern to integrate the pastoral and academic aspects, and this is helped by a 'pastoral curriculum'. The rapid emergence of active tutorial work in schools is an index of this. Such innovations, it should be noted, have sprung not from the DES or the Schools Council, but from the schools themselves; it has been a 'bottom-up' development. The way in which comprehensive schools are so fervently embracing a curriculum content that assigns importance to personal and social skills is, in part, in imitation of the comprehensive schools' elder brothers, the colleges of further education. In recent years they have been very aware of the needs of their new clients, recruited largely because of youth unemployment and the Youth Training Scheme (YTS). That so many 'non-academic' pupils now enter the colleges with an obvious lack of life-skills is an implicit condemnation of the education these clients received in the comprehensive school. But many schools have been quick to grasp the point and it can be argued that the pioneering work of the Further Education Unit (FEU) has been at least as influential in the comprehensive school as in the colleges of education.

Once comprehensive schools take personal and social education seriously, once 'life-skills' are seen to have a legitimate place on the curriculum, schools are ineluctably drawn to various forms of community studies. Members of the community, such as employers and trade unionists, are now being welcomed in the schools; and teachers are taking pupils out of the school into the community. Does this mean, it might be asked, that comprehensive schools are evolving into community schools? Yes and no, for the changes in curriculum, and the tendency to invite community visitors into the schools as well as taking pupils out into the community, remain very firmly within the teacher's control. Such innovations can be introduced with no threat to the position or power of the professionals. As I have noted, the trend to greater parental involvement has been very much slower precisely because such a development has enormous implications for the distribution of power. Thus, it might be said, the comprehensive school adopts the philosophy of community education when the teachers' power remains unaffected, but rejects those parts of the philosophy when the teachers' power is put at risk. Community *participation* in the comprehensive school is acceptable; community *control* of the comprehensive school is not.

The philosophy of community schooling has failed to evolve in parallel with the profound changes in secondary education and elsewhere within the education system since the 1960s. Much of our basic thinking about the community school/college is linked to the rural or small town setting, where it makes sense to meet the wide range of educational and recreational needs on a common site. But in many towns and cities it is more difficult to design a system of community colleges, often because of the complexity of current provision which the community system must replace. In inner London, for example, there is a wide acceptance of parental choice in relation to secondary education, and in consequence it is not unusual for the Inner London Education Authority's secondary schools to recruit their intake between forty and sixty feeder primary schools, which means that the school's catchment area is exceptionally wide. In what sense can such a school be a community school?

A more fundamental problem springs from the confused way in which we have designed our educational system. In part it assumes that clients need different institutions according to their *age* (infant schools and adult education institutes), and in part differentiates between institutions according to the clients' educational *levels* (primary education, further education and higher education). A system organized around age inevitably leads to duplication between institutions; a system based on levels is more rational today, but presupposes that clients of different ages are happy to learn together and that teachers are willing to teach mixed-age classes. Community schools and colleges should organize by level, but in practice there is still a very low degree of age integration in these institutions.

The community education movement has never really come to terms with its own title. The movement has long agonized over the *concept* of community[6] but little progress has been made. Precisely what *is* 'the community' once we leave the rural or small town setting? The answer was relatively easy in Morris's Cambridgeshire: all those who lived within the catchment area of the college, and that consisted of one or more self-conscious and reasonably stable residential communities with their own histories. Most of the clients were part of the community while at the college, and they subsequently returned to the community. But this conception of community-as-residential-area is not easily transposed to urban settings that have no clearly delineated residential communities and where the population is highly mobile. For whom the college is intended and who should rightfully control the college are questions which become difficult to answer in a simple way.

It is easier to define the community for which the college is preparing inner city clients, provided we are willing to adopt a pluralist model. In contemporary urban life most citizens are destined to belong to multiple communities, not a single community. As adults they will belong to overlapping sets of communities organized round a variety of interests: family and kin, neighbourhood, occupational, recreational, religious, political, ethnic, and so on. Far from adding up to a common community, many of these smaller communities conflict with one another. Elsewhere[7] I have argued that an important task for a community school is providing people with the skills of resolving conflicts between such communities while retaining high solidarity within each community. It is a task we have hardly begun to confront. The task of educating *for* the community currently attracts much interest, but it is difficult to connect such endeavours with the problems of resolving the governance *of* the community college.

One suspects that if the community education movement is to realize its goals, it may well have to abandon the word 'community', for it is now becoming an encumbrance which restricts its own evolving philosophy and traps it into finding distinctive forms of governance. It could do so without in any way abandoning its basic principles, which are about accessibility to all, about educational institutions needing to reflect the interests and needs of members and about the priority of clients over professionals or politicians. If we followed such a course, we could forget about labelling schools and colleges as 'community' institutions, which has become such a curious obsession. Too many institutions, in my experience, mistakenly underestimate their powers to implement the principles of community education, merely because they lack the word 'community' in their title, and then once they have acquired the label, they actually fail to put many of those principles into practice. It is a harsh judgement, I recognize, but labels can inhibit as well as facilitate change and development. The central principles in community education have little to do with labels; they can be put into practice without reference to labels. More alarming to me is the attitude that underlies the demand for a community label, for too often it betrays the 'bottom-up' principle which is at the heart of community education.

At the present time most commentators observe a clear trend, under the Conservative government, towards increased centralization or 'top-down' solutions to current problems. This tendency not merely weakens local control and autonomy, as well as the power of the professionals at the local level; it also threatens to stifle 'bottom-up' developments. The classic case is reform of the examinations system at 16+. Local authorities and examination boards in London and Oxford developed plans which might potentially transform the nature of assessment in secondary education. In late 1983 the secretary of state was converted to these ideas and outlined national development plans costing £10 million. His approach was warmly welcomed in educational circles, but some detect here signs that a firm central hand is being placed on the tiller of the reform of assessment, one which will soon be steering the ship of change in its own preferred directions, which may not be at all those of the original pioneers.

Centralization is deeply inimical to the principles of community education and to community control of educational institutions, and the community education movement is powerless to resist the tide of centralization. Education is a highly political sphere of life, but the community education movement is itself apolitical. No doubt it is in some respects advantageous to be so since teachers, who are as mixed in their political allegiances as the rest of the population, tend to avoid explicitly politicized education movements. The community education movement has avoided an explicit political philosophy and instead harks back vaguely to Henry Morris in the hope that these ideas will be palatable to all, whatever their party political preferences. Without a more explicit political philosophy, however, it cannot address contemporary issues which are themselves highly politicized. Of course such a political philosophy need not be party political. We may adopt Oakeshott's[8] definition of politics as 'the activities of attending to the general arrangements of a set of people whom chance or choice have brought together' by which any philosophy of the community must, at least in part, be a political philosophy.

The community education movement does, I believe, have an implicit and unacknowledged political philosophy on which it can potentially draw: it is *anarchist.* Anarchism is not within the political vocabulary of most British people; the term 'anarchy' is still used as a synonym for chaos or disorder. Our European neighbours are more familiar with the political philosophy of anarchism. Contrary to the popular stereotype, anarchism is committed to principles which command much support in contemporary Britain: first, a massive decentralization programme; and secondly, a belief in fraternity, or the capacity of people to co-operate for the common good through voluntary associations. These are evidently close to the principles of community education and the notion of community control of education institutions. The best-known exponent of educational anarchism is Ivan Illich, who might be seen as part of the long tradition of Christian anarchism. Illich's anarchism is always implicit, whereas Paul Goodman, on whom Illich drew so extensively, was an explicit anarchist. It is perhaps because Illich's anarchism was implicit that he attracted so much attention in the 1970s, for his appeal could be to libertarian socialists *and* the libertarian right.

Illich exercised a curiously weak influence on the community education movement, perhaps because he failed to link his ideas with the movement. Illich's plans for a radical decentralization of the education system in *Deschooling Society*[9] were not very practical. It is difficult to see how his 'networks' or voluntary associations could ever replace schools until society as a whole was 'deschooled' and he gives no guidance on how this was to be achieved. Moreover, Illich constantly side-steps the issues of power and control as well as community development.

Since Illich's anarchism was implicit, it failed to alert community educators to the political philosophy which lies behind his writing.

Anarchism has a long history, which goes back to the English writer William Godwin[10] whose remarkable treatise was written in the shade of the tyranny that overtook the French Revolution. This led him to the insight that governments will use educational systems for their own purposes and thus to make what is an astonishingly prescient attack on any idea of a national education system. Against this he counterposed his ideas of educational institutions as voluntary organizations devoted to rationality, freedom and fraternity rather than as centralized instruments of indoctrination by the state. His own 'bottom-up' philosophy is clear:

> It is our wisdom to incite men to act for themselves, not to retain them in a state of perpetual pupillage. He that learns because he desires to learn will listen to the instructions he receives and apprehend their meaning. He that teaches because he desires to teach will discharge his occupation with enthusiasm and energy. But the moment political institution undertakes to assign to every man his place, the functions of all will be discharged with supineness and indifference.

Anarchist principles are alive today in the undervalued work of Colin Ward.[11] The practice is also alive in the preservation of Croxteth School in Liverpool by parents and teachers, despite its official closure. The community education movement has drawn too little on this fund of anarchist principles and practice.

But it may legitimately be asked, what has the educational anarchist to say about the governance of schools? Godwin announces the basic principle from which one might proceed:

> It is earnestly to be desired that each man should be wise enough to govern himself, without the intervention of any compulsory restraint; and, since government, even in its best state, is an evil, the object principally to be aimed at is that we should have as little of it as the general peace of human society will permit.

Godwin would, I suspect, be somewhat contemptuous of current concern about the governance of community schools/colleges[12] since, to him, it is too locked into questions of representation and consultation, too much like the devices of central government writ small. Rather, I believe, Godwin's anarchist approach is to make the key issue quite simply this: how can we educate people, so that they do not need any government? In other words, how can we give people the skills and capacities to organize their own lives through voluntary associations, so that government can be reduced to a minimum?

The answer, according to the nineteenth-century anarchist writer Michael Bakunin, is by the transfer of authority from teacher to taught. Successful teachers make themselves redundant because they have given away their knowledge and skills to their pupils. We should, says Bakunin, progressively do the same with our general authority, for this is the essential condition of self-management that allows us to dispense with government:[13]

> All rational education is at bottom nothing but the progressive immolation of authority for the benefit of freedom, the final aim of education necessarily being the development of free men imbued with a feeling of respect and love for the liberty of others. Schools should be free from even the slightest appreciation of manifestation of authority. They will not be schools in the accepted meaning, but popular academies in which neither pupils nor masters will be known, but where people will come freely.

This anarchist approach to community education, then, declines to answer the narrowly defined question of who should govern our education system, for it begs the question of whether or not the education system needs to be governed. The only response to educational centralization, whether it comes from the political left or right, both of which Godwin feared, is the creation of people with the capacity to generate, in the spirit of Croxteth, educational institutions which subvert the centralizing tendencies of governments.

The anarchist community educator is not satisfied with greater local and non-professional or non-political participation in the government of education and is sceptical of consultative machinery. 'Anarchy is order: government is civil war' proclaimed the anarchist Proudhon, who understood that any government, by its differential distribution of power, is inherently divisive and corrosive of individual rights, whereas anarchism stands for the diffusion of power and the capacity of individuals to use voluntary organization to meet their needs. From this point of view the 'liberal' community educators of today are caught in a contradiction between their rhetoric and their paternalist approach to governance. The anarchist and the community educator share the conviction that the urge to self-management and the drive to mutual aid are inherent in human nature under favourable conditions. The anarchist goes on to insist that those conditions require the dissolution of government. For the anarchist, then, present trends in the government of community education, which are more participatory than in other sectors, are but a temporary stage in the movement from a formal, governed 'top-down' system towards a network of informal, 'bottom-up', de-professionalized voluntary organizations, by which education is no longer a means of shaping the character of clients in the interests of those in power, but rather a liberating experience that meets personal needs, generates individual autonomy and facilitates social co-operation. In its anarchist form community education represents the most significant challenge to the government of education.

NOTES: CHAPTER 16

1 C. Poster, *Community Education: Its Development and Management* (London: Heinemann, 1982).
2 My favourite example is from *Secondary Education*, a report of the Advisory Council on Education in Scotland (London: HMSO, 1947).
3 *A New Partnership for Our Schools* (Taylor Report) (London: HMSO, 1977).
4 E. Midwinter, *Education and the Community* (London: Allen & Unwin, 1975).
5 A. H. Halsey, 'Schools for democracy?', in J. Ahier and M. Flude (eds), *Contemporary Education Policy* (London: Croom Helm, 1983), pp. 191–210.
6 D. Clark, 'The concept of community education', *Journal of Community Education* (1983), vol. 2, no. 3, pp. 34–41, vol. 2, no. 4, pp. 31–6.
7 D. H. Hargreaves, *The Challenge for the Comprehensive School* (London: Routledge & Kegan Paul, 1982).
8 M. Oakeshott, *Rationalism in Politics* (London: Methuen, 1962).
9 I. Illich, *Deschooling Society* (London: Calder & Boyars, 1971).
10 W. Godwin, *Enquiry concerning Political Justice* (Harmondsworth: Penguin, 1978); originally published 1793.
11 C. Ward and A. Fyson, *Streetwork: The Exploding School* (London: Routledge & Kegan Paul, 1973); and C. Ward, *Utopia* (Harmondsworth: Penguin Education, 1974), and *The Child in the City* (London: Architectural Press, 1977).
12 'The school and the community', *Secondary Heads Association Review*, vol. 78, no. 243 (1983).
13 G. P. Maximoff (ed.), *The Political Philosophy of Bakunin* (New York/London: The Free Press/Collier-Macmillan, 1953), p. 334.

17

A Community Service: Strengthening the Institution II

TIM BRIGHOUSE

Most people share a common interest in their own development and that of their children; most want to have a say in how they are organized and governed, and most are interested in their immediate locality and the fortunes of the country: neighbourhood and nationhood, seldom anything in between. Counties these days still exist largely for those interested in cricket, and most people have little interest in abstractions like local government and local authorities. Consider the different responses to a threat to local government in general (for example, rate-capping) and a threat to close the local school, and the differing impacts on the MP and local education authority (LEA) members – both in the size of their mailbags and the potential size of their majorities. The thesis of this chapter is that it is essential for the education service to be emphatically local and that the rate and extent of central government incursions into local affairs is dangerous and to be resisted. The most effective way, it will be argued, of dealing with this and preserving and enhancing the vitality of education is to put responsibility for it as far as practicable into the hands of those who use it and work in it in community schools and colleges. Central and local government have important roles of course, but these should be concerned with establishing frameworks, distributing resources and monitoring standards, and not with prescribing content or process or pace.

Whether education is to be a national or local service should be tested against the principle of providing the most effective way of unlocking the talents of youngsters and adults in a society where the preservation of a truly democratic way of life is regarded as important. Democracy and education have long been linked in the development of the British system of public education. Indeed the thinking behind universal education must, in part, have been the better to discharge democratic duties. Robert Lowe's dictum 'we must educate our masters'[1] followed a second Parliamentary Reform Act, heralded an Education Act and preceded universal manhood suffrage by fourteen years and votes for women by almost fifty. The link between education and democracy was very much alive in the days of the last war as the last great Education Act of 1944 was being constructed:[2]

> Until Education has done far more work than it has had an opportunity of doing, it cannot have society organised on the basis of justice: for this reason, there will always be a strain ... between what is due to a man in view of his humanity with all his powers and capacity and what is due to him at the moment as a member of society with all its faculties undeveloped, with many of his tastes warped and with his powers largely crushed. Are you going to treat a man as what he is or what he might be? ... that is the whole work of education. Give [the man] the full development of his powers and there will no longer be that conflict between the claim of the man as he is and of the man as he might become. And so you can have no justice as the basis of your social life until education has done its full work ... and you cannot have political freedom any more than you can have moral freedom until people's powers have developed, for the simple reason that, over and over again, we find that men with a cause which is just are unable to state it in a way which might enable it to prevail ... There exists a mental form of slavery that is as real as any economic form. We are pledged to destroy it ... if you want human liberty you must have educated people.

The ease with which the Axis dictatorships had been able to mould the minds of the young through their highly centralized systems was fresh in people's minds at the time of the passage of the 1944 Act. Indeed the education world in the years after 1944 devoted more time to the subject of the duty given to the Minister of Education under section 1 of that Act (to control and direct) than to any other subject. The former Education Officer for Manchester, Lester Smith, said at the 1949 North of England Conference, 'it represents a mighty leap into the dark, as near an approach to authoritarianism in education as we have had since the Church States of the seventeenth century'.[3]

As late as the early 1970s Sir William Alexander repeatedly referred to the awful dangers of Hitler's Germany in arguing against centralist moves in England, and later still he resigned from the Assessment of Performance Unit on the same principle. Whatever the reasons, for generations the British have been convinced that the localization of the education system and principles of democrcy are inextricably interlinked and that the greatest possible care has to be taken in achieving the right balance between central and local power.

The case for a devolved system also reflects essential beliefs about the purpose and process of education. Those who espouse such a set of beliefs and theories incorporate the following, that:

(1) knowledge – itself a combination of information and skill – grows from learning and direct experience or by means of the imagination;
(2) each person's interpretation of supposedly inherited culture is slightly different and the culture in consequence changes continuously;
(3) the need in society is to tolerate the rich diversity of individual talents

and habits which then serves high standards of self-discipline and a complicated accommodation of different sets of values and practices;

(4) there should be an accommodation of different methods of teaching and learning with an emphasis on self-learning;

(5) the institutions of society and the methods by which it governs itself change and should be encouraged to change.

Whatever arrangements for the delivery of the education service pertain they ought to depend to some extent on a view of the curiculum and the education process. The case for a devolved system is particularly strong when the process of education and training is closely and simply examined.

Consider: the purpose of education is surely to unlock, in so far as the individual will allow, inherent talents and socially useful skills to the full, to allow the acquisition of the relevant information the individual needs at any one moment to become or remain an autonomous person, to acquire and develop socially useful attitudes and to encounter – one hopes eventually to promulgate – ideas towards the further development of mankind. That is the purpose of schooling, the aim of adult education and the youth service and the goal of further and higher education. The business of those who run the system is to sweep away the boulders that obstruct such a process.

So far so good. The next issue is the curriculum. What is it and where does it happen and who has a hand in it? The government's answer is simple. The curriculum is a list of subjects, the school or college is where it happens and the government, the local authority and the school are the partners who determine it. Such answers have their roots in the thinking that went into the 1944 Act when information and skills were more limited and attitudes more certain and shared. The government's answer on the curriculum, however, is of limited value for a number of reasons.

Attitudes are clearly reinforced by people as well as subjects. Skills transcend subjects, so that the clear observation of students in our schools is of some skills being endlessly reinforced and practised (for example, memory and writing) and others scarcely, often only by serendipity, encountered (for example, the skills of working in groups). Information is as readily available from the media, the home, or the local community as from the teacher, and is certainly not confined to the classification of subjects which owes as much to a picture of higher education at the beginning of the century as it does to the present state of knowledge and ideas. In short, the simplistic definition is inadequate. The curriculum is quite simply the cultural backdrop against which the information, skills, attitudes and ideas are developed. This happens in the *totality* of a human being's existence. The school or the college is the specialist place where it is orchestrated but the home, the street, the holiday and the media contribute to it. And the people who have a hand in it ought to be the grandparents, the parents, the teachers and the young themselves in a wider local economic community. It would seem a bizarre proposition that central government should determine the nature of children's education in the sense of defining all that was socially useful for them to learn. And if it should, would it be for the children in private schools as well as those maintained by public money?

It could be that the very success of the education process during these last hundred years calls into question the constitutional arrangements of our society and will shortly demand some reassessment of what powers should be exercised at the centre and what at the periphery. Unless our society wishes to move to a more authoritarian, centralist, or totalitarian approach to its governmental arrangements, it will seek continually to protect the local determination of how the young are taught and how they are brought up.

The evidence of the last few years is that the central government juggernaut is rolling inexorably with only feeble resistance put in its path. That is not for the want of trying on the part of the local authority associations and individual authorities, and the issues are well understood by people in the local government world, both officers and members. However, they are virtually unknown and certainly not understood by people generally, the users of the services and those who pay for them. People in general simply do not have an interest in such things as targets, penalties, cash instead of volume, rate-capping, the proposal to hold back half of 1 per cent of the education budget to be controlled from the centre, and a quarter of further education expenditure to be controlled by a central government agency – unless the significance is spelled out very carefully. And even then they will not march on shire hall let alone the Houses of Parliament in the cause of something called 'local government', as they would and do when their local school is under threat, or even when a fraction of a teacher is removed from its staffing establishment. If we are going to protect the service as a local one, sensitive and responsive to local needs, we must find a way of making a more direct connection between provision and use: we must give far more responsibility to the institutions and to those for whom the institution is the unit of loyalty. And if the curriculum can be regarded by common consent as the means by which the education process happens, and if the proper determinants of it are those most immediately involved in it, we must consider ways of arranging the education system that the maximum autonomy and minimum dependence is encouraged.

It is considerations such as these which have brought into sharp relief the movement in the last twenty years towards community education and have lent it a new force and definition. During the previous thirty years the concept of community education had largely lain dormant outside the tiny handful of authorities which had espoused the ideas of Henry Morris and their realization in Cambridgeshire. The original motivation was the concern to revitalize the declining rural areas which had become impoverished in the postwar slump of the 1920s and were served by an inadequate network of small and unsanitary elementary schools. Morris contrasted the facilities of the towns – better elementary schools, the vast majority of secondary schools, libraries, recreational, cultural and social facilities – with those of the threadbare and neglected countryside. His aim was nothing short of building up a 'rural civilization' and his medium was the village college which would provide for the educational, recreational and cultural needs of the entire community, house welfare services and what we would now call the careers service, and become the natural centre for the whole population of the catchment area. He and his later disciples[4] rejected the traditional notion that education is something that is done to people between the ages of 5 and 16 and will last the recipient throughout life.

As these boundaries between school and adult students are removed a number of fundamental challenges are being made to the notion of school and what it is for. Who is a student? Who is a schoolchild? How does one study? What, why and when does one study? Who determines the curriculum? What restrictions may teachers reasonably place on students? What is work? What is play? Who shall we learn from? There are implications here for the teachers and their schools, for the LEA and its systems and for the government and its constitutional arrangements. First, the school and teachers.

The teacher immediately acknowledges the role of others in the process of education, for example, the parents. The community educator would cheerfully recognize the educative role of many others in the community and the learner himself. All he would claim for himself as a teacher would be a certain expertise in the process; perhaps diagnostic skills based on training and years of experience with countless youngsters; perhaps in consequence a more successful prescriptive talent, so that the next step in developing a skill, acquiring relevant information, or reinforcing a useful attitude may be suggested by the teacher; and perhaps a full development of those interpersonal skills which spring from a genuine liking for others, so that the teacher is seen to be simply more successful at *assisting* the education process than others are. The parent, the local craftsman, the local industrialist, the child, other children and the retired can all add to the repertoire of the resources available to assist in the educational process of community education. And they may determine its direction. The community educator sees her school or college not so much as an island of learning, but as one, albeit imporant, part of the rich tapestry of learning and sharing within a wider community. Above all, she has the role of animateur.

A community educator will be committed to education as a lifelong activity: the social education of the young school-leaver, continuing education and the university of the third age; the flavours are different, the sense the same. This is a deeply ingrained belief which stems from the certainty that educational insights are not linear, gradual, or predictable, nor are they linked necessarily to developmental stages, but are sparked unpredictably by differing circumstances and different people. All the community educator has to do is to have high expectations and a knowledge of the mind (and the mind's power), so that the learner can be encouraged towards autonomy. A community educator is mistrustful of institutions and time labels, and in development work within a community will be seeking to enable people to identify needs for themselves, and then if possible meet those needs by themselves. A community educator knows that labels such as 'junior', 'secondary', 'higher' and 'school' encourage the mistaken belief that education can only be undertaken, or indeed finished, at a particular time or place, whereas she apprehends that learning takes place in the most unlikely places: in a train or on a walk, in a pub or a house. Learning comes from experiential activity of one form or another in or out of the school, college, or university. The teacher therefore demonstrates an interest in the students' total experience, not just within the school, the subject, or the course. When shall we dare to leave behind the outmoded model of teacher omniscience which has its roots in the Middle Ages, when 'to know a little' was the source of considerable power? Today of course this is no longer true. The teacher is not the filler of empty vessels – a kind of intellectual drawer of water – for the true teacher knows his own ignorance and can motivate the student towards self-learning.

For the school within which the teacher works there are immense implications. And there are at present severe disadvantages. Other than village schools hard by the church, the pub and the shop, most of our children and our adults are educated in institutions which are essentially *apart from* rather than a *part of* their urban communities. David Hargreaves remarked, 'you can compare most in their isolation only with two other forms of institution, namely the open prison and the mental hospital'.[5] Certainly the daunting drive, the confusing doors, the forbidding injunction to report to an unidentified office are unwelcoming, not to say threatening obstacles, to many people. The corridors, the printed notices on the doors all too often at variance with the architect's intentions for the design of the school or college are strange signals. So what can be done to welcome the local community and connect it to the school?

First, and most important, must be an attitude of encouragement and openness which must too clearly be seen at the highest levels – in the commitment of the LEA to such an approach realized through the appointment of headteachers with a brief to develop their schools in this way. Then there are decisions about where to site schools (a diminishing option in times of falling rolls but opportunities do still exist) in order to ensure that they are physically at the heart of the communities they serve. There are plenty of superb examples of these carefully placed urban community schools. In rural or suburban areas many schools are approached by drives and surrounded by open land some of which could be used for housing – and increasingly LEAs find themselves having to realize such capital assets as spare land – thus bringing the community nearer to its school. The scope for creating a visually attractive and welcoming environment in and around the school is boundless and these things are prerequisites for ensuring that people become proud of their local school, value it as a learning resource in its widest sense, and develop a jealousy and concern about its reputation and continuing well-being, which ultimately will provide the best insurance for the quality and future of the school.

These things will signal powerful messages to the local community, but schools have in any event the ability to communicate in ways open to no other local government service and few other organizations of any kind. Until relatively recently society and communities were stable but since the war housing and planning policies, industrial and religious changes have undermined this stability: the 'one-industry' town and the dominant church have gone in most communitues, but the school so far remains and has access through its pupils to most homes in the area directly or indirectly. So in addition to its many informal media of communication, a school could, for example, start a newspaper (and nowadays with improved printing techniques, newspapers can be quite attractive and have been successful in a number of areas).

Good communications are of course vital to the systems of a successful school but neither they nor openness of approach, nor a belief in the principles of community education or the most dedicated and skilful team of well-motivated professionals, will of themselves ensure the survival of a local service. In order to handle successfully the combined pressures of contraction, the continuing drive for more accountability and the growing demand for more relevance in the curriculum without succumbing to centralization fundamental changes are needed in the way institutions are governed. The English system is deliberately diffuse. The historical reasons for this – the role of the church as the main provider, the diffidence of government initially to become involved in the concept of a national service, the role of the boards and then the local authorities as providers – were confirmed in the 1944 Act not just because of the 'political' need to preserve traditional partnerships, albeit with some change of role, but because of the recent spectre of totalitarianism. But the emphasis on checks and balances inevitably obscured accountability. The William Tyndale School episode provided an extreme example of the problem, and the length and detail of the inquiry demonstrated the difficulty in disentangling the intertwining strands of responsibility of the various partners. So there needs to be a clearer definition of accountabilities in the management of institutions, and this should start from the premiss that most decisions about matters directly affecting the school from curriculum content to the use of *all* its resources should be taken at school level.

The conclusion of this chapter is an attempt to reconcile three strands. First, there is the educational rationale for the delivery of the curriculum as it has been defined; secondly, there is the need to have regard to the logic of 100 years of a better-educated electorate; and finally, the *real politik* of party political dogfighting.

The possible rearrangement of educational responsibilities and duties which would reconcile these apparently diverse objectives would be a very locally based school service coupled with a regionally based further and higher education system. For in order to reflect the community basis of the curriculum and the needs of a better-educated democracy, and to secure the freedom of speech and action long associated with our way of life, there now needs to be a changed distribution of powers and duties in the education service. The power of central government would be restricted and the minister's present right of 'control and direction' embodied in the Act should be removed at least so far as examinations and the curriculum are concerned. Central government, however, would properly retain rights of funding and direction of advanced further education and provide funds, in discussion with the regional authorities suggested below, for training needs. Essentially therefore there should be three levels to the new arrangement – central, regional and school districts.

The regional authorities which should be charged with looking after the economic life and well-being of their region, in consultation with central government, would need to have powers within the region for training needs.

Hence they would control further education provision. There would be concurrent powers and obligations on district and region so far as *éducation permanente* or continuing education is concerned. Their requirement in law would be for there to be an 'agreed' policy. Similar shared powers for special education provision would obtain. Once again the emphasis should be on an 'agreed' policy between the districts collectively and the regions. Cases of dispute would be referred to national level. Once the policy was determined, it would be binding on each party.

At the most local level of the school district there should be some property and tax-raising powers supplemented by a grant from the regional government. Such a funding system – the region would need to supplement the local taxes by a regional income tax used for a wealth equalization formula – would take care of all local government services including social services, education, planning, housing, environmental policy in addition to health and other public utilities. The school district's powers would be to determine the curriculum, the distribution of resources among the various headings, teaching and non-teaching staff, books and equipment: the school district would run its school meals service and control buildings and grounds and with the regional support provide new plant. It would employ teachers but on salaries negotiated regionally. In-service training and professional development would be a duty shared and agreed between the school district and the regional authority with some national funding support and of course influence.

In the interests of education being on rough terms of equality with some other major services it seems essential that the districts are in fact coterminous at both metropolitan and shire level with the present district councils, which in the main seem both efficient and sensitive to local needs. Because these districts would be quite large in terms of criteria for the curriculum and local communities, thought might be given to requiring each to maintain a certain number of school boards – in effect, larger governing bodies than obtain at present covering the whole age range and provision. Such boards would have charged to them the responsibilities for local management envisaged in the Cambridgeshire devolution plan.

It would, however, be impossible for the districts envisaged to provide sufficient expertise in advisory and inspectorial functions. It will be necessary to overcome the disadvantage of small size and avoid parochialism in such debates. All successful practitioners need a professional umbrella of support and development which is the hallmark of successful local education authorities. Some of the metropolitan districts and one or two of the smaller counties are already under severe disadvantage in this respect. In order therefore to promote a wider professional fellowship there would be the need for an agreed professional development policy in funding between district and region. Adivisory teachers would be employed at the district level, drawn from the teachers on a rotating basis, and the advisers would be seconded to the regional authority which should also have separately exercised powers of inspection. The region therefore – in practice, a substantial seat of government perhaps embracing 5 million population – would be charged with agreeing policies on special and continuing education with the districts, and agreeing plans with national government and subsequently making provision for advanced further education and training in its area. The region too would negotiate salaries, provide external examinations and validate institutions in the district through its advisory and inspectorial powers.

Finally, national government's role would be restricted to a share in the plans and provision for higher education and training and providing a forum for a central advisory council to promote national debate about educational issues and good practice. All the need for interference, control and direction would be removed to the interface between district and region. Freed of its present substantial and increasing role in governing and directing detail of so many of its citizens' local services, national government's considerable talents would of course be reserved for strategic direction of the economy and the law, and for stimulating public debate and for taking care of its citizens in national affairs.

In 1948 a leading education officer of the time said that 'a touch of central control and direction wouldn't come amiss ... after all the tradition of freedom in this country is so strong that no latterday Strafford could come along and put a rule of "Thorough" across'.[6] That of course was 1948 not 1984.

NOTES: CHAPTER 17

1 Robert Lowe, in B. Simon, *The Two Nations and the Educational Structure 1780–1870* (London: Lawrence & Wishart, 1964), p. 355.
2 Lord Butler, *The Art of Memory* (London: Hodder & Stoughton, 1982), pp. 144–5.
3 W. O. Lester Smith.
4 Harry Rée, *Educator Extraordinary: The Life and Achievement of Henry Morris: 1889–1961* (London: Longman, 1973).
5 David Hargreaves, speech delivered to a teachers' conference in Larkmeads School, Abingdon, Oxfordshire, 6 January, 1982.
6 John Leese, *Personalities and Powers in English Education* (Leeds: E. J. Arnold, 1950).

18

A Local Service: Strengthening the LEA

JOHN STEWART

A school is not an island. The governance of education is that of a complex of institutions and services. The school is not the whole of education, but it is the archetype of education. The school is a separate institution. It has a way of life of its own. To a large extent it is self-managing. It has its own system of management, its own culture and its own practice.

The capacity of self-management is a capacity to be encouraged. The school that can itself learn, can itself innovate, can itself adapt and improve its management is likely to be the most effective in education.

The school is, however, not an independent institution. It is set within a wider system of education. The government of education focuses upon that wider system, and places the school within that system. The government of the education system constitutes and maintains the school, sets conditions for its management and, in effect, sets the conditions for its accountability. The requirements that the system of government places upon the school draw their rationale from perceived needs of society. The system of government elaborates those needs by the conditions under which schools are required to operate.

These conditions can if overelaborated destroy the quality of self-management in schools. A system of government that went beyond the perceived requirements of society to, for example, detailed specification of curriculum, class organization and teaching method would be destructive of those very qualities that make an effective education institution. The task for the government of education is not to educate; and the process of government does not encompass the process of education itself. Education is itself carried out in the classroom or in the home, in the lecture-room or in the library. The task of government is to provide the facilities for, and to set the conditions and to state the requirements for, the process of education.

The system of government can be finely or loosely articulated. It can define generally or in detail. The danger of too general a definition is to overextend the autonomy of insitutions and to weaken their accountability to society.

The danger of too specific a definition is that the process of education ceases to be self-managing. It would lack the capacity to learn, to adapt and to develop itself.

A LARGE-SCALE COMPLEX COMMUNITY SERVICE

The government of education is the government of a large-scale complex community service. It is those characteristics that have formed, and should form, the governance of the education system.

A large-scale system cannot be governed as a totality. It has to be broken down into components if it is not to be overwhelmed by the sheer scale on which it has to operate. Complex services are not easily governed or easily understood. They have to be governed in uncertainty, both of present knowledge and of future circumstance. In uncertainty government must seek a capacity for learning that comes not from uniformity, but from variation.

A service that is directed at the community has to be responsive to the differences and to the conflicts, both as regards needs and values, that are found in and between communities.

The government of education needs a form of government that permits variety and differences in response, recognizing the differences between communities. That variety and that difference are themselves critical to learning.

A large complex community service needs a structure which while recognizing national imperatives also allows for points of authoritative decision-making at local level. The simplicities of a national structure could not match the complexity of governing education.

It is said that education is 'a national service locally administered', and that is one possible mapping of the government of education. Equally plausible would be the statement that education was an institution-based or school-based service, occasionally influenced by local authorities and occasionally influenced by central government.

The reality is that the education service can properly be regarded as a school service, a local authority service, or a national service. The education service has many actors, none of which have substantive power; power lies not at one point, but at many points. Indeed power is elusive. There is a power to act, to move and to change, but it is a power that normally requires many actors; not a single actor at a defined point of decision, but a complex of decision-makers.

The phrase 'a national service locally administered' is dangerous, both because it conceals this reality and because it diminishes the role of local authorities. The local authorities are and always have been more than units of administration. Under the Education Act 1944 both the secretary of state and the local education authorities (LEAs) were given significant roles.

The myths summed up in the phrase 'a national service locally administered' were not wished upon reluctant local authorities by a dominant centre, but strongly claimed by the LEAs. It was in presidential talks to the

Society of Education Officers that most emphasis was put upon the phrase. To an extent the phrase fulfils the same functions as the 'myth of statutory constraint', that is, the belief that virtually the whole of education expenditure is mandatory. The myth of 'a national service locally administered' and 'the myth of statutory constraint' support each other. They fulfil a role in protecting education expenditure and the working of the education service from pressures, within the local authority, for reductions in expenditure and for changes of policy. A national service constrained by statute is a service protected by the education professionals, from the reality of local political choice. Both myths played a functional role for the education professional.

The reality of over 100 local authorities, each making decisions, some innovative, some maintaining and some changing gradually, is not a story that makes for simple history. To argue that the system tends to move towards uniformities through trial and error, through the learning that spreads by the folkways of the world of education, is not dramatic:[1]

> [The] broad uniformity in standards of education that exists throughout the country appears to be due at least as much to pressure by parents, professional influence and, in adult education, direct demand, as to statutory requirements and departmental inspection. The provision for education has steadily increased since the end of the second world war and greatly exceeds the provision being made some 25 years ago, without any change during that time in the basic statutory requirements which were laid down in the Education Act of 1944. The underlying threat of the use by Ministers of statutory default powers, where they exist, or of new legislation to enable Ministers to rectify gross lapses by local authorities below acceptable standards, may also be contributory factors towards uniformity. Because of the mixture of pressures and influences it is not possible to distinguish a minimum standard in education which can clearly be said to be mandatory. Rather there were generally accepted but undefined standards which can be discerned from the varying practices of local authorities.

Although this passage is concerned mainly with the issue of minimum standards, it conveys the complexity of the process of decision-making in the education service. Uniformities are chosen uniformities, emerging from the complex of pressures. Minimum standards have emerged and not been imposed.

Extended to other fields of education policy, ministerial influence cannot be denied. It is the influence of a key actor, whose views receive attention and are, after all, widely reported. It is the influence of an actor at a key point in the network, drawing upon and contributing to the learning of innovation.

My concern is not to deny the role of minister and department, for they have been important actors in the government of education. But that does not make it 'a national system locally administered'. There is rather a policy community in which there are many actors; history may be written by the centralists, but many contribute to its making.

The movement from a period of growth to contraction has shown that the role of local authorities goes far beyond mere administration. Central government has not been able to secure from local authorities adherence to its policies. If local education were limited to local administration, then local authorities would have had to carry out those policies. Yet the reality is that local authorities have not done so.

Local authorities, called upon by Shirley Williams, as the last Labour Secretary of State for Education, to expand their expenditure on teacher training did not do so; the traditional process of ministerial speech and circular did not have the expected effect. That process was dependent on the world of growth. In that world a ministerial speech was powerful support to the chief education officer, in his claims upon the element of growth, in a local authority's budget. It was effective because it assisted in the budgetary process at local level. An additional claim on reducing resources was of no assistance in the changed world of expenditure cutback.

If local government had been merely the means of administering nationally determined policy, then the Department of Education and Science (DES) would have been able to secure that allocations made in the public expenditure process were spent as specified. It is argued that it was its inability to do so that meant additional funds for training required because of growing unemployment were allocated not to education departments through the DES, but to the Manpower Services Commission (MSC) through the Department of Employment.

However, the real failure of central government to impose its policies on the LEAs has been failure to achieve the reductions in total local authority expenditure on education that it was seeking. Local authorities have budgeted for higher expenditures on education than those sought by central government. In a period of declining rolls they have not reduced their manpower to the extent required by central government. Despite grant reductions and special provisions to penalize local authorities for spending above government targets, local authorities generally have chosen to raise the level of rates rather than reduce expenditure to the extent required.

The argument may be challenged. There is a widespread belief in the education service that education has been unfairly treated by local authorities and made to bear cuts far beyond those intended by central government. Those who hold such beliefs will not accept the argument based on general local government targets, rather they will say that although the government has set targets for local government expenditure that require cuts, they never intended that such cuts should fall so severely on education. That, they will argue, has been due in too many local authorities to the bias against education.

Reality is very different from this dreamworld. Far from treating education more harshly than intended by central government, local authorities have protected the education service by budgeting to spend more than wished for or intended by central government. Local authorities in 1981/2 and 1982/3 together planned to spend nearly £1 billion or 5 per cent more than planned by central government. Even if school meals and transport are left out of account, local authorities budgeted to spend over those two years £725 million more than required by central government. The process of alleged overspending has continued since.

The 'national service locally administered' has proved to be a local government service operating within a national framework of legislation; it has, then, proved to be what it has always been. Central government could not secure that the expenditure on education was reduced to the extent it required. Nor could it secure that that expenditure on education is allocated as it wishes. Both these decisions remained with local authorities.

THE CENTRALIST ADVANCE

Central government has sought to increase the range of instruments available to control or influence the local authority. Certain of these changes can be regarded as the construction of new instruments to replace instruments whose influence had depended on the period of growth.

It was not merely that in a period of growth the circular and ministerial statement met a ready response from local government. The main influence was exerted through the use of loan sanction controls over capital expenditure, but that influence ceased to have major significance with the ending of the period of growth in school population as well as in expenditure.

The proposal to introduce limited specific grants can be seen as the forging of a new instrument to enable the secretary of state to give impetus to new policy initiatives. Specific grants are part of the mythology of local government, arousing passion both from those who support and those who oppose them. Back in a golden age – or so it can seem in the legends of the education service – there was once a specific education grant which had the magic quality of increasing as expenditure increased, since it was a percentage grant. In the legends as told by others in local government the magic, if magic there was, was black magic, the percentage grant being seen as a force for division within the totality of local government. Specific grant has become a symbol of good or evil, triggering automatic reaction in support or opposition – often without considered thought.

The changes that have had the greatest potential effects have been the changes in local government finance. These changes have not been stimulated by education policy, but by the government's objective of controlling local government expenditure. The introduction of the block grant targets and penalties, and legislation to provide direct control through rate-capping, are all measures intended to bring the expenditure of individual local authorities into line with the requirements of central government. The measures have moved from ever-greater influence to direct control over what is likely to be an increasing number of local authorities. As the number grows one will then be able to describe the education service as a national service locally administered. It will, however, be a service in which central government will have direct control over finance without the clear responsibility for policy outcomes that depend on finance. A national service locally administered will have been built on financial control and not for education ends. The threat makes it the more important to reconsider and restate the case for strong local authorities within the government of education.

There are two elements in the tendency to centralization within the government of education as outlined in this book. The first is an education drive based on a ministerial concern to change the direction of the education system. The second and the more significant is a financial drive based on a government concern to cut-back local government expenditure. This has led to the government introducing measures to control directly the level of local expenditure through rate-capping.

It is the right to determine its own level of expenditure in general, and its level of expenditure on education in particular, that has guaranteed the capacity of the local authority to exercise significant local choice. Local choice over expenditure implies the capacity to take initiatives and pursue policies which may not be required by central government. Control over their own budget and an independent source of revenue in the rates have formed the instruments of local choice which has its legitimacy in separate elections. It is the removal of the financial basis of local choice that makes education measures of centralization more significant. The limitation on finance enforces conformity on education issues.

A centralized system of government is inappropriate to the government of a large-scale, complex community service. Only a belief in the infallibility of the centre would justify such a centralized system. A complex community service – and, above all, in a changing society – requires learning as the prime requirement in its governing.

It is from the diversity of response, which implies a diversity of expenditure patterns, that learning comes. From the uniformity of a centralized system there is no basis for learning. Innovation and advance in education has not come from the centre, but from individual authorities and schools, from which others including central government have then learnt.

There is a presumption of established truth in the ministerial model for the government of education that sits uneasily with the reality of a process of learning in government. There is a terrible vanity in a minister, remote from schools, teachers and parents, who believes he has the truth, which must underlie the government of education. There is a critical difference between decisions in central government which have to be taken on the files about authorities and schools, unknown and unseen, and decisions in local authorities which are made about schools known and visited. There is a terrible vanity too in those who, at the centre, believe that they should alter the views of local councillors and officers in Manchester or in Tameside about the organization of schools in a local area.

The government of a large-scale service means that centralized government is remote government. At the centre the required quality is an awareness of ignorance. Yet long hierarchies breed organizational vanities that are protected by the secrecies of decision-making at the centre. Decisions at the centre can appear as simple decisions, precisely because they are abstracted from local knowledge.

Decisions at the centre are protected decisions. They do not have to be exposed and dealt with at parents' meetings. Time and again one is told by national politicians that public meetings have died, but to the average chairman of education large-scale public meetings are part of the commonplace of the government of education.

The remote government of centralized education concerned with imposing uniformities of policy or the sterile formulae of grant-related expenditures on the diverse circumstances *and* wishes for education is inappropriate to the government of a large-scale, complex community service.

THE CASE FOR LOCAL GOVERNMENT

The case for local government within the government of education is that it provides a legitimate point of independent authority for decision-making within the national framework of education.

Decisions on the government of education are quite rightly political decisions. They are concerned with the requirements for accountability for the professional process of education, with both the conditions for that process and the requirements of that process. They are concerned to set education within the requirements of the community and to interrelate education with the many other aspects of community life. All these issues involve critical value judgements made of the needs of the community. In our society these decisions are deemed to be political decisions.

The system of government has to be related to the limits of political capacity, for the latter is limited both by time and by the capacity to encompass issues. *Local* government of education is a critical element in government, enabling more decisions to be brought within political capacity, by spreading political power. The alternative is that the rich variety of circumstance and difference that makes educational reality has to be reduced by abstraction and simplifications to the limits of ministerial capacity. Politics reflects differences in values, beliefs and assumptions. A centralized system seeks to impose on those differences a false uniformity.

It is the diffusion of power that legitimates the capacity for innovation and differences that is present in the local government of education. A chief education officer who can persuade his councillors has established a justification for different approaches, be it to in-service training or to methods of school government, in a way that would be impossible if he was not the officer of an independent point of elected authority. On the authority of elected councils educational advance was built by Morris, Clegg and Newsom, as it is still being built by many of their successors.

The local government of education is about the government of difference – not merely the response to difference, but the creation of difference. The creation of difference of approach is not to be regretted in the government of education, for it is from difference that learning comes in the government of complex community service.

The local authority role in the government of education provides a capacity for authoritative decision-making close to the process of education itself. Decisions are formed and made by councillors and officers about schools and other education institutions which are not geographically or organizationally remote. They are decisions unprotected by the Official Secrets Act, or hidden in private minutes of Cabinet subcommittees. They have to be defended locally to parents and teachers. The pressures of local politics are very real and very immediate. Local decision-making in the government of education is, or should be, decision-making on a scale that can be known and understood and in a setting that is visible and within reach.

There are those who see centralization as inevitable and desirable. We live in a society in which the governing elite almost inevitably thinks in centralist terms. The little village of the centre that is Whitehall, or perhaps in this context Elizabeth House, has a powerful call upon those concerned with the government of education.

Too easily the redress for local problems is seen as national redress; the thinking of political parties is too dominated by the ministerial model of political change. We have a strange logic based in centralist thought which means that if there is a failure in action by a local authority, that is immediately seen as a justification for central government intervention and new measures of centralization. A failure in action by central government is not, however, taken as a justification for reducing central government powers. There is a strange logic of centralization that, in effect, assumes the automatic superiority in capacity of central government, whereas the reality is that central government merely has the capacity to make mistakes on a greater scale than a local authority.

Thus many in education have been deeply concerned at what they see as the growing disparities in education expenditure between local authorities and look to national action to secure redress. There are and always have been such disparities, yet the nature and the cause of those disparities must be understood before action is taken. Growing differentiation in education expenditure can come about because a number of local authorities increased expenditure at a time of general standstill or cutback. Disparity in this instance would be the disparity caused by a number of local authorities setting new and higher standards of education expenditure. Growing differentiation in expenditure can equally have been caused by a number of local authorities cutting back on educational expenditure more severely than other local authorities. Disparity in this instance would be caused by a lowering of standards of education expenditure.

In practice, growing differentiation can be caused by both factors. Disparity in education expenditure is therefore a complex concept. To object to disparity is not enough; it has to be made clear whether the objection is to the lowering of standards or to the improvement of standards, or to both.

Undoubtedly the concern of the education service is with the lowering of standards caused by cutbacks among authorities already considered as low spenders. There may be hope in the education service, that the Department of Education and Science (DES) would find ways of encouraging the 'underspenders' to increase expenditure. Whatever the intentions and hopes of the DES may be, the realities of Treasury control must be faced. It would be a strange scenario indeed that saw the Treasury committed to a strategy of encouraging increased expenditure by any local authorities.

Indeed most of the underspending authorities have cut precisely because they have been set targets by central government that require cuts. Yet we are so dominated by centralist thought that many saw these cuts created by central government's own interventions as requiring new central government intervention.

This chapter does not deny a role for central government. It accepts the need for central government to set the framework within which local authorities can carry on the local government of education. However, it is critical that there should be a significant area of governmental discretion at local level with the elected authority and the independent financial resources to exercise it.

Central government should not seek to overdetermine the government of education. The government of a complex service imperfectly understood at the centre cannot be governed by overdetermined processes. Local authorities need organizational, financial and statutory space to develop.

Consider for a moment the debate on minimum standards. It is often argued that central government should determine minimum standards for the education service (this is in many ways the converse of present policies which are, in effect, setting maximum expenditure standards). There is a distinction between setting minimum standards in a particular situation because in certain local authorities educational standards had fallen below an acceptable level and setting minimum standards as a matter of principle over all aspects of education expenditure.

There is an illusion that there are already widespread nationally laid down minimum standards. The illusion exists because there are minimum standards in practice. They are, however, the minimum standards that emerge from local choice within a complex series of pressures. If those standards are within limits of acceptability, why seek to overdetermine through a system of nationally laid down minimum standards, seeking to confine what is an ever-changing and responding pattern of choice?

What is a minimum standard? It is unlikely to be a standard of output, for how does one enforce it? Minimum standards, then, become input standards or levels of expenditure. It means in the end that central government is moving to determine particular combinations of staff, equipment and maintenance required by schools, when some education authorities are seeking to give their own schools greater freedom in those matters.

In the good government of education the centre would intervene but sparingly. It should eschew overall control which specifies inputs and parameters in detail because such will overdetermine. It will specify the necessary, it will debar the unacceptable, it will influence and it will take initiatives, but it will not overdetermine because that will prevent real advance made in different ways by the many local authorities. A task of the centre is to assist the learning made possible by variety.

REVERSING DIRECTION

The current need is to strengthen the capacity of local authorities in the government of education if the tendency to centralization is to be reversed.

The key change that is required is not a change in the government of education alone because the main threat of centralization is not in the government of education, but in the financial accountability of local government. Rather than pursuing the policy of ever-weakening the accountability of local authorities for their own expenditure decisions, that accountability should be strengthened.

Changes in the Basis of Local Government Finance

There is a need to create a system of local government finance which ensures that expenditure decisions (including educational expenditure decisions) are clearly borne by taxes paid by local electors, with grant restricted to the equalization of resources in relation to need. At present only about 22 per cent of tax-borne local government expenditure is borne by the local electorate through the domestic rate. Elsewhere[2] I have argued that local government finance should be based on

(1) the retention of the domestic rate;
(2) the transfer of the non-domestic rate to central government as an appropriate national tax;
(3) the reduction of grant to the amount required for equalization purposes, probably about 25–30 per cent of expenditure on average;
(4) the introduction of a local income tax to replace grant and the transfer of the non-domestic rate to national taxation.

It would be a matter of local choice how far public goods or private goods were consumed by the local community and the costs would be spread by local income tax and the domestic rates among a wide range of electors.

The Functions of Local Government

There is the need to build the role of local government as the basic unit of community government. This involves a review of the functions of local government, so that it embraces the range of functions relevant to the local community and for which local choice is important.

It is of great importance for the role of education in local government, and for the role of local government in the government of education, that local government and, in principle, one main authority is charged with the government of a series of interrelated community services. In the first instance the case for the local government of health as a large complex community service parallels the case for education. It is also of critical importance to avoid the growing fragmentation of the government of education itself to place, at the very least, the training responsibilities of the Manpower Services Commission under local government control.

Statutory Review of Duties; Powers and Conditions

There is a need to review the range of statutory duties and conditions placed upon local authorities to establish whether they overdetermine local choice. In particular, it can be argued whether the legislation specifiying the school-year and school-day is required in its current forms.

Equally it can be questioned whether the extent of the power exercised by the secretary of state over the organization of schools within an authority is required. Random interventions in situations imperfectly understood are classic examples of overdetermination. If there are necessary conditions to be met by school organization, they should be stated with the authorities free to implement any school system that does not breach those conditions.

At a time when the main influences are centralizing and the main part of those influences derive from the government's drive to control public expenditure, it is important to state a case for the local government of education within a national framework. That case has been developed in relation to the characteristics of education as a large-scale, complex community service requiring a diffusion of power, a diversity of response and a responsiveness in locality.

If that case has weight, there is a need to reverse current trends and strengthen local government's role in the government of education. That requires, first and foremost, a positive approach to the problems of local government finance, designed to strengthen local accountability and to highlight local choice.

If local government is to play the role demanded in the government of education, local government must be prepared to look critically at itself. Those responsible for education in local government must reject the mental limitation of an approach based upon an image of 'a national system locally administered' and accept the deeper challenge of the 'local government of education within a national framework'.

NOTES: CHAPTER 18

1 *Local Government Finance: Report of the Committee of Enquiry* (Layfield Report), Cmnd 6453 (London: HMSO, 1976), annex 12.

2 G. W. Jones and J. D. Stewart, *The Case for Local Government* (London: Allen & Unwin, 1983).

PART FOUR

Conclusions

19

An Alternative View of Education and Society

STEWART RANSON and JOHN TOMLINSON

> The grand, and leading principle, towards which every argument unfolded in these pages directly converges, is the absolute and essential importance of human development in its richest diversity. (Wilhelm von Humboldt, 1767–1835, *Sphere and Duties of Government*)

The distinctive pattern of government in education established by the Education Act 1944 distributed powers and duties between the ministry, the local authority, the teachers and parents. This settlement created a partnership, so that neither centre nor locality, nor the profession, should dominate. Nevertheless, for much of the postwar period it was appropriate to describe education as a decentralized service with the local authority and the teachers as the influential partners. This was entirely appropriate given the broad consensus between the partners that the pre-eminent objective of the service should be the personal development of each young person. This suggested that as much discretion as possible should be allowed to the prime relationship between teacher and student. Power was devolved as well as diffused in education.

A series of changes during the 1970s have transformed the context of education and government. Falling school rolls and public expenditure cuts have focused the service upon the management of contraction. Parents and industry began to challenge the content and performance of schooling and demanded a more accountable service. But overlaying these problems, which have preoccupied the partners directly, has been the impending consequences for education and society of structural changes in the nature and availability of work. The accelerating growth of youth unemployment together with the initiatives of the Manpower Services Commission (MSC), described in Chapter 9 by Geoffrey Holland, have altered the face of education and training policies for young people. A new partner had made its presence felt.

The contributors to this book have described the strains caused by this changing context. The Department of Education and Science (DES), as

Edward Simpson recalls, was expected to give a lead in the planning and direction of educational change, yet lacked the necessary policy instruments satisfactorily to steer the service. Many local authorities were quickly confronted by considerable problems of managing a contracting service by reorganizing schools and redeploying teachers while being deprived of the necessary resources or appropriate administrative structures. For the teachers there has been the prospect of diminished career opportunities, compounding, as Sayer argues, 'the confusions, crossed lines of management, and inappropriate systems which tug at the teacher in different directions at all points of a career'. Schools will require improved procedures of educational accountability if they are to face a period of falling school rolls with any confidence.

The partners have experienced directly the pressures of change. For the local authorities, the profession and the parents the problems of coping with a transformed world have been further complicated by the secretary of state and the Department. The story of educational policy-making related by this book is one of a march towards central planning and direction. The centre took a very clear view of its responsibility under section 1 of the Education Act 1944 to 'control and direct' the education service through a period of change and set about developing the necessary steering capacity to implement central policy.

Encouraged by Prime Minister Callaghan's Ruskin College speech in 1976, the department has clarified its policy objectives for the service: to rationalize provision, so that a more efficient service serves more directly the economic needs of the nation by preparing young people with more practical skills and vocational attitudes for their future station in employment. These policies have been promoted with unusual vigour by the DES. Shirley Williams, as secretary of state, together with the minister and the Permanent Secretary, Sir James Hamilton, began a remarkable policy launch in 1976–7 with speeches in Parliament and at education conferences intended to reshape the attitudes and practice of their education partners. Mark Carlisle continued to promote the importance of rationalizing 'surplus capacity' and made important decisions about examinations at 17+ and 18+, while Sir Keith Joseph's Sheffield speech, in January 1984, has formed the most significant recent statement of educational policy.

Much of the focus of central initiative has been, as both Norman Thomas and Denis Lawton describe in their chapters, upon the curriculum. The 'secret garden' has been entered and taken over by the secretary of state. Whereas curriculum development had been the responsibility of teachers, schools, examination boards, and nationally of institutions such as the Schools Council, which represented the interests of all the partners, now it would become more firmly under the control of the Department. First, the Further Education Unit was created and appointed by the DES to drive forward programmes of curriculum development in the post-school sector but especially in vocational preparation. Then the Schools Council, which more than any other single institution embodies the idea of partnership, was replaced by two centrally appointed committees, separating examinations from the curriculum. The Examinations Committee is nominated by the secretary of state and entirely funded by him. The Curriculum Committee is half representative of the local education authorities (LEAs) and half nominated, jointly funded by the DES and LEAs. But its range of work is to be restricted to what the DES sees as more its own prerogative. As the secretary of state put in a letter of instruction to the chairman of the Curriculum Committee on 30 January 1984, immediately before the first meeting: 'the formulation of curriculum policy lies outside the Committee's remit.' The rhetoric still spoke of partnership. Sir Keith Joseph's letter to Professor Blin-Stoyle goes on: 'I am sure that in discharging its responsibilities for curriculum development, the Committee will wish to take fully into account the curriculum policies now being developed by the Government in consultation with its education partners.' But the next sentence reads, 'the most recent statement of these policies is in the speech which I made at the North of England Conference on 6 January'.

A different adjustment to the notion of the partnership in relation to the curriculum was made by the DES Circulars 14/77, 6/81 and 8/83. They introduced a linear accountability of DES–LEA schools for the content of the curriculum and the way in which it was made operational by teachers. Moreover, whereas the relationship between the LEA and the schools appears to involve reciprocal obligations, the relationship between the LEA and the DES is firmly one-way. Thus the LEAs can be criticized for failing to resource schools to match agreed objectives. But the LEAs appear to have no way of bringing the centre to share in the responsibility for resources. The procedures now required of LEAs subsequent to the publication of an HM Inspectorate (HMI) report on a school appear to embody the same view: LEAs must report to the DES on how they intend to remedy deficiencies reported by the HMI, but the secretary of state's responsibilities are not mentioned.

The DES has taken firm control of the examination system. Plans to reform examinations at 16+, 17+ and 18+ form, as Denis Lawton has demonstrated in Chapter 10, a principal strategy of determining and redirecting the curriculum. By centralizing control of examinations, the criteria which inform them and the councils which validate certification, the secretary of state has finally wrested control from the hands of the teachers whose discretion over forms of assessment (CSE, for example) had grown since the 1960s. Records of achievement, which might be teacher-led, are at the insistence of government to be criteria-referenced. How far this will prove possible, and how far if it does not the records of achievement will continue as policy, remains to be seen.

The place of the teacher is to be squarely in the classroom. Teachers' preparation and training for classroom practice is also seen, as John Eggleston comments, as an essential area of DES intervention. Powers held by the secretary of state and used sparingly in the past are to be asserted. In-service training has also been brought considerably under central direction through various systems of direct grant to the LEAs and providing bodies. The White Paper on *Teaching Quality* in 1983 proposed a national approach to the management of the teaching force, while the Open University/DES project on the Selection and Appointment of Headteachers

(POST) has also brought the secretary of state into a field hitherto cultivated solely by LEAs and governing bodies.

All this, seen in the light of Burnham Committee proposals for linking salaries with conditions of service (which are believed strongly to have the support of the DES), suggests a radical switch towards a teaching force centrally trained, managed and paid in most important respects.

The secretary of state has intervened directly in the planning of institutional arrangements. Through the Education Act 1980 the secretary of state has used his discretion to determine the character of major secondary reorganization plans preferring wherever possible for 'schools of proven worth' to retain their sixth forms. In the local authority higher education sector the idea of a central government planning agency was resisted and the National Advisory Body has formed a strong central planning agency. How far the LEAs will actually have any measure of policy involvement with 'their' colleges seems increasingly problematical.

By introducing a series of strategic changes to the curriculum, examinations policy, institutional arrangements and the teaching force, the DES has been able to develop the necessary steering capacity for the management of educational change. Control of finance would complete the levers of intervention. Although the department failed to win its own education block grant, it has nevertheless been able, as Tony Travers points out in Chapter 13, to make use of the constitutional victories achieved by other Whitehall departments: block grant, target multipliers and now rate-capping provide the panoply of powers to regulate much of local expenditure. More recently the DES has succeeded in taking legislation through Parliament that would provide for some of the specific grants capacity which they covet so dearly. These grants are to fund significant initiatives which the DES wishes to give priority. The LEAs can gain extra resources through these grants but only if they submit projects which have the approval of the secretary of state and his officials. This strategy has been practised with considerable success by the MSC.

The DES is committed to shifting power over educational decision-making towards the centre. To facilitate this they have tried to develop 'what the Germans call "instrumentarium" through which ministers can implement and operate policy'. The department has drawn upon a wide variety of strategies and instruments to facilitate its policies: 'education is such a complex, pluralist, institution that to achieve one limited goal you have to make five or six interrelated moves: it's rather like playing a fugue using the device of theme and counterpoint' (a secretary of state). The instruments have embraced, as outlined below, bureaucratization, procedural advice, pressure and regulation.[1]

(1) *Bureaucratization.* The department has introduced a more organizational structure into a disparate and diffuse educational system. The relations with the LEAs representatives have been formalized through the central consultative Expenditure Steering Group (Education); the HMI have been encouraged to play their role *within* a framework of directions established by the department; and territorial officers have been encouraged to play a more

assertive role in relations to the LEAs. Significantly in the field of curriculum and examinations new organizations have been created and tied in direct dependence to the DES (there was no means, the DES complained, of 'coercing' the secretary of the Schools Council, and there was a need for a more 'submissive staff').

(2) *Procedural advice.* The department has tried to persuade the LEAs of the virtues of, for example, institutional rationalization by providing for them manuals of practical advice about methods and procedures of rationalizing schools and colleges: 'our task is to confront LEAs with the severity of the situation and the need for rationalisation ... we must identify options for them, tell them how to approach the problems methodologically – by defining the client groups for them and the courses which should be provided: we aim to give practical advice to LEAs.'[2]

(3) *Pressure.* Circulars have been used by the DES to request information from LEAs about progress of local policies on institutional reorganization or upon curriculum planning. The circulars place the LEAs under pressure while providing the department with important information and knowledge about local developments: 'knowledge about the education service is a source of power and influence to the DES.'[3] Officials hoped that when such information was connected to negotiations about rate support grant, it would place the LEAs under considerable pressure. Information provided about surplus capacity under Circular 2/81 would be built into assumptions about grant need; smaller grants calculated on the basis of lower LEA institutional costs would encourage the LEAs to close surplus schools if they had not already done so.

(4) *Regulations.* The department has used its ultimate powers of legislation (the 1980 and 1981 Education Acts) to extend its potential for direct control and regulation of the LEAs. Two provisions in the 1980 Act are significant, in sections 12–16. The need for most LEAs to reorganize their schools and submit proposals to the secretary of state brings the department centre-stage in a crucial policy area. Section 12 increases the capacity of the centre to intervene in LEA proposals, despite the restraining words of Circular 2/80, while section 15 provides the centre with a mechanism to regulate the admission limits of each school over time: 'this is a major addition to the powers of the Secretary of State, in this case to regulate the reduction of school places'.[4]

The DES therefore has formed a strongly interventionist strategy in response to the transformed economic and demographic context. Its policies and instruments have been directed to creating a more efficient service during a period of resource constraint but, more significantly, to reorienting the purposes and content of schooling. As one official has commented, 'this is a more fundamental centralization than we have seen before'.[5]

Yet this story of centralization and the apparent emergence of a new *dirigiste* department and secretary of state is only part of a more complex series of changes. We need to account for a number of changes which seem to take power away from the DES by decentralizing initiative. The discretion of parents has been strengthened, and so has that of governing bodies. Section 8 of the 1980 Act requests the LEA to publish information about each of its schools including information 'as may be required by regulations made by the Secretary of State' on the performance of schools as indicated by their examination results. Such information would help parents to express a preference for a particular school.

Also through the 1981 Act parents are given an equal right alongside professionals (doctors, psychologists, nurses and teachers) to say what they think is necessary for their handicapped child. Indeed enshrining that status for parents in legislation may prove to be the most important aspect of the 1981 Act.

The position of governors in the government of education has been strengthened by the 1980 Education Act and the promise of further reforms contained in the recent Green Paper, *Parental Influence at School.*[6] But whereas the 1980 Act introduced elected parents as part of a partnership in school government, the Green Paper will give parents a majority on governing bodies thus breaking the traditional control held by local authority nominees. The governing body under these new arrangements will have a duty to 'determine the statement of the schools curricular aims and objectives' and will now be in a position to decide upon the appointments of their headteacher.

These several strategies of the DES appear inconsistent in their effects: some changes have led to greater centralization of decision-taking in education, while other initiatives seem manifestly to decentralize influence. The apparent contradiction is clarified when we understand the principal intention of the centre to alter significantly the balance of power within the education partnership. The department has endeavoured to strengthen the centre at the expense of the LEA and the profession. With these partners effectively subordinated, the need for institutions and forums which permit discussion and exchange of ideas diminish in importance.

For the centre to reassert itself as the pre-eminent influence in education it had to displace the LEA which, some have argued,[7] was the key partner in the planning and provision of postwar education. The authority and discretion of the LEA has now however been consistently eroded by the imposition of central controls from above, while the ground beneath its feet is simultaneously undermined by the encouraging of shifting consumer preference. The local authority's capacity to plan its provision coherently according to local needs is systematically weakened and destroyed. The juxtaposition of hierarchy and the market-place leaves, as Chris Price argues in Chapter 1, little policy space in which the LEA can live and breathe.

Looked at from the point of view of the DES, the increasing control of resources together with the growing steering capacity over the curriculum and examinations all amount to a considerable expansion of the centre's authority: 'looking at the education service as a whole it seems that the DES acting on its own initiatives and in context of more general government policies, is now in the process of expanding its power and influence at the expense of the LEAs.'[8] To this should be added the incursions of the Audit Commission and more especially of the MSC – into youth training, adult education, the Open Tech and, more dramatically, in the White Paper,

Training for Jobs, which proposes to set up the MSC as a National Training Agency to have responsibility for 25 per cent of the work-related, non-advanced further education in LEA colleges. When we also include the change in capital expenditure control from the starts programme to cash spending and dramatic curtailment of rate support grant proportions from 69 to 56 per cent on average, together with the constraint upon opportunity to raise rates locally, then as Jack Springett, William Stubbs and Tony Travers emphasize in this book, looked at from the point of view of the LEA, all these developments in all the sectors of their work over the past eight years constitute a transformation. There seems to have been a concerted and successful attempt to weaken, diminish and defeat the most significant partner of the 1944 settlement, namely, the LEA, which was the strategic provider of educational services and opportunities to young people.[9]

With the developing economic crises and the structural revolution in employment driven by the new technologies, the education system is being reconstructed. A new system of tasks, institutional arrangements, curriculum offerings and administrative arrangements is being introduced, shaped by the organizing principles of economic need and social control. The code is one of place and vocation, drawn from the utilitarian philosophies of the nineteenth century. The key is provided by administrators in a centrally steered system. The department is supplanting the LEA as the determining agency in education. Perhaps most obtrusive of all, this painful contraction and reorientation is being constructed within a prevailing philosophy of denigration of the public sector. Restriction of expenditure is a moral crusade in the eyes of many, which has a higher value than the notions of equality of access to education and public service by members and officers which underpinned the period of growth and partnership between central and local government.

In the redirecting of education we can witness the lineages of a new social order. The metaphors of man and society which inform it, however, are not ones which inspire us with any hope in that future: they deny basic rights to individuals and create a fractured foundation for the development of late-twentieth-century society and polity. The state's reordering of education contradicts the fundamental organizing principles – educational, social and political – of the postwar social order. Alternative beliefs and assumptions are possible which build upon the social contract of that earlier period. We shall discuss these principles in turn.[10]

PERSONAL DEVELOPMENT THROUGH EDUCATION

During the earlier educational epoch from the mid-1950s to the mid-1970s the organizing principle of the educational system was personal development and child-centred education. The code was one of opportunity, of raising expectations and of expanding horizons. There has been tension in educational thinking between the values of personal justice and economic efficiency. During much of the postwar period, however, the belief prevailed (exemplified by the Robbins Report) that the educational needs of the individual and the manpower needs of the nation could be reconciled through the progressive expansion of educational opportunities. In subordinating the needs of the individual to the economic needs of the nation government is doing what Bourdieu[11] would call 'symbolic violence' to education. Its dominant paradigm of vocationalism is being imposed arbitrarily upon the natural task of education to fulfil equally the potential of all young people.

By overtly determining to differentiate young people, to define what they may or may not experience or how they may develop, the centrally led reconstruction of education is contradicting the central principles of the previous period. We would follow C. B. Macpherson[12] in the implications of his argument that the organizing principles which inform the restructuring of the education service deny a liberal tradition in our society which has its roots in J. S. Mill. This tradition – a reaction to the crude utilitarianism of that period – drew upon a conception of man as possessing unique powers and capacities for activity and creativity, and argued that it was the duty of society to maximize each individual's powers and potential:[13]

> the moral principle implicit in that value judgement is the principle that all individuals should equally be able to use and develop their natural capacities. The transfer of powers contradicts that principle because it denies the greater part of men equal access to the means of using and developing their natural capacities.

An education service committed to the personal development of young people based upon a belief in their active, creative potential could harness constructively the aspirations of a new generation.

AN OPEN SOCIETY OF EQUAL OPPORTUNITIES

The right to develop one's personal powers and capacities requires a society in which all are entitled to equal opportunities to develop these capacities. It presupposes a more open, equal and fraternal society than we have yet managed to construct, much more so than the closed society that now envelops us. It also presupposes a significant place for education in society.

These presuppositions are, argues Gellner,[14] the preconditions of all advanced societies. An advanced, mobile and differentiated labour force must share, if it is to hang together at all, a common language and culture. The modern economy demands an integrated people; its efficient operation would be obstructed by the deep social and class divisions which prevail in pre-industrial societies. The key institution is education, expected to socialize citizens into one nation, one culture and indeed 'into the same *high* culture'. Literacy is no longer a specialism as for the cleric in the pre-modern world, but a common idiom, a shared medium in the modern world. Education provided not only the skills required by the advanced society, but the qualities of social integration which are a precondition for their use.

In practice, as Shipman argues,[15] although 'there has been a dissemination of culture and some social mobility', education has managed only to soften the edges of a class-divided society. Greater educational opportunities have not, alone, been able to create a more open society. Achieving greater equality of life-chances will require government to challenge more directly the sources of inequality in the distribution and ownership of wealth. Nevertheless, in spite of the disappointed (although overambitious) hopes that education could transform society single-handed, Halsey, Heath and Ridge can conclude their study in *Origins and Destinations* thus:[16]

> expansion can bring us higher standards more fairly shared. Education has changed society in that way and can do more. It does so slowly against the stubborn resistance of class and class-related culture. But it remains the friend of those who seek a more efficient, more open and more just society.

DIFFUSED POWER AND DIVERSITY IN THE POLITY

The recent attempt by government to undermine local government and centralize power in Whitehall or in its nominated quangos denies historic traditions in our constitution, embodied particularly in the postwar government of education, to protect both the devolving and diffusion of power in society. We would argue that those traditions are required more than ever to underpin the government of education and of a changing society.

The case for decentralization is well made by Stewart; in a society undergoing structural change there can be no certain solutions to the problems experienced. A changing society requires a plurality of political institutions which can provide an increased political capacity to resolve problems by allowing a much wider participation in the government of society; a diversity of response that allows opportunities for learning; and a capacity for responsiveness to local needs and circumstances:[17]

> the response required of government is less certain, less sure. This is not to be regretted, but welcomed as opening up a style of government less dependent on imposed certainties and more on learning from the community.

In our society the institutional capacity for participation, diversity and local responsiveness has been provided by local government in partnership with the centre.

Most of the important postwar innovations in education, whether it be in the curriculum or in institutional change, have as David Hargreaves notes in Chapter 16 grown up from the roots, encouraged by strong local political institutions. The education service, if it is to protect and develop its diversity of response, its capacity for learning and its local responsiveness, will need to be a driving force within a strong local government: 'local government is no passing luxury in our society: it is a guardian of fundamental values. It represents first and foremost a spread of political power in our society.'[18]

OPPORTUNITY AND CITIZENSHIP IN THE SOCIAL CONTRACT

The form of the current reordering of education, marked by its stratifying of access and curricular experience at a time of social and economic transformation, may be placing at risk a central principle of postwar settlement – common citizenship. The social concordat established during and after the war and building upon the principles of Keynes, Beveridge and Butler that all should have equal access to standards of health, housing, security and education created the foundation of one national community enjoying the same civil, political and social rights. These principles of citizenship would be, Marshall argued,[19] a significant means of 'class abatement'.

Education was central to the postwar contract and the creation of citizenship. Industrial capitalism would be rendered tolerable not by the safety net of welfare, nor only the prospect of decent health and housing, but through the dignity of citizenship as symbolized in the common prospect of employment together with an equal opportunity to develop potential and thus the capacity to participate in complex ways in the governance of society.

The contemporary metaphors of educational change indicates the forging of a social order devoted to the Platonic principles of hierarchy, inequality and place. People are being developed instrumentally to suit the supposed needs of economy and society. We need, however, to reaffirm the principles embodied in the earlier social contract and deny the prevalent utilitarianism which subordinates the happiness and development of particular individuals.

We require a theory which affirms with Rawls[20] the 'inviolability of persons' and, in particular, the development of their natural powers and capacities. Only a new concordat can embody the principles of justice and citizenship for all: an equal share of liberty and equal opportunities, and only those inequalities which benefit the worst off in the community. It is a contrast which strives to weaken the principles of self-interest and strengthen the principles of community and fraternity which constitute our membership of one polity[21] and which underpin, as Halsey[22] has argued, the development of liberty in society. Education will have a central contribution to make to the renewal of common citizenship and to the capacity of our society to adapt to, and to shape, a period of change.

We now turn in this book to the respective conceptions of how best to constitute a government of education that will fulfil the organizing principles of a new, more just and less class-divided social order.

NOTES: CHAPTER 19

1 See extended discussion in S. Ranson, 'Contradictions in the government of education', *Political Studies*, vol. 33, no. 1 (March 1985), pp. 56–72.
2 Ranson, research sponsored by SSRC into 'Central–local policy planning in education'.
3 ibid.
4 ibid.
5 ibid.

6 *Parental Influence at School* (London: HMSO, May 1984).
7 M. Kogan, *The Government of Education* (London: Macmillan, 1971).
8 S. Ranson, SSRC research, op. cit.
9 cf. S. Ranson, 'Rationalising systems and opportunities in education', in S. Ranson, G. W. Jones and K. Walsh (eds), *Between Centre and Locality: The Politics of Public Policy* (London: Allen & Unwin, 1985), pp. 187–206.
10 cf. S. Ranson, 'Contradictions in the government of education', op. cit.
11 P. Bourdieu and J. C. Passeron, *Reproduction* (London: Sage, 1977).
12 C. B. Macpherson, *Democratic Theory* (Oxford: Oxford University Press, 1973).
13 ibid., p. 19.
14 E. Gellner, *Nations and Nationalism* (Oxford: Basil Blackwell, 1983), pp. 139–43.
15 M. Shipman, *Education as a Public Service* (New York: Harper, 1984).
16 A. H. Halsey, A. F. Heath and J. M. Ridge, *Origins and Destinations* (Oxford: Clarendon Press, 1980), p. 219.
17 J. D. Stewart, 'Decentralisation and local government', in A. Wright, J. D. Stewart and N. Deakin, *Socialism and Decentralisation*, Fabian Society, no. 496 (May 1984), p. 13.
18 G. W. Jones and J. D. Stewart, *The Case for Local Government* (London: Allen & Unwin, 1983).
19 T. H. Marshall, *Class, Citizenship and Social Development* (Chicago: University of Chicago Press, 1964).
20 J. Rawls, *A Theory of Justice* (Oxford: Clarendon, 1972).
21 M. J. Sandel, *Liberation and the Limits of Justice* (Cambridge: Cambridge University Press, 1982).
22 A. H. Halsey, 'This way please for the Open Society', *Times Educational Supplement*, 11 January 1980.

20

Government for a Learning Society

STEWART RANSON

> Social institutions – property rights and the organisation of industry and the system of public health and education – should be planned as far as is possible to emphasise and strengthen not the class differences which divide but the common humanity which unites. (R. H. Tawney, *Equality*, 1931)

Education has a crucial contribution to make as late-twentieth-century society enters a period of historic transformation. The rapidly emerging post-manufacturing society will ensure that the fundamental issue becomes one of human surplus capacity. Work, the means by which most have contributed to the value and wealth of their community, may now become a privileged activity. What value men and women are in future to contribute or to be seen to possess in themselves is now in question.

Education, as we have seen from the earlier chapters in this book, will have a particularly significant part to play in creatively shaping the response of society and polity to such changes by: providing opportunities for *all*; creating the conditions for a learning society; and sustaining challenge in the polity. By contributing to the personal development of individuals as well as to what Habermas[1] calls 'communicative rationality' in society – reaching agreement through reasoned argument – education can enrich the fabric of our late-twentieth-century experience. How the issues of surplus capacity will be resolved and what impact education will have upon them will depend much upon how we understand and organize the relations between government and society. The crisis between central and local government has been deteriorating since the mid-1970s and the ways of understanding the crisis have themselves been changing over time. Initially the problem was caused by confused administrative arrangements. The Layfield Report, however, conceived the crisis as reflecting more significant issues of control and accountability: 'few people, if any, know where the real responsibility rests'.[2] Yet Layfield was aware that the problems of accountability themselves represented more lasting social and economic concerns, and that 'underlying all these were the human and social considerations which are the reasons for local government'.[3] Deeper questions about the relationship of state to society underlie the crisis.

The state is a structuring of power and values. The organization of government, law and finance embody society's dominant beliefs about the distribution of power and control and about whether power should be concentrated or diffused. Yet those beliefs about the organizing of power themselves reflect values about the form that economic and social relations might take in civil society. The organizing of government reveals conceptions about its role; the relations between public and private; and understanding of citizenship; and the contribution which individuals and groups may make to society and the polity.

The structuring of power and values embodied in government and the polity have changed over the postwar period.[4] Much of the postwar period can be characterized as a 'social democratic state', which had a positive contribution to make to the modernizing and reform of postwar economy and society. The stress upon meeting individual needs as well as upon the attempts to consult local interests strengthened the role of local authorities as the principal arm of government in the social democratic state. This contrasts strongly with the 'liberal nightwatchman' state which has emerged with vigour since the late 1970s. Beliefs that the state is a bureaucratic burden and that public service is mistaken activity have led to the progressive contraction of public expenditure. Efficiency has replaced need as the directing criterion, while the polity is conceived in terms of aggregated individuals rather than as a community. The attack upon democratic local government and upon education opportunities follows naturally as power is restructured.

An alternative structuring of power and values is needed. The task is to reconstitute a form of government which develops but goes beyond the principles of the social democratic state.

GUIDELINES FOR THE GOVERNMENT OF EDUCATION

The principles which might inform the design of the future government of education should be developed, I contest, in relation to five essential issues – what should be

(1) the relation between public and private in education?
(2) the relation between market and non-market?
(3) the relation of central to local government?
(4) the relation of education to other services?
(5) the interrelationship of sociodemographic communities?

I shall discuss each issue in turn and the principles arising from them.

Public Education and Personal Development

Educational services should be publicly owned. We have already outlined the qualities that we should like to see inform any future polity and society. Such a society would, we hoped, be open, participative, egalitarian in provision of opportunities and respecting of fellow citizens. The processes and organizational forms of education will be vital if these aims are to be realized. Education can facilitate or frustrate the open society. Private education offends those principles of polity; it divides the educating of young people, so that those in the 'independent' sector acquire a hidden curriculum of closure, a closed world behind the boundaries of protected exclusiveness. Can respect and fraternity be developed in the polity when young people are segregated in their educating along the class divide? The motive for establishing private education is pre-eminently one of reproducing privilege and advantage.[5] Tawney's response is apposite:[6]

> [in] a civilized community ... its members shall treat each other, not as means, but as ends, and that institutions which stunt the faculties of some among them for the advantage of others shall be generally recognised to be barbarous and odious. It will aim at making power not arbitrary but responsible, and, when it finds an element of privilege in social institutions, it will seek to purge it.

Guidelines for the government of education need to begin by removing the boundaries of privileged ownership. Education is a public good.

Rationality in Planning

If we are to ensure effective schooling, then decision-making cannot be left to the random choices of individuals in the market-place. A number of writers have recently focused upon the paradox of unintended consequences in decision-making, especially about public services.[7] To pursue self-interest is self-defeating when we aim to make decisions about education or health. Private decisions produce collective consequences which frustrate our original aims. Decisions about institutional arrangements, resourcing, staffing and social composition are the ingredients of effective schooling and these cannot be put together sensibly from an aggregate of private choices. Rationality presupposes public dispositions of co-operation and interdependence which follow from qualities of relationship and shared understanding in society and the polity. In the public realm selfishness is folly. The process of educating can dissolve these confusions, but this process can be facilitated if these principles are embodied in the very organization and government of education. The supposed virtues of the market-place – experiment and diversity – are protected through progressive decentralization of control.

Progressive Decentralization

The relations between central and local government should be guided by the principle of progressive decentralization in order to allow people to participate more fully in the government of their society. And yet if our principles of polity and society are to be accomplished, some controls will be required at the centre. We need to be clear about the tasks to be undertaken as well as an understanding of the limits of government at different tiers; in short, we need a theory of power which analyses the distribution of powers to different tiers to fit their appropriate responsibilities.

We need a multidimensional approach to distributing power and authority in education, as follows:

(1) *The centre* – would be responsible for the infrastructures of public policy in education: the institutional framework of comprehensive education – public and non-selective; – resource re-distribution; promotion of good local practice; and a monitoring role for the HM Inspectorate.
(2) *Locality* – would be responsible for system maintenance and development; effective education requires a number of dimensions – institutional, resourcing, staff development, balance of intake, and so on – to be planned and managed from the level of the local authority; there is an important networking and team-building role as the unit of provision becomes inter-institutional; and there is an important role for the locality to evaluate and monitor performance and to practise accountability to several publics.
(3) *The institutional level* – having responsibility for personal development and thus for developing the curriculum, teaching practice, assessment and counselling; it is the level of experience, discovery and, hopefully, raised horizons; increasingly this presupposes inter-professional collaboration and close ties with the community as well as with employers; and it is the arena in which to encourage community participation and 'communicative action'.

The burden of power distribution is towards decentralization. The public within and through education must feel more identity with, and ownership of, the service than hitherto. The welfare state provided services *for* people; it was a paternalistic state. Public welfare may have been less vulnerable to an ideological assault and the ensuing expenditure cuts if it had been less alien in its provision. In future the provision has to be more accountable to the public, but also more democratic with the public. School and college can become vehicles for a local polity extending the community's experience of democracy, for being educated by democracy.

Integration of Services

Integration of service disciplines rather than specialization should inform the structuring of government of education at all levels. A number of chapters in this volume, especially Barry Taylor's, have argued strongly for the importance of greater co-ordination between sectors within education. The divisions between secondary and further education, together with the isolation of the adult, youth and careers services, can only diminish the quality of provision to young people. At national level a reorganization is necessary to integrate the Manpower Services Commission (MSC) into a unified Department of Education and Training/Personal Development, while at local level most authorities need to rethink the organizational arrangements of their education departments to facilitate co-ordination.

The energies and capacities of young people to explore their learning environment depends as much upon conditions beyond school: their health, and housing and social welfare; and as important as teachers to personal and educational growth are doctors, social workers, housing managers and librarians. The capacity to respond to, and to shape, local needs and demands calls for strong local government which eschews the traditions of professional rivalry and the fragmentation of knowledge implied.

A future reorganization of local government is needed to reintegrate the health service under local democratic control. If such a change were beyond the art of the possible, then a move to promote, at least, an independent education service could not be sustained given our overriding criteria: the progressive fragmentation of services seems an odd way to proceed towards their integration. The boundaries between service bureaucracies need to be diminished rather than reinforced.

The most important organizational development task, at local level in particular, is to encourage a process of networking between services and professionals. In the 16–19 sector, for example, local networks need to be established to keep track of young people as they move between 'learning sites'. The careers service has a particularly strategic role to play here in co-ordinating the advice of disparate educators to help the counselling of personal progress.

Unifying Town and Country

The final guideline for the government of education reaffirms the principle proposed by the Redcliffe-Maud Report of unitary local government that would integrate town and country. This principle is even more apposite in the 1980s as a period of change begins to accentuate even further the differences in modes and standards of living, and of culture and politics, between town and country. At present the city region travel-to-work areas allow many to draw their life incomes from the urban area and retreat to the leafy, low-rated county villages for home and leisure, escaping the local taxes which would contribute to redistribution and the renewal of the inner city. Town and country are in danger of becoming geographical masks for a class-divided society.

As Dunleavy[8] has argued, we need to explore further the 'distributional impacts' of particular forms of local government. The 1974 reorganization retreated from the recommendations of unitary local government and divided functions between counties and districts in a way that perpetuated the separation of geographic communities. A further reorganization can recall the principles of Redcliffe-Maud and contribute significantly to making connections between communities and thus the capacity to learn from one another.

THE SCENARIOS REVISITED

Our five principles provide a basis for evaluating the scenarios of educational government already presented in this book.

The Centralization Scenario

If we are in agreement with Maurice Peston and Barry Taylor that education is a national service, and especially with Peston's egalitarian intentions (see

Chapter 14), then we must concede some of their arguments for centralization of control. It would be inconceivable for there to be no education provided in a part of the nation or for one local community to terminate schooling at age 11 or 13. It would be unthinkable to have no national redistribution of resources to ensure that poor areas with low rateable values provide comparable levels of service with wealthy areas (for instance, Wales *vis-à-vis* Westminster).

Peston and Taylor nevertheless overextend the powers and responsibilities of the centre. Although it may be appropriate for the centre to establish broad parameters for the nation's education – the framework of a public and non-selective comprehensive education, resource redistribution and monitoring – it is entirely inappropriate for the centre to intervene in local planning, curriculum development, or classroom practice which are best developed and negotiated locally between members, professionals and the community. To overcentralize is not only inefficient, it is ineffective, incapable of delivering what it promises. If the centre cannot *know* the detail of local or individual need, it cannot be sensitive or responsive to them.

Overcentralization will stifle initiative and change at a moment when our society most requires those qualities. More important, the argument for centralization is plainly undemocratic if we mean by that a form of government which seeks to involve the interests and energies of ordinary people. It is a bias towards local initiative, participation and ownership which is needed at this historical moment. If people are committed to services because they identify with them, feel part of them, and understand their complexities, they will be more reluctant to lose them and more willing to resource them. The planned central paternalism of the past – when services were handed down to be gratefully received – has held people at a distance, not only their enthusiasm but their understanding, and left services vulnerable to challenge and contraction. A national service locally administered is no more effective and certainly a no more democratic arrangement. To administer central policies is to make local authorities an agent of the state with little real discretion – local *government* implies some capacity to choose policies to meet local needs.

The Decentralization Scenario

Decentralization promotes the interests of the working class whose needs, David Hargreaves has argued in Chapter 16, have been neglected in previous structures of education. Only a radical shift towards greater accountability to the community can ensure learning experiences and practices which meet the needs of disadvantaged sections of society. Perhaps the most significant claim for decentralization is made by Tim Brighouse (see Chapter 17), who returns us to the fundamental idea of an intrinsic interdependence between education and democracy which influenced the 1944 Education Act, as well as earlier legislation, and has its roots in the philosophy of J. S. Mill. Education is a precondition for democracy because it produces informed participation, and because there can be no political freedom, as Butler envisaged, unless each person's powers and capacities are fully developed. Democracy is also a precondition for education, for the responsible exercise of decision-making is an educating process (and for the Athenians, for example, the goal of civilized education).

There are a number of problems with the presentation of the decentralist model. It lacks an understanding of effective provision and it is naïve about power. First, its selective understanding of effectiveness in education. To incorporate the community is indeed a priority for the service but not at the expense of the contribution of the centre, or most important, the local authority, whose system planning and development are a prerequisite of effective schooling. There is in Hargreaves (see Chapter 16) the mistaken individualist assumptions that effective education could emerge from private decisions or from the spontaneous transactions of individuals.

Hargreaves openly displays his distrust of institutions and of the beneficial capacity of government. The distrust of institutions is consistent with Hargreaves's professed anarchism but sits oddly with his community tradition, which believes in the positive potential of schools to *create* a sense of community in place of anomic experience. The mistake in the work of Illich and others is to deny that institutions are probably a precondition for fraternity rather than its obstruction.

The most important institution in this respect is government. The notion of eliminating government is naïve because any society cannot avoid the task of determining access to, and the distribution of, power; that is, it cannot avoid 'politics'. As Weber put it, '"politics" for us means striving to share power or striving to influence the distribution of power, either among states or among groups within a state'.[9] To advance an argument about power seems unfair to Hargreaves, who begins in the most *realpolitik* fashion proposing correctly that the government of education has always been a power struggle and a battlefield in which working-class interests have usually been defeated. But if those interests are to be advanced, we need countervailing centres of power, and we need to distribute power with some care. To demolish government is to make people vulnerable to other centres of power in civil society, and to demolish local government is to abandon the institution which has more than any other responded to the needs of the disadvantaged in our society. The irony of the institutional autonomy model advocated by Tim Brighouse (see Chapter 17) and by Halsey,[10] is that it is really no different from the centralization model; both seek to weaken or eliminate the local authority and then haggle about the division of functions between the remaining two tiers. The decentralization to institutions model is a mask for centralization in the government of education. Our third scenario proposes that the middle tier of local government is crucial both to the balance of power in society and to the development of services to meet the needs of people. It is to this argument that I now turn.

The Localist Scenario

John Stewart in Chapter 18 forms a sophisticated discourse on power and the conditions of power for a society that must learn to adapt to a period of uncertainty and change. But there is also a greater need for definition about the distribution of powers and responsibilities between the tiers. Both Stewart and Edward Simpson, for example, accord the centre the right to establish 'the framework' for education, yet Simpson would include in his framework control over policy for the curriculum (see Chapter 2).

More seriously, however, Stewart's chapter is incomplete in its analysis of the purposes of power. His purpose is both to devolve power in order to prepare the conditions for learning in society and to facilitate the intrinsic value of distributing power in the polity. We need, however, to get behind these questions to explore more fundamental ones. At the heart of our current changes are uncertainties about the nature of society and polity themselves; uncertainties about who is to do the learning (is it to be community government for the community, or with or by the community?), and who is to choose. It is only when we have formed some view about how we conceive the public, the community, that we can form a view about the distribution of power within the polity. We need a view about citizenship and what it means to be a citizen within the community. These questions are prior. A conception of the polity, together with a theory of society (its existing structures of advantage and opportunity), produce an analysis about the purposes to which power is to be put.

Such an analysis can suggest an argument for the use of power at separate levels to create the conditions for community, for membership of the polity, and to create a public that is a polity. This would require a less formal, less neutral view about 'public' and 'private' or about social diversity, and a more assured view about the need to redistribute power and advantage to create the conditions for membership, for citizenship and thus for a learning society.

PROPOSALS FOR THE GOVERNMENT OF EDUCATION

Responsibilities and powers can be distributed to each tier of education – the centre, locality and institution – so that each can make an appropriate contribution to the overall aim of maximizing individual powers and capacities through a system of comprehensive and equal opportunities.

The Centre

Drawing upon the principle of integration the centre will be defined as the Department of Education and Training (DET), with the MSC being dissolved and its functions amalgamated with those of the Department of Education and Science (DES) to form one department that can minimize duplication and enhance accountability.

The role of the centre is to establish the broadest preconditions, the infrastructures, of educational equality: by establishing dimensions of the framework, by redistributing resources, by monitoring performance and by promoting the aims of education. I shall begin with the classic view of the role of the DES as one of *promotion*. Recent work[11] reinforces this interpretation of the department as having an effective impact upon the climate of opinion in education 'through a rather intangible but very real shift in the balance of prevailing values'. What is to be promoted? The centre has a useful contribution to make in promoting good ideas, innovations and practice which have been developed by teachers and local authorities. The centre can help circulate the exciting innovations which invariably grow up from the roots, as Hargreaves has pointed out earlier. The centre can also facilitate this distilling and crystallizing of good ideas and practice by recreating and servicing the important advisory councils whose great reports (Newsom, Robbins, Plowden, and so on) provided a progressive influence in postwar education. The function of these councils is, at key moments, to draw together the disparate policy community in education to create a common language and shared understanding of policy issues.

The promotional role for the DET needs, however, to be more fundamental than a focus upon a particular sector of educational policy. Its prime promotion, perhaps even over the next two Parliaments, would be to use its proven capacity to shape opinion and values by promoting the very notion of public education, of one public in education. Research and departmental papers, together with assertion across the political spectrum, agree about the entrenched influence of class upon educational achievement. If the department could promote the abandonment of independent, private privileged education, it could promote the value of community and help to dissolve the barriers of a class-divided society.

The role of promotion will in this way support the department's main contribution in establishing the infrastructure of public comprehensive education. Part of the institutional framework has already been created with the opening of comprehensive schools in secondary education but needs to be completed by further institutional changes. The most important would be the forging of a new settlement between the state and the private and voluntary sectors. Richard Pring[12] has described, fairly exhaustively, the various ways in which private schooling is subsidized by public funds. There are the obvious forms of state subsidy through the assisted places scheme and the Youth Training Scheme (YTS), but there are also more disguised forms of subsidy through the charitable status of independent schools which exempt them from paying taxes (on profit from fees) or national insurance (exemption from the employers' surcharge) and gains them rate relief. Even more indirect support comes from the charitable status of non-educational institutions which can support private schools, or the corporate sector purchasing fees and places at such schools for their employees. A new settlement would begin by offering financial incentives to the private sector to join the public sector, would reduce progressively such subsidizing of independent schooling and conclude by legislating for the end of private schools and the duty of parents to send their children to public, comprehensive schools.

Butler's compromise between church and state in 1944 was a major achievement. But there is a growing understanding of the need for the state to review the settlement with the voluntary sector because of the problems caused by falling school rolls, and because of the growth of a multifaith, multicultural society. The *Times Educational Supplement* has said that there is a need to 'prepare the ground for new legislation later in the decade'.[13] This journal and others[14] argue that there is a need to establish a new settlement to establish democratic accountability and control over voluntary schools, so that they cannot operate hidden selective admission policies, seeking parity between the county and voluntary schools without abolishing religious rights and freedoms. Yet there are others,[15] examining the emerging multicultural society, who wonder whether denominational schooling does not paradoxically deny its essential faith and is divisive in its effects: schools run separately for Anglicans, Catholics, Muslims, or Hindus would be 'inherently divisive and seek to perpetuate tensions and strife'.[16] The report calls for the churches to abolish their independent schools in the interests of a more united society.

The integration of the private and religious interests would create the proper foundation for a truly public comprehensive education. This would be rounded out by the centre preparing legislation to complete secondary reorganization, by requiring local authorities to submit integrated plans for comprehensive education and training for 16–25-year-olds and by preparing plans for the unification of universities and polytechnics in a comprehensive higher education sector.

The Level of the Institution

This level is constituted increasingly by inter-institutional relations. The age of the autonomous school and college, Peter Newsam once pointed out, has passed. Not only does effective provision now depend upon the local authority managing the institutional system and staff deployment more closely than before, but the very nature of educational experience now takes young people between schools and colleges and schemes and workplaces. The unit of educational provision at this level increasingly forms a network of community organizations dependent upon inter-professional collaboration (indeed one of the winners of the recent School Curriculum Awards was a school which had developed 'learning networks' with its local environment).

The prime responsibility of institutions as always is to encourage and enable personal development. If education is a process of opening out, of becoming aware through experience which sparks ideas and reflection, then it is a process which emerges from the transactions of student and teacher. Education is a journey in which the limits of one's understanding and being are engaged, tested and expanded. The task of facilitating personal growth and reflection can only work out from this level of the educational system (the recent absurdity has been that civil servants suddenly came to believe they were educators rather than administrators supporting education). The exploring of experience is mediated by the curriculum, by counselling and modes of assessment which are best shaped by teachers, trainers, youth workers and careers officers working in direct relation to the needs of young people.

The particular responsibilities at this level follow from this understanding of the educating task. First, *the curriculum*. In order to encourage opportunities for personal development curriculum planning will increasingly need to form a process of negotiation between the interests of the student and the professional seeking to ensure balance and variety in learning – a whole curriculum for whole people as the exciting Hargreaves Report[17] would describe it. Such a curriculum would embrace the development of cognitive skills, *knowledge* and problem-solving; *experience* both in the community and at work; and creativity through the arts as well as through social relationships.[18] Curriculum planning should encourage, as George Tolley has suggested, a 'portfolio' of skills experiences and knowledge, for *all* young people. Comprehensive education presupposes equal access to a broad curriculum that enables a rich mosaic of personal development.

Professionals are concerned increasingly to develop the curriculum in a modular form which allows education experience to accord with individual need and facilitates the guiding objective of *progression* in learning, especially important given our aim to develop continuing education for adults who need to return to continue and update knowledge and skills.

The concern to negotiate personal development changes the relationship between learner and professional and brings inevitably counselling and guidance to the forefront of the educating process. Guidance seeks to help young people 'take charge' of their decisions and choices surrounding their own progress and development and thus to make students take part in the review and assessment of their progress and achievement.[19] The process of assessment in this context requires a more sensitive and complete record of achievement that is sensitive to the breadth of capacities displayed by the student. Such profiles can then be used to celebrate the achievement of the learner, to improve self-image and thus becomes a positive 'formative' influence of assessment. This process of negotiated assessment, of achievement and of guidance about future progress seeks to create a sense of self-reliance rather than dependence in learning and this grows out of a tutorial relationship that expresses the qualities of trust, equality and openness.[20]

The implications of this understanding of the educating process are far-reaching for examination-based traditions of assessment. The instruments and measures of examinations and tests can only make sense, Goldstein has argued,[21] in relation to what is taught and experienced. It implies, he proposes, a much more localized and professionally moderated process of assessment. Comparisons nationwide and over long time periods are probably meaningless. One of the most important recent developments in developing assessment to meet this new framework of thinking on personal development is the Oxfordshire Certificate of Educational Achievement (OCEA); this seeks to broaden the basis of assessment by providing for as many pupils as possible a portfolio of assessment including examinations, graded tests and profiles. This multidimensional assessing expands the spectrum of achievement reviewed and encouraged.

The learning experiences indicated in these developments of curriculum, assessment and counselling often imply closer ties with the community. The skills and experiences of members of the community can be drawn upon by schools and colleges as part of the learning network to extend the curriculum, to lend counselling support and become an essential precondition for pupil achievement.[22] A learning society can grow in and around the school or college. Members of the community together with parents can work in partnership with professionals to expand the learning experience in particular school networks. More widely, members of the community can be drawn significantly into the consultative process about the development of local education; and not just as required by existing law to consult local interests about institutional closure or amalgamation, but about the driving force of the new educational ideas. Kindling argument and understanding of the education process in this way could enable schools and colleges to engage the energies and enthusiasms of local communities, so that they can become a significant element in the negotiating processes of the government of the community. We need to deepen participative democracy[23] and the institutional networks of education can become vehicles for such energies and communicative action.

The unit of local democracy, however, must remain the local authority if there is to be fairness between communities and the needs of all are to be responded to in the locality.[24]

The Local Authority

Many of the most significant roles in the government of education will fall to the local authority. It was so in the settlement of 1944, in which local government was made the centrepiece of a national system (cf. p. 2). Local government was to be the providing authority – building and maintaining its institutional system, staffing the schools, supplying them with books and equipment and, most important of all, responsible for the curriculum. If anything, these functions need to be strengthened if the conditions for the learning society are to be created.

Those scenarios which argued for greater centralism, or institutional autonomy, sought to erode or replace the authority of this strategic tier of government. The need for strong local government, however, derives from an understanding of the task of educating in the modern world as well as the demands of democratic accountability for a learning society. The key roles/functions of local government therefore comprise the maintenance and development of the system of local education (providing the framework of institutional arrangements, networking and resourcing), together with responsibilities for evaluation and accountability.

The role of maintaining and developing the system of local education is a traditional function which takes on renewed significance during this period of change. Many authorities will have to complete the process of comprehensive reorganization, particularly as we are envisaging the end of private education and the integration of independent sector students, in ways which will enhance the comprehensive principle. But the institutional framework has to be revised in quite radical ways if equal opportunities are to be provided – especially in the expanding tertiary sector and beyond if the need for continuing access to education and training throughout life is to be fulfilled:[25]

> It will require the development of provision for all adults to join in formal or informal ways at various levels, times and stages of life: when, where, how and what the individual needs. We need to break away from ... a rigid delivery system of fixed entry points, of hours in the day, terms, academic years and self-contained levels and entry qualifications.

At the heart of this elaboration of the system of local education, however, are policy developments in curriculum and assessment. The institutional changes are informed by the new beliefs about the learning process. The most important recent expression of this need to transform local education processes is provided by the Hargreaves Report of the Inner London Education Authority. The significance of this report, however, lies as much in its mode of working as its refreshing educational ideas. It showed the authority's officers and advisers observing and working with teachers and celebrating good practice in schools. The role of the authority implies discussion and negotiation between the several local partners to education in order to create a framework of values and beliefs about the learning process which can be embodied and realized in local practice.

Networking and resourcing complete the 'systemic' functions of the local authority. The local authority will have a key role to play in providing the conditions for inter-professional networking, giving time, resources and support as well as helping to make the connections where necessary. Part of the local authorities' skills will be those of recognizing and reinforcing the professions which have a tradition of networking. It may be that some services which have been perceived as 'peripheral' – the cinderella services of careers, of youth and community – now have the skills to play a strategic role in keying in disparate activities which could benefit from shared experience. Watts[26] and Bazalgette[27] have argued that the careers service has a particularly strategic role in facilitating inter-agency collaboration to ensure effective guidance networks for 16–19-year-olds.

If the educational systems, processes and networks are to run effectively so that opportunities are provided equally for all, then the distribution of resources will be critical. In many authorities there will need to be processes of positive discrimination in favour of disadvantaged areas and institutions; cf. Sheffield.[28] Equally, if people are to be encouraged to take advantage of opportunities for continuing education, then local authorities will need to develop more radical systems of grant support.

Essential to the democratic government of education for a learning society will be a service that is accountable. This function which can be seen to overlay and inform the other functions is the most vital performed by local government. Accounting for the performance of local education to its several publics involves an authority in seeking to evaluate (thus to understand) and to transform that performance over time. Discourse and action are interrelated in the management of accountability.

THE ACCOUNTING OF PERFORMANCE (THE DISCOURSE)

To give an account of educational performance is first to *describe* that performance in terms of pupil achievement (in, say, examinations or creative work) or the costs of producing those results. But to describe performance always implies some *evaluation* in terms of measured-against standards and expectations. A judgement of performance may follow with praise or blame (sanctions) apportioned.

It is important that local authorities should be 'held to account', be answerable in this fashion. They should be held to account to parents, the community and employers, to the consumers of the service for what has been accomplished.

An account can only make sense when accompanied by a scenario of what was to be attempted and any limiting conditions needed to be taken into account. The difficulty for local authorities is that different scenarios or 'paradigms of performance' reflect the competing understandings of possible achievement which are presented by different partners to the service – parents, professionals, employers, and so on. To account therefore is to seek to persuade others of the virtue of one's story, to be drawn into discourse; it is to try to renegotiate ideas and 'assumptive worlds' about what achievement is and what causes it.

Therefore, for many local authorities to report is always also to persuade and negotiate because they seek a paradigm shift in the understanding of, and accounting for, educational achievement. Winning the argument, or reaching agreement, is a precondition for being able to act upon performance.

THE ACTING UPON PERFORMANCE (ACTION AND CHANGE)

Paradigms of performance indicate paradigms of action and attempts to transform the conditions of performance. The accounting function of the local authority leads back into the function of maintaining and developing the local education system. The radical paradigm pursued now by some local authorities suggests that the conditions for effective performance depends upon local authorities mediating and negotiating changes at the level of the institution in terms of curriculum and assessment but also, crucially, in the direct strategic work of the local authority itself: in positive discrimination of resources and, most controversially, managing the 'balance of intake'. A number of studies[29] have suggested that balance of ability and class in schools was the best predictor of school effectiveness after family background had been taken into account. The social composition of schools may be a vital precondition for progress in learning.

The government for a learning society needs to help classes within that society to learn from each other. Changes in social structure and in the communicative relations between classes can be seen to be a precondition for the learning society. The government of education, it seems, has to encourage social change to facilitate educational progress in young people, yet in so doing it enhances the learning of one and all. We have come full circle to considerations of the values and power in society which underlie the structuring of government.

CONCLUSION

The form of government established tends to reflect the dominant images of society that people wish to create. In an earlier era the dominant images of the social democratic state were often paternalistic providing services for people, while the dominant images of the liberal/authoritarian state deny any conception of community as anomic consumers pursue self-interest even to irrational consequences.

The future of post-manufacturing society is uncertain, yet if all are to contribute, to develop their powers and capacities, there will need to be sharing of work, leisure and wealth. This can only be realized if members of a society can identify themselves as members, as part of one polity. Sharing in the benefits of the post-manufacturing society presupposes common citizenship that enables all to participate democratically in the shaping of the future. This suggests the need for a more open, communicating, learning society.

The structuring of government, and the government of education in particular, can enable the development of the learning society. It will need to distribute and devolve power to allow participation and the expression of ideas, and through education fulfil personal capacities, so that all can contribute their creative potential.

The distribution of powers and responsibilities to each tier of government will, I have argued, provide the conditions both for individual progress and learning in the community. Local government is the tier of government which can best support the pressures of a more open, participative polity and society, mediating the discourse between communities of interest and enabling communication which forms the basis for understanding and action. The local government of education is, as has been expressed elsewhere, 'the jewel in the crown of the education system'.[30]

NOTES: CHAPTER 20

1 J. Habermas, *Legitimation Crisis* (London: Heinemann, 1976).
2 *Local Government Finance: Report of the Committee of Enquiry* (Layfield Report), Cmnd 6453 (London: HMSO, 1976), p. 46.
3 ibid., p. xxiv.
4 cf. S. Ranson and K. Walsh, 'Understanding the crisis of government relations', in S. Ranson, G. W. Jones and K. Walsh, *Between Centre and Locality: The Politics of Public Policy* (London: Allen & Unwin, 1985), pp. 1–19.
5 M. Shipman, *Education as a Public Service* (New York: Harper, 1984).
6 R. H. Tawney, *Equality* (London: Unwin, 1931), p. 90.
7 See D. Parfitt, *Reasons and Persons* (Oxford: Clarendon, 1984); J. Elsten, *Ulysses and the Sirens* (Cambridge: Cambridge University Press, 1979); and A. Sen, 'The new economic gospel', *New Society*, 26 July 1984.
8 P. Dunleavy, *Urban Political Analysis* (London: Macmillan, 1980).
9 M. Weber, *From Max Weber* (London: Routledge, 1948), p. 78.
10 A. H. Halsey, 'Democracy for education', *New Society*, 28 May 1981.
11 See H. Glennerster, *Planning for Priority Groups* (Oxford: Martin Robertson, 1983); and J. D. Stewart, 'Local authority', *Times Higher Educational Supplement*, 27 May 1983.
12 R. Pring, 'Privatisation in education', *RICE*, 7 February 1983.
13 *Times Educational Supplement*, 22 January 1982.

14 See C. Benn, *Education*, 4 December 1981, p. 426; and Socialist Education Association, *The Dual System of Voluntary and County Schools* (London: SEA, 1981).
15 J. Chadderton, *Education*, 6 March 1981, p. 203.
16 World Council of Churches Report, cf. *Guardian*, 20 January 1982.
17 *Improving Secondary Schools* (Hargreaves Report) (London: ILEA, 1984).
18 S. Ranson, 'Policy priorities and plans for the 14–19 age group', in R. Pryke, S. Ranson and S. Butters, *Management of Change in the 14–19 Sector* (Exeter: Devon County Council, 1984).
19 J. Miller, B. Taylor and A. G. Watts, *Towards a Personal Guidance Base* (London: Further Education Unit, March 1983).
20 See Miller, in Pryke, Ranson and Butters, op. cit.
21 Harvey Goldstein argued this in his keynote lecture to the Annual Education Statistics Conference, INLOGOV, Birmingham, November 1984.
22 J. Rennie, Community Education Development Centre.
23 G. Hodgson, *The Democratic Economy* (Harmondsworth: Penguin, 1984); and D. Blunkett and G. Green, 'Building from the bottom', *Fabian Society*, no. 4a, 1 October 1983.
24 J. D. Stewart, *Bureaucracy and Decentralisation in the Delivery of Local Services* (Birmingham: INLOGOV, 1984).
25 *Comprehensive Education for Life* (Coventry: Coventry City Council, 1983), p. 46.
26 A. G. Watts, *Education, Unemployment and the Future of Work* (Milton Keynes: Open University Press, 1983).
27 J. Bazalgette, *School Life and Work Life* (London: Hutchinson, 1978).
28 B. Webster, 'Decentralisation in Sheffield', INLOGOV occasional paper, May 1984.
29 M. Rutter, B. Maughan, P. Mortimore and J. Ouston, *Fifteen Thousand Hours* (London: Open Books, 1979); and P. Clifford and A. Heath, 'Selection does make a difference', *Oxford Review of Education*, vol. 10, no. 1 (1984).
30 D. Hargreaves, *Education*, 27 July 1984, p. 74.

21

The Education System Restructured

JOHN TOMLINSON

> The control of education is the wholesomest and most ennobling form of local government. (John Tomlinson Brunner, *Public Education in Cheshire*, 1897)

How might the government of education be reformed so as to serve the needs of individuals and society as perceived in the economic and cultural analysis developed thus far? How should we order an education system which is to meet the needs of a pluralistic society in the midst of economic change so profound that it alters the meaning of citizenship and calls for resilience in both individuals and groups? How can the formal educational structure use and enhance the values of an open society and further the principles of open learning? Indeed how can the government of education itself be helped to use the principles of good education by being adaptive and open to learning in an environment of uncertainty?

Reform of structures, though necessary, is not sufficient as experience has shown. The argument presented here therefore involves purposes and relationships as well as mechanisms. In summary, it brings into play the rights and duties of parents and pupils; the definition of the professionalism of teachers; the role and status of the school or college; the position and purpose of the local authority and local education authority (LEA); and the position and purpose of central government: the whole being predicated upon a view of personal, social and economic needs at this period.

The witnesses who have written in this book, all of them senior practitioners in the education service, have testified to the stronger part played by central government since the 1970s. Moreover, as promotion of policies has been replaced by intervention or direction, instruments additional to those available to the Secretary of State for Education have been brought into use. Since the question of what should be the appropriate role for central government in the government of education is seen by so many as crucial, it is worth reflecting for a moment on this perspective before developing the full argument for new structures and relationships.

The role of central government in the education service needs to be defined so as to respect the principles proposed. But there can be no doubt of the need for a strong involvement by central government. At crucial stages in the development of the service the centre has given a lead and it should be no surprise that a generation after the Education Act 1944 the centre is again active. As earlier chapters in this book have shown, there have been important stages in the development of the service where the dynamic has been largely based at the centre, and others where the bulk of the money required for change has come from the centre. But in both the role expected of the LEA was clear and accepted.

What is objectionable about the recent and current activities of central government in the education service is that they are inappropriate in many of the principles adopted (hierarchical, *dirigiste* and causing fragmentation); do not respect the position of the LEA (appealing over its head to the market and the institution); and yet nevertheless require considerable effort and innovation by the LEA while at the same time, and for mainly other reasons, there is both a cutting back of central government grant and a demand that the authorities themselves cut back, enforced from the centre through a system of penalties – and now a limitation upon the power to raise revenue in the locality.

The reaction of the LEAs and the profession to the 'great debate' and to the climate of criticism of the late 1970s was constructive not pusillanimous. Moreover, they agreed in most essentials with the analysis and views expressed by government itself (both before and after 1979), and HM Inspectorate, industrialists and parents. It must be admitted as a possibility that had government chosen to maintain the tradition of calling for new objectives and new ways of working, the LEAs and profession would have responded appropriately given reasonable resources.

Whatever may be thought to be the achievements attributable to the new stance of central government towards the education service, the position after eight years of increasing conflict between central and local government is neither satisfactory nor stable.

The annual conference of the Council of Local Education Authorities (CLEA) in 1983 opened with a resolution urging partnership between the LEAs and government, and deploring the strains in it caused by government actions. It was moved by the ACC (Conservative) and seconded by the AMA (Labour) and passed unanimously. In his address to the conference Sir Keith Joseph emphasized the importance he placed upon the idea of partnership. By the time the CLEA met in 1984 there had been the White Paper, *Training for Jobs*, the Education Support Grants Act, rate-capping and the Act paving the way for the abolition of the metropolitan county councils. The talk now was of 'betrayal of trust' by the secretary of state and government and of a 'constitutional crisis'. An ACC representative observed that 'There is a real danger that we may drift into a situation where government intervention might make it virtually impossible to conduct a responsible and locally accountable education service'. Another spoke of 'a government of ideologues intent on wrecking the education service'. All were conscious that the crisis was not only about education, but also (and perhaps mainly) about local government. The annual meeting of the ACC, a week earlier, had agreed without division a motion supporting a draft charter of local self-government drawn up by local and regional authorities of the Council of Europe.

Ironically 1984 was also the year in which fell the fortieth anniversary of the Education Act 1944. It was notable how commonplace in the commentaries was the acceptance that the partnership and the essential spirit of the Act were broken beyond repair: 'The sense of disillusion in local government is nowhere more apparent than among education committee members of all political persuasions.' Whether central government had overstepped Butler's unwritten mark because of the weakness of local government or through its own new determination was no longer relevant: either or both made the notion of partnership an anachronism. Thus the extremes of language reached in the current rhetoric; it betokens deep concern and sometimes approaches the edge of despair.

But the situation cannot be allowed to rest there. If no conscious co-operative effort is made, the damage to individuals, social cohesion and economic prospects will become irreversible. The remainder of this chapter proposes the outline of a governance for education suitable to these times. Certain principles of organization would require recognition and realization.

AN EDUCATION 'BILL OF RIGHTS'

This would approach a statement of the rights of individuals (as parents, pupils, or students, and as adult citizens) to claim access to learning for themselves and their children. It would be coupled with a recognition that such rights also confer duties upon the claimant. It would place a duty to provide appropriately upon the public education authorities.

There would need to be an acknowledgement that the demands made upon the service should be subject to a test of reasonableness; and on the other hand, an acknowledgement that the appropriate provision of education should not necessarily be through institutions. There would need to be procedures for the resolution of conflict.

Such a general statement of the position of the 'citizen as learner' would do much to remove the anomalies which have arisen from the application of market economics to education supply and demand; and re-balance the relationship between teacher, pupil and parent.

THE PROFESSION OF TEACHER

The role expected of, and offered by, teachers has changed in response to new insights into how humans best learn and developments in family and social structures. So far these changes in expectation and response have been attended to piecemeal as, say, part of the relationship between schools and the public over objectives and curriculum, or the introduction of new teaching methods, or in national or local discussions of 'extraneous' duties.

There is a need to make a powerful statement of where the teacher stands in our kind of society. It would facilitate and inform – but not pre-empt – subsequent discussion or negotiation about particular aspects of the teacher's work.

Such a definition of professionalism for teachers would accept:

(1) The need to negotiate (and renegotiate) the curriculum of learning with the polity (the community via its representatives – ministers, LEAs, governors, parents, workers and employers), or in its later stages with the student himself (in recognition of his growing maturity and to help achieve the objective of autonomy).

(2) The duty to create opportunities for learning which permit the pupil or student to acquire the knowledge, skill, value, or attitude required by the curriculum.

(3) That since points 1 and 2 cannot be achieved solely by the individual efforts of individual teachers; an appropriate measure of collective responsibility as the whole staff of a school or college is accepted – thus allowing a learning plan which:

  (*a*) has the required balance between areas of human experience;
  (*b*) has coherence when received by the pupil or student, so that learning in one area reinforces or permits learning in another;
  (*c*) is progressive, so that a dynamic is provided;
  (*d*) takes account of the 'hidden curriculum' of values and attitudes, so that the whole ethos of the school is consonant with and promotes the aims of the school.

(4) That the teacher neither can be nor should wish to be the sole mediator of the child's learning and personal development; that the parent should be seen and welcomed as a partner with unique knowledge of the child and a continuing part to play in his or her upbringing; and that members of the local community have many skills and much knowledge and experience which can be pressed into the service of the curriculum objectives of the school.

This view of professionalism sees the teacher as the expert leader of thought and analysis working with parents and other adults to the benefit of children. He/she must take responsibility for the learning which is created and for recording and evaluating its results. Yet the teacher is not working alone, but rather as the orchestrator of the resources, human and physical, of the whole community. And humility, in the face of human variety, will be the teacher's greatest strength.

Such a view also places upon the national leaders of teachers a new role to speak for a unified body in all its professional aspects. A Teachers Council, separate from trade union activity, would be a necessity.

In this way the open society, through the sensitive leadership of professionals and using the techniques of open learning, may take part in and accept some of the responsibility for its own learning and the intellectual and social nurture of its children. The young are reconnected progressively and appropriately according to their age, aptitude and ability to the adult world, from which they have had to be excluded for their own safety and care since the advent of the Industrial Revolution. Issues of motivation, especially in the adolescent, and of the connection between school and community can be approached practically and optimistically. To those who regard the potentially overmighty professional as a threat to the open society, rather than one of its animateurs, we admit of the danger but retort that to place the client at the centre of attention (rather than the teacher or institution) is to return to where Hippocrates began.

Where failure and conflict occur in the web of teacher–pupil–authority relationships (as they will from time to time), explicit and equitable procedures for review and resolution will be needed.

AN APPROPRIATE ROLE AND STATUS FOR THE INSTITUTION

For this view of the working of schools and colleges to be realized certain aspects of their organization and government need to be clarified including the constitution and powers of the governors, the role of the head, and the relationship between the institution and the LEA.

The guiding principle should be the maximization of the opportunity afforded teachers with their community to realize their curriculum objectives within the resources given the LEA and the principles of education adopted by the LEA. The clarification and definition of these roles should aim to promote the principles of collective as well as individual professional responsibility and co-operative action with parents and others expressed in the previous section of this chapter.

This country has been foremost among the 'school improvement' movement. There is a considerable experience among teachers, advisers, administrators and local politicians of how schools may be more connected with their communities and locality, both using its richness to help realize the aims of the school and giving something in return. This movement has also been a main vehicle for the enhanced professionalism of teachers. The self-critical, self-developing school working interactively with its community is a model already available, should we wish to promote it.

THE LOCAL EDUCATION AUTHORITY

There should be a democratically elected body given responsibility for the development of policy in its area and allowed to raise resources unfettered by central government or any other authority than the decisions of the local electorate.

This is required because:

(1) the kind of schools and colleges envisaged will need a hospitable and imaginative local matrix within which to operate. The LEA would, for example, be responsible for the recruitment and in-service training of

teachers, and the management of the teaching force; the development of policy on a broader scale than the school locality; the general direction of the curriculum and its progressive improvement; the encouragement and evaluation of schools and colleges; and non-institutionally based educational activities and advisory and psychological services.

(2) It is undesirable that schools should receive resources and all the advice and support they require directly from a single central authority. The system required would be rigid because it would have to work according to strict rules, could have little contact with schools and communities and would therefore be inefficient and ineffective. Such concentration of power and responsibility could lead only to ossification and occasional large-scale disasters.

(3) It is necessary on this analysis of the importance of giving voice to and mobilizing the needs and resources of individuals and communities that a level of intermediate operation, between central government and the institution, should be created on a scale which allows general participation in planning for, and meeting the needs of an identifiable area.

(4) Schools must relate to wider community planning.

Above all, the LEA would be the driving force behind policy analysis and development within a defined area according to the changing social and economic structure of that area.

The LEA as developed in this country is arguably the most efficient and effective way in which to provide for local control and improvement of a service within a national framework. If the innovations provided by LEAs are considered, it will be seen how far they are already reaching forward towards the kind of open, interactive system based on a new view of professionalism which we have argued is essential.

The School and the Community

Three strands are identifiable and reinforcing one another to open up the school. Adult education (in the intellectual tradition of Tawney) and community use of schools (in the traditions of the Folk High School and the Cambridgeshire Village College) have encouraged schools to allow the adult community to make use of the school 'out of school hours'. Now the demands of a wider view of the education of children are making teachers want to use the people and the locality in the pursuit of the 'ordinary' education of their pupils. Thus the community–school relationship has become fully reciprocal and a powerful instrument potentially within our grasp. Pre-school and primary education often pioneered such developments and offer some of the most developed approaches. The idea of a curriculum 5–16 beckons.

None of this was planned or promoted by central government. Yet arguably it has more relevance for the successful education of children and the mobilization of communities in pursuit of their own needs than any other current mechanism available.

Professionalism

The relationship between the professional and his client is one that teachers in this generation strenuously have applied themselves to. The need to make the child or adult the agent of his/her own learning has been acknowledged to arise from our nature as a species in which learning is the essence of growth since so little of the knowledge and skills which we need for our development is provided innately through inherited factors. It has had a profound effect on the approach of teachers to their work as have parallel changes on the approach of professionals in health care and social work. Moreover, this extended view of professionalism has embraced the adult(s) also responsible for the child, and has not only recognized but worked to enhance their role. The relationship between teachers and children and their parents in, for example, the best pre-school and infant education is a revelation which points the way to the future.

Interdisciplinarity

The new professionalism in education has not stopped at the teachers' boundary. It has learned the importance of working with other professionals and the hard lessons of how this can be done effectively. To observe teachers working for the young handicapped child, for example, is to see the very best practice by highly trained and competent individuals who know the limits of their skills and enjoy the experience of co-operating with others in the interests of their clients.The same philosophy and practice can be found in pre-school education, careers and counselling services, school health and welfare services, the youth service and many other aspects of education. They have grown out of practice and through local encouragement.

Training

Many of the most imaginative forms of in-service training have resulted from local experimentation. Teachers may be learning alongside colleagues from the police, probation, health, social work and libraries. Teachers may be taking workshops or master-classes with leading teachers. Teachers and the pupils in their ordinary care may be working together in a residential setting on the ordinary subjects of their curriculum but with the stimulus of the absence of time constraints and the presence of other gifted adults (many of them not trained as teachers).

These patterns for the development of a profession which needs to acknowledge and then learn how to receive the methodology of the new professionalism described here have already been pioneered by LEAs and their collaborators in teacher training.

The Creation of Networks

The LEAs have promoted myriad ways of working which connect schools and fieldworkers (home visitors, adult tutors, youth workers, prison educators, psychologists and advisers) with the many organizations existing in the community which are to do with confronting social and individual problems and require learning and information. The interconnected 'information society' creating groups to solve its own perceived problems is embryonically already in existence. Pre-school services, youth service and training and adult education, together with librarians, social workers, health visitors and many others, are already working with and through self-determining action groups. The self-educating, self-connective and self-developing society is appearing in the interstices of the formal education system. Monolithic, hierarchical and bureaucratic impositions will only hinder its further development.

The case for a locally elected and responsible education authority with power to develop policy and practice seems, on the face of the economic and cultural analyais, incontrovertible.

THE LEA: IN OR OUT OF LOCAL GOVERNMENT?

Where should it lie? Inside local government or separately, as a directly elected, single-purpose authority? It would be best within local government. The paradigm is still Redcliffe-Maud's unitary, multipurpose authority. If that is now utopian, something as near as possible should be adopted. But in view of the way in which local government has developed since 1974 certain other preconditions need to be stated:

(1) The services administered along with education must be cognate. They should allow a single policy body to contemplate the needs and development of a range of social services which have relevance for one another – education, health, social work, libraries and housing are a minimum; police and probation services are desirable too.

(2) The scale of the authority must be sufficient to permit a necessary range of administrative and professional advisory services and 'sufficient mass' for a rich offering of in-service training and professional argument and activity in the interest of a powerful, self-developing community of learning and policy development.

(3) Local government must willingly accept that in interpreting national policies and developing local initiatives their prime responsibility is to provide services suitable to local needs and circumstances, and that the applicability of party political activities, management systems, or financial procedures must all be judged by reference to the extent to which they serve or undermine this responsibility.

If for reasons connected with the rest of local government and other connected services these conditions cannot be met, then it would be better to have a directly elected, single-purpose LEA which could be of sufficient size to play an appropriate part in both school and further/higher education.

THE CENTRAL GOVERNMENT

As part of this articulation of the rights and duties of the citizen, the profession of teacher, the role of the institution and the nature and purpose of the LEA, the way forward so far as the centre is concerned might be as follows.

A statement of the overall plan and strategy which can then be scrutinized and following discussion acknowledged and adopted by the three partners to the service. This is not to deny central government the right to have such a plan or to determine its general thrust and priorities; but to acknowledge that unless it is understood and accepted by those who must make it operational, there is no chance that it will succeed.

The elements of the overall plan are already clear in, for example, the secretary of state's Sheffield speech of January 1984; the decisions over examinations at various levels; the White Papers, *Teaching Quality* and *Training for Jobs*; the Green Paper, *Parental Influence at School*; and the national statement on the school curriculum. Taken with the 1980 and 1981 Education Acts, they constitute a major reshaping of much of the service. Little public discussion of many essentials has occurred; and no admission is made of the lacunae or how they may be supplied (16–19 as secondary rolls reach their nadir; the relationship of education to the new 'non-work' economy; the need to extend pre-school and primary education on a more family-centred model; the size and purposes of higher education and their importance for schools and LEAs; and much else).

There is some justice in the cynical view that throughout the 1950s and 1960s, when apparently educational practice and objectives were driven chiefly by the pursuit of the personal development of pupils (since criticized as neglectful of the true economic interests of society), the truth was that the schools were training and distributing young people into the reality of job opportunities. They stayed on or left school; and if they did not take higher education, they went into the local labour market. The difference in the 1980s is that there are not enough jobs and therefore the system has broken down. We are witnessing two reactions, both politically cynical. On the one hand, the education system is accused of failing to prepare young people adequately for work and a vocationalization of curricula in school and the new training structures between school and 'work' are being imposed, mainly to mop up the frustrated and unemployed. On the other hand, no long-term thought is given to the likely character of a high-technology economy, the kind of labour market and opportunities it would create, the kind of informal 'non-work' economy that would have to exist in parallel with it, or the kind of social readjustment necessary in the exhausted localities and therefore of the kind of education system which would best support all this.

It will be necessary to have some national means of providing a basis of consent for the view of education and training we are to adopt in the heralded high-technology, post-industrial society; that is to say, we shall need a national aspect to 'The Learning Society' as much as its local aspects. The many initiatives of government can only form the starting point: the framework will always need evaluation and adjustment and life-blood from the fields of action. Something akin to the Central Advisory Council will have to be created. It must be regarded by all the partners as the point of contact and alliance, not the tilting-yard. The mark-II Schools Council, with its important constituencies of industrialists and parents as well as teachers, LEAs and government, could have been the embryo, but government did not think there was time for discussion of their intentions at that stage and perhaps lacked the desire for it. However, unless consent is given, there will be no success.

Such a process of challenge and response between government and its partners is the only realistic way of defining the role of government, which must properly change its profile according to the urgencies of social and economic change. Let any who remain in doubt reflect on this. Many of the radical changes in school education brought in since 1980 – for example, 16+ examinations, 17+ pre-vocational examinations, widening the sixth form curriculum, records of achievement and new approaches to teacher training – were the outcome of discussion during the 1960s and 1970s in the sort of representative councils now discarded. They created any basis of consent which may exist. What is now being done to confront the issues that will face us in the 1990s and to begin to build the necessary understanding? Those who strip the assets of their predecessors have a duty towards their successors.

A general statement can be made of the service which it might be appropriate for government to attend to; it would include the following aspects:

(1) the length of compulsory education;
(2) the manner of its delivery (full-time, part-time, or a mixture and when: within the same ages for all, or at the individual's discretion beyond a certain age?);
(3) the general curriculum objectives (but not the means of their realization, which is to say the methods of teaching and of internal school organization);
(4) the size of the teaching force and the broad curriculum for its formation;
(5) the objectives of the post compulsory system of general education and vocational training;
(6) the size and objectives of the higher education system;
(7) the capital and revenue resources appropriate to these ends, taking account of demography, provided centrally up to an agreed proportion and acknowledging both the share to be provided locally and the additional element of discretionary local expenditure.

The kind of model proposed here, which is based on definitions of individual, institutional, professional, and central and local government rights and duties, requires also the means of ensuring justice for individuals and respect for the public interest. This is not a new notion within the education service, but it would need development. The role given the Secretary of State for Education by section 1 of the 1944 Act should be retained (it would be reinforced by concepts such as an entitlement curriculum); all parties concerned would have to accept some restraints upon their powers and procedures for review by their peers or other bodies; and the courts would be called upon when law (for example, the bill of rights) needed interpretation.

The crisis for education of the 1980s has not come about particularly because the Department of Education and Science and other parts of central government started to take initiatives; nor because there was a determination by central government to restrict local government expenditure; nor because central government advertised its distaste for the public sector and thus for public service including the public education service on which 96 per cent of our parents and children rely; nor because public and teachers felt there was a need for new objectives and new ways of working; nor yet because the number of pupils in school fell by a third and the consequent contractions were painful and hard to manage. It came about because all these contributing factors happened at once, amid an embittered political climate.

If the system is to be able to carry the weight now required of it and to have the flexibility to adjust to both demographic change and new social and economic objectives, then the partnership of the centre, the LEAs and institutions needs to be reconstituted. And at each level there must be a meeting of politicians, other laity and professionals appropriate to the task. At the centre the HMI give continual advice and intelligence to ministers and officials; a National Education Council would call up a wider representation of the profession and community. The LEA, properly resourced, has shown that the education committee can provide for policy-makers (elected members, churches and parents and other laity) to meet professionals. And LEA professional administrative and advisory officers can provide for daily maintenance of the system and its development on agreed lines of policy. Likewise at the school and college a two-part process is already at work in the best examples. The governing body provides a formal meeting place for polity and profession and should have clearly defined duties and responsibilities. The 'collegiate school' taking responsibility for its development on agreed lines, the evaluation and recording of its work and giving account of itself is already a reality in some places.

This three-tiered system, allowing politician and profession a proper relationship and having at each level its tasks, duties and responsibilities defined and agreed, is now lacking but sorely needed. And supporting it all, there must be an acknowledgement of the areas of independence of each tier, and resources allowed for its exercise.

The resilience and adaptability of such a system will come chiefly, as it has hitherto, from the LEA and the locality, from the day-to-day engagement with reality. Without that, and without the underlying and dynamic philosophy of open learning in an open society, this formulation would only be another prescription for the reinforcement of elites and ossification. The essence is that the system uses its own best weapons on itself: hence the crucial part to be played by the LEA.

The consensus which supported the partnership from 1944 until the mid-1970s and which was born of implicit agreement about the ends and means of education and the priority to be attached to it in an expanding economy will not reappear of its own accord in the new circumstances of the 1980s. But since a totally centralized or totally devolved education system are both impractical and undesirable, the consensus must be recreated and kept alive by an act of will. The principles on which it should be based and the mechanisms by which it can be achieved have been demonstrated. The aim must be to recreate the partnership in what Edward Simpson calls an 'agreed, respected and durable form'. It is desperately important that action should be taken soon, if we are to match the system to the tessellated, self-actualizing but suffering society now around us.

Index